THE BOOK OF HIGHS

250 ways to alter consciousness without drugs

BY EDWARD ROSENFELD

QUADRANGLE
THE NEW YORK TIMES BOOK COMPANY

to D. & G.-W.

*". . . how hard it is
to keep the mind open to surprises!"*

L. L. Whyte in *Internal Factors in Evolution*

PICTURE CREDITS

7 NASA/*The New York Times;* **10, 13** *The New York Times;*
23 *The New York Times;* **25** Dover Books;
34 Gerald Oster; **49, 60, 61** *The New York Times;*
80 Gary Azon; **87, 88** *The New York Times;*
108 Lottie Jacobi; **112** Marty Fromm; **113** American Psychological Association; **115, 121, 123** Steven Bernbach;
140, 145, 146 *The New York Times;* **148** Oxford University
Press, Elinor Greenberg; **152, 153, 155, 157** *The New York
Times;* **158** The Japan Society; **161, 163, 164, 166, 169, 172, 173,
179, 183** *The New York Times;* **189** Black Star; **190, 192, 197,
201** *The New York Times;* **203** *Scientific American;* **204** William Ittleson; **210, 211** *The New York Times;* **218** Wide World
Photos; **226** USAF/*The New York Times;* **230** *The New York
Times;* **237** Edmund Scientific; **248** *The New York Times;*
249 Gay Gaer Luce; **251** *The New York Times*

BOOK DESIGN: BETTY BINNS

ACKNOWLEDGMENTS

A book of this scope requires the aid of many people. I
received much help and guidance. I will attempt to give credit
to some; there are numerous others who go unnamed, but not
unremembered.

The first recognition goes to Frances Cheek, whose idea this was
to begin with and who shared that idea so selflessly.

My gratitude goes to Bernie Aaronson (and the entire group at
The New Jersey Neuropsychiatric Institute), Susan Alexander,
Reza Arasteh, Greg Austin, Jeff Berner, Adam Crane, Richie
Davidson, Rockie and Jeremy Gardiner, Dolly Gattozzi, Midge
Haber, Harry Hermon, Charles Honorton, Mozart and Annette
Kaufman, Stanley Keleman, Alexandra Kirkland, Stan Krippner,
Gay Luce, Eric McLuhan, Ralph Metzner, Marni Miller, Gerry
Oster, David Padwa, Milo and Celia Perichitch, Don Plumley,
Ilana Rubenfeld, Pyrrhus Ruches, David Sarlin, Steven and
Gabriel Simon, Deborah Steinfirst *nee* Lotus, Klaus von Stutterheim, John Wilcock, Karl Yeargens and Gene Youngblood.

Without the very special help of others this work would never
have been possible. Elly Greenberg has typed, endured and given
much needed support. John Brockman has been a
helpful and wise friend. Peter Matson's hard work has made
this publication possible. Bob Masters, Jean Houston and Bill
Wine shared unselfishly of their own work in the area of
altered states of consciousness. Charles Tart's book of readings,
Altered States of Consciousness, has been and continues to be
an expansive model.

Bennett Shapiro provided help, suggestions and encouragement, as he has been tirelessly doing for more than two
decades. Marty Fromm gave me and continues to give me the
greatest gift of all: myself.

Section 34 is reprinted by permission of: Hokuseido Press for
material from *The History of Haiku,* Volumes One and Two,
by R. H. Blyth, © 1963, 1964; and New Directions for material
from *Collected Poems* by Kenneth Patchen, © 1967, 1968.

Section 154 is reprinted by permission of: Japan Publications
for poetry by James Hackett, © 1969; and The Paris Review,
Inc. for poetry by Jack Kerouac, © 1966.

Library of Congress Catalog Card Number: 72-90448

International Standard Book Number: 0-8129-0329-3

Contents

Getting High and Staying There

by Andrew Weil
author of *The Natural Mind*

Altered states of consciousness have become so respectable in the past few years that they are now known simply as ASCs—a sure sign that they are in fashion among scientists. Conferences on them are proliferating (one took place recently at the Smithsonian Institution in Washington, D.C.), and month by month ASCs carve out a bigger niche in medical literature. But despite the accumulation of scientific data, we still do not know what it is to be high or the significance of our seeking that state so persistently.

The desire to have peak experiences, to transcend the limitations of ordinary consciousness, operates in all of us. It is so basic that it looks like an inborn drive. Almost as soon as infants learn to sit up, they begin to rock themselves into highs. Later, as young children, they learn to whirl into other states of awareness or hyperventilate out of ordinary reality. Still later they discover drugs.

There has been much talk lately of alternatives to drugs. The present book describes a great many techniques for getting high, none of them making use of drugs. If we could teach people other methods to achieve highs, the drug problem would take on more manageable proportions. But what is wrong with drugs? They certainly work for many people, and, if used with the respect and care they demand, are no more dangerous than many agents in common, legal use in our society.

Some object to drug-induced highs on a puritanical level: it is too easy to get pleasure, let alone religious ecstasy, by swallowing a pill. One ought to work or suffer for that reward. I doubt that any drug user will be convinced by such an argument, especially if his pills do the trick for him. A more convincing argument borne out by the experience of many users is that drugs sometimes do not do the trick. They may trigger panic states and depressions instead of highs. One can take steps to ensure that a drug experience will be good, but there is always a possibility that unforeseen factors will supervene. The drug itself does not contain the experience it triggers. Highs come from within the individual; they are simply released, or not, by the drug, which always acts in combination with expectations and environment—set and setting.

Drugs reinforce the illusion that highs come from external chemicals when, in fact, they come from the human nervous system. The practical consequence of this illusion-making tendency is that users find it hard to maintain their highs: one always has to come down after a drug high, and the down can be as intense as the up. The user who does not understand this may become dependent on drugs because the easiest way to get out of a low following a high seems to be to take another dose of the drug.

I make no distinction between legal and illegal drugs here. Coffee, an innocent "beverage" in the eyes of many persons, is as dependence-producing as any illegal drug in just this way. The stimulation it provides is offset later by lethargy and mental clouding, usually in the morning. In full-blown coffee addiction a person cannot get going in the morning without his drug, and the more he consumes, the more his need increases.

Moreover, the more regularly one uses a drug to get high, the less effective it becomes. Many marihuana smokers find that their highs diminish in intensity the more frequently they smoke; chain smokers of the weed do not get high at all. And users of psychedelics, heroin, and amphetamines often look back on their earliest drug experiences as the most pleasureful.

The value of drugs is their ability to trigger important states of consciousness. People who grow up in our materialistic culture may need a drug experience to show them that other modes of consciousness exist. It is notable that the increasingly widespread interest in meditation, intuitive understanding and spiritual development was spurred by drug-triggered highs giving a glimpse of these other realities. The problem is that drugs cannot be used regularly without losing their effectiveness. They do not maintain highs.

And so there is much searching for other ways of getting high and staying high. Some people say they are looking for more natural methods. But it is difficult to say just what is natural and what is not. Firewalking as practiced in northern Greece may be a terrific high. It is also dangerous when not done correctly; those who try it without proper preparation wind up with badly burned feet. Is it more or less natural than taking mescaline?

The distinction between drug and non-drug methods of getting high might not be very useful, because it is just another product of our current national obsession with drugs. Any technique making use of something material or external to the individual will tend to produce dependence, will tend to lose its effectiveness over time, and will limit one's freedom to get high. Any method requiring things, for example, ties a person to his things—whether they be glowing coals, biofeedback machines, or tabs of LSD. A better distinction would be between methods that one can use by oneself anytime, anywhere and methods that require something else. The person who can get high by himself is at a great advantage.

Even if we could convert most of the drug takers in our country into meditators, chanters, or whirling dervishes, I am not certain we would end the dissensions. I think that many people who seem to be anti-drug would be suspicious of any methods used to get out of ordinary awareness. Meditation, for instance, despite all the support of orthodox religion, is often erroneously regarded as an avenue to passive withdrawal from the world and would doubtless stir up much opposition if it were practiced openly on a larger scale. To the rational, straight side of our consciousness, the search for better highs may look like simple hedonism and a shirking of all responsibility.

No doubt some persons are just out for new thrills and pleasures. But the drive to get high that appears in earliest infancy cannot be there for no reason at all; it is too basic a need. And many nonordinary experiences are not pleasureful—they are powerful, different, strange, even terrifying. Still, we call them "highs" because somehow they seem fraught with positive potential and the capacity to change us for the better.

If we look over an extensive catalog of methods for getting high, one common trait stands out: they all are techniques of focusing awareness, of shaking us out of habitual modes of perception and getting us to concentrate on something, whether a sound, a sight, an unusual sensation. Possibly, what we call a high is simply the experience of focused consciousness, even if the focus is on something we would normally consider painful or unpleasant. And possibly, when our ordinary consciousness is focused on anything, we can become aware of what is ordinarily unconsciously perceived: our internal organs, for example, or other persons' minds, or even things beyond ordinary time and space.

Concentration is the key. In "normal" states of mind our conscious energies are scattered. Our attention wanders aimlessly from thought to thought to external sensations to internal sensations, to the past to the future to snatches of tunes to hopes and fears to images to objects. Nearly all systems of meditation require preliminary practice at concentration, at stilling the restlessness of the ever-observing mind. Meditation is nothing other than directed concentration. Concentration is power.

Sometimes we enter states of concentration spontaneously, without making any efforts. An intensely pleasureful, painful, or unusual stimulus can draw our single-minded attention so completely that we simply find ourselves in an altered state of consciousness. All of us have the capacity to enter these states, and all of us probably spend time in them even if we are not aware of it. And the states are natural whether the means used to achieve them are peculiar or not. In this sense it is natural to be high and natural to want to be high.

In fact, being high might be the most natural condition of all. The euphoria of a state of focused awareness is almost always accompanied by a conviction that it is the way things are "supposed to be." Instead of learning to get high, we may have to unlearn not being high; by ridding ourselves of the learned habits of worrying, fearing, and scattering mental energy, we get down to that core feeling of joyful transcendence that is the basic state of the human nervous system.

Far from leading to withdrawal from the world, meditation and other self-reliant methods of getting high tend to make us better able to function in ordinary reality. The better we get at getting high and staying there, the more we integrate the conscious and unconscious spheres of our mental life. This integration is the key to wholeness (health) of body and mind.

We are caught up in a fever of experimentation with methods of changing consciousness, much of it generated by the young. There will be much wasted effort, some casualties. But out of it all will come a generation that will know how to use its consciousness more and more fully—a generation that can build a truly high society.

A. W.
Tucson, Arizona
March, 1973

PART ONE

JUST YOUR SELF

Awareness

1 Concentration

The development of concentration—that is, our ability to direct our attention at will, is germane to many of the techniques and methods described in this book. We usually go through our days paying little attention to our environment. It is only occasionally that we actually "take in" a particular object, image, thought or person. We fail, almost always, to concentrate.

Concentration means learning to focus; it means training ourselves, through practice, to "stay with" the object of our attention despite distraction; it means staying with a subject and "mastering" our relationship with the subject. (This does not mean mastering the subject! Real concentration indicates a relationship of equality, an I-Thou relationship with the subject.)

Our attention should be directed toward the field, both interior and exterior, of our environment. That field is made up of Gestalten—literally, configurations or patterns. In order for these configurations to become meaningful, part of the pattern serves as background so that another part of it will stand out as the foreground. Life itself is a continuum of such changing and transforming figure-ground interactions.

To concentrate means to establish a clear Gestalt, so that the foreground figure stands predominant—clear of the background. Being able to stay with the figure is concentration. Powers of concentration can be developed through practice. Pick a thought, idea, object and/or person, and stay with it. Devote your attention to it. This is surprisingly difficult. You will generally notice how your attention wanders. Bring the subject back into focus and stay with it. Remember, the process is more important than the subject of concentration.

Try an experiment: concentrate on one of your fingertips. Carefully examine the lines that are etched there. Treat them as though they were a maze, and choose a beginning and end. Don't resist when your attention fades; stay with your experience. Find out what happens to your concentration when it wanders.

ACCESS

Christmas Humphreys's book, *Concentration and Meditation*, is a good general introduction. The first four exercises in *Gestalt Therapy*, by F. S. Perls, R. Hefferline and P. Goodman show how to go about concentrating, from the phenomenological point of view. Other aids may be found in this book under Meditation (No. 10), Yoga (No. 145), Buddhism (No. 152) and Gurdjieff (No. 161).

2 Philosophical awareness

Philosophy may be thought of as speculative inquiry into our nature. Through philosophical awareness we focus our attention on the questions and problems brought about by the "facts" of our existence; through philosophical awareness we may be able to effect a relationship with certain manifestations of our lives.

What is it to be alive?
What is the meaning of life?
Who am I?
Am I real?
Who are you?
What is the world (Earth)? Solar system? Galaxy? Universe?
What is knowledge?

One of the major problems in dealing with questions like these is our language. To answer the question:

"What is the meaning of life?" an answer must be constructed that begins: "The meaning of life is . . ." Since our language reflects our reality, what we are able to *describe* can circumscribe what we are able to *experience*.

What is written above is illustrative of the traps that we encounter in attempting to cultivate philosophical awareness. The experience of the Austrian philosopher Ludwig Wittgenstein (1889–1951), is a profound example of some of the difficulties of philosophical thought. His two major published works contradict each other. The first, *Tractatus Logico-Philosophicus* (1921), provides a general and ultimate philosophical theory. His second work, *Philosophical Investigations* (published posthumously), rejects any such general theory and examines many individual cases without general comment. As he wrote: "In philosophy we do not draw conclusions . . . philosophy only states what everyone admits."

The *attempt* to reach conclusions in philosophy, though often frustrating, can be liberating. The *I Ching* says: "Perseverance furthers."

ACCESS

Philosophers of the West are covered in Bertrand Russell's *History of Western Philosophy*. Many Eastern philosophies are referred to later in this volume. Contemporary philosophical trends are reviewed in the works of Colin Wilson, in *The Age of Complexity* by Herber Kohl, and in Susanne Langer's *Philosophy in a New Key*.

3 Sensory awareness

We receive information from and about our environment through our senses. The primary senses are:

Vision (eyes)
Hearing (ears)
Smell (nose)
Taste (tongue, mouth, and nose)
Touch (skin and tongue)

Our senses continually process an amazing amount of information. Here again, the Gestalt theory of figure-ground formation is important to our understanding. When we open our eyes we observe and focus our visual attention on one subject. The other objects in that same visual field form the background against which that figure stands out.

There are many different methods, techniques, and exercises which can help us to develop our sensory awareness.

The best way to develop the senses is to find out what it's like to live without them. This is called sensory deprivation. Sight lends itself to this experiment best. Select an environment that you know very well—your house, room, or someplace equally familiar. Close your eyes or wear a blindfold, and sightlessly examine your environment. Pay attention to those senses you use when you cannot see. You will depend on your sense of touch to feel your way around; you may also use your sense of smell; * you will hear sounds that you rarely pay conscious attention to.

Another experiment is to isolate a block of time, say 5 minutes, during which you will be performing some everyday task or activity (changing your clothes, going to the bathroom, coming home from work, etc.). Pay careful attention to everything that you touch during this period. If you are wearing clothing, examine every point and surface where your skin and clothing touch. Do not *do* anything with your observations. Stay with what you are feeling.

Now try the same experiment employing the senses of smell and hearing.

We usually associate tasting with food, but there are many other possibilities. We always have some taste in our mouths: our own, clothing, pens, glasses, etc. Try paying attention to them and pay special attention to

* Unless the mazes used for rats are thoroughly sterilized, the rats smell their way through them.

the way utensils such as saucers, bowls and silverware affect the taste of food by their own separate tastes.

You might select a variety of spices to taste—parsley, sage, rosemary, thyme—and spend 5 minutes with each; taste and stay with the experience of salt, butter, oil and catsup; try butter and caraway seeds or make up combination concoctions of your own.

By experiencing your senses, rather than possessing them, you will revitalize your sensory awareness. You do not *have* senses; you *are* your senses.

ACCESS

A good introduction to sensory work is provided in the article "Report on Work in Sensory Awareness and Total Functioning," by Charlotte Selver and Charles V. W. Brooks, which appears in Herbert Otto's *Explorations in Human Potentialities*. Exercises 6 and 13 in *Gestalt Therapy* by Perls, et al., can be helpful. Bernie Gunther has developed a variety of techniques for opening up new channels of sensory awareness. Some of the best include his instructions for touching, tapping, slapping, shaking, lifting, and stretching, as described in *Sense Relaxation* and *What to Do Until the Messiah Comes*. Also see *Joy* by William Schutz.

4   Biological awareness

We often forget that we are an animal species. Our powers of communication have become so great and vast that we have forgotten how recently we left the trees. What is necessary is perspective. A trip to the zoo or, better, a weaponless safari, will remind us that we are biologically linked to the other species on our planet. Better organized than some, less peaceful than most, lacking in spontaneity yet exceedingly intelligent—still, we are animals. We are MEAT. We are flesh and cells and neurons and blood, organs and bone and marrow. We are hair and muscle and teeth and secretion and waste. What are we made of? What are we made from? How do we keep making?

Reduce experience to the cellular level. Learn about cells and *be* your cells; rather, be *cells*. Be invisible!

Feel your needs, feel your revulsions. Experience your levels and all of your strata. Flow like blood; leap and charge like a nerve impulse across a synapse. Be aware of how you process nourishment and eliminate toxins and continue to be.

Imagine anthropologists from another world observing and visiting us. What might they find? What words would they use to describe us?

ACCESS

For the topological and geological groundwork consult Gray's *Anatomy* and Royce's *Surface Anatomy*. For "meat" considerations see Michael McClure's *Meat Science Essays*. An extraterrestrial anthropological report is contained in Arthur C. Clarke's *Report on Planet Three*. For cellular awareness, see Kees Bokes's *Cosmic View*.

Biological systems of man

5 Visceral awareness

We are systems, and we take totally for granted the fact that hundreds of thousands of "parts" are acting synergistically to keep us in action.

Our systems include:

the skeletal
the muscular
the sensory
the circulatory
the respiratory
the gastro-intestinal
the genito-urinary
the endocrine
the nervous

Glands, networks and organs all work cooperatively for your maintenance. All operate without your instructions and without your knowledge.

To get in touch with how your insides work, find out what *makes* them work. Find out as much as possible through your own concentration. Listen for the pumping of your heart. Zero in on the heat of your liver. Pay attention to the contractions of your stomach. Feel the changes in tension as your urine leaves your bladder.

Know your body.

Be a body.

ACCESS

For some assistance in this area see Access for No. 251.

6 Rhythmic and cyclic awareness

The rhythms and cycles that we experience in our lives are part of a delicate universal balance. Most of our changes, like sleeping, waking, becoming hungry, eating, etc., are connected to the permutations in our solar system, especially those involved in the relationship between the earth, the sun and moon. Other rhythms include those influenced by cosmic rays, electromagnetic fields, gravity, and planetary motion. The most important rhythm, the most meaningful cycle on earth, is the circadian or daily rhythm. The word circadian comes from the Latin *circa dies*: about a day. There are two daily cycles; the solar day, which has 24 hours, and the lunar day, which has 24.8 hours.

Rhythms and cycles direct your sleep and dreams. They vary your body temperature as much as two degrees during each circadian cycle. Your blood, blood sugar, urine, hormones, energy, and stress all flow to prescribed rhythms.

Sense and feel your rhythmic cycles, stay in touch with them. Be your rhythms. Feel your body temperature at 99 degrees F., at the peak of your daily cycle. Know that when you sleep your temperature is near 97° F.

The adrenal hormones function so that dinner has a more pronounced aroma than lunch or breakfast. Noises sound louder at night and bright lights are easier to tolerate after you've slept. As the day progresses your steroid levels decrease your ability to make sensory discriminations diminish.

The moon controls many aspects of life. The tides obey the pull of the moon as do the menstrual cycles of women. At the beginning of this moon cycle there is a buildup of tension as well as an increase in bodily fluids. After the periodic cycle is complete, there is a release from this tension and a sense of well-being.

Police have noted that crimes of violence and passion increase during the full moon and the new moon.

Energy levels also change with the seasons. Tune in to your body's storing and spending of energy. When you are depressed, examine your sleep cycle; check your internal clock. Become aware of all your bodily rhythms.

ACCESS

See Gay Gaer Luce's *Body Time* and Ward's *The Living Clocks.*

7   Ecological/planetary awareness

We must realize that we are living on the surface of a planet. Though we may leave that surface and go elsewhere, we have yet to escape the influence of Earth. Even when we go to the moon we are still a vital part of the ecological system of planet Earth.

The universe may be thought of as a macrocosmic aggregate of our lives. Individual life, with all its sensations, feelings, emotions, thoughts, ideas, intuitions, movements, cellular interchanges, events, interrelationships and decompositions, is a small but whole universe, a microcosm of the greater universe in which life exists.

Earth from space

We live in a small envelope of protective (and destructive) gases that surrounds the outer surface of a medium-sized planet. That supportive envelope also maintains a variety of vegetables and minerals which in turn maintain us in our universe. The key to this system, as to all systems in the universe, is the relative transformation of energy. Prior to man's acute post-tribal awareness of energy, he had no problem maintaining a balanced relationship with the planet's energy transformations. But since the beginning of urban culture, certain activities of man have upset the balance of many Earth systems. It has only been in the last century, especially since the initiation of a global electronic environment, that urban man has begun to receive visible, audible, smellable, tangible and tastable evidence that his actions have affected the balance of nature.

We have destroyed the old ecology; it will never live again. We are creating, without conscious ecological direction, a new environmental system that will eventually destroy our species. If man is to survive, a new, consciously created, anticipated, participatory, planetary ecology must be achieved, for it has become impossible to "return" to the old Earth ecology.

ACCESS

All of the works of Buckminster Fuller and John McHale are essential in this area. Especially helpful are the World Design Science Decade Documents (1–6). The best introduction to current thought in ecology is *The Subversive Science*, edited by Paul Shepard and Daniel McKinley. Boeke's *Cosmic View* covers the entire universe, macrocosmically and microcosmically, in forty simple but wonderfully effective pictures. For a view of the ecological situation under our feet see Rudolf Geiger's *The Climate Near The Ground*. Barry Commoner reviews contemporary problems of ecology and speaks forcefully about their solutions in *The Closing Circle*.

8 Semantic awareness

The limits of my language are the limits of my world.
Ludwig Wittgenstein

When we communicate our ideas, thoughts and opinions to each other, our words carry powerful messages. These messages may not be communicated through pronunciation or grammatical structure; but they are always present in *how* we say what we say. A good example of this is the salutation "Hi, slow-poke!" jokingly spoken by the jealous observer to the runner just finishing a workout. Obviously, here the message is in the literal meaning of the words. The speaker has revealed his secret jealousy.

Other indicators of semantic awareness are: attention to whether our language is general or specific; whether it judges or shows objectivity; and whether the attitude contained in our words shows an open or a closed stance.

A good experiment is to set aside one day for taking everything said to you exactly at face value. Even when people are kidding you, respond as though they are giving you a sermon. If someone says something sarcastic or facetious, treat it as though he has shared his most profound insight with you. The point of this experiment is to show that people almost *always* say exactly what they mean, even when they conceal it in sarcasm or facetiousness.

Another good experiment is to set aside a day in which you take pains to make every sentence you speak a complete one. Every sentence you hear should also be complete. If someone says something to you in an incomplete sentence, take it upon yourself to finish it.

Still another language game is to be aware of every exaggeration, every disproportionate allusion, and every overstatement. Remember that we mean what we say and we are what we say and how we say it.

ACCESS

The works of Ludwig Wittgenstein, though difficult, are among the most intense and thorough considerations of language that we have. A good general introduction is *The Meaning of Meaning* by C. K. Ogden and I. A. Richards. *Science and Sanity* by Alfred Korzybski is more specific and outlines a method of awareness, General Semantics. Benjamin Lee Whorf's *Language, Thought, and Reality* examines man's behavior and view of reality as a function of his language.

9 Self awareness

The preceding entries all deal with self awareness. Not yourself, but your *self*. Anything that alters consciousness, with or without drugs, provides the potential for increased awareness of your self.

Ride in a car at 60 m.p.h. It seems quite fast at the beginning. Maintain a speed of 60. Your awareness of it will slowly diminish. Then slow down to 30 m.p.h. and accelerate back up to 60. Another way to increase awareness of the constant 60 m.p.h. speed is to change what you see. Instead of looking ahead onto the road unfolding before you, look down at the road directly beneath. The "slowness" of 60 m.p.h. quickly disappears.

So it is with your self. When we continue our usual lifestyles, repeating the same actions over and over, getting tied into habits, not paying attention to either the fine details or the overall general patterns and trends of existence, we don't notice who is *living* the life. Pay attention, concentrate, tune into the meaning of your existence. Your life is *real*. Experience yourself as an animal, part of the species, a biological phenomenon filled with cells and systems and organs, rhythmically crawling, walking, running, rolling, and flying around the surface of the planet. Become ever more aware of how fantastic your universe-presence is. Blake said, "If the doors of perception were cleansed every thing would appear to man as it is, infinite." As it is.

ACCESS

The methods, techniques, and approaches discussed in this book are meant to be helpful. I have found a combination of phenomenology, existentialism, altered states of consciousness, Zen Buddhism, Gestalt therapy, and planetary awareness to be helpful. Other combinations may help you. Different strokes for different folks.

Positive techniques

10 Meditation

Meditation is essentially:

sitting quietly, doing nothing;

or, perhaps better:

quietly, doing no-thing, here/now.

The fundamentals of all meditation are centered in your self, wherever you may be—still, on the move, or doing nothing but that which you are doing at that moment.

Make or do? How do you do other than do?
                                    John Brockman

A simple sitting meditation procedure is described below. There are many to fit different temperaments. Try out as many as you can and pick the one that suits you best.

Find a place where you won't be disturbed, a comfortable spot where you will be able to sit for at least thirty minutes. Many believe that more difficult, arduous positions, like the crossed legs of the full- and half-lotus are more helpful during meditation. (In full lotus one sits with the legs crossed so that the outside of the right foot rests on the inside of the left thigh and the outside of the left foot rests on the inside of the right thigh. In half-lotus only one foot is placed on one thigh, with the other leg crossed beneath.) Others have found that meditation can be accomplished proficiently even while sitting in a chair. It is important to keep the spine straight but not rigid, and perpendicular to the floor.

Meditation at the San Francisco Zen Center

After getting into this posture fold your hands in your lap. You might find that your meditation will be enhanced if, when putting your hands in your lap, you place your palms upward. Many religious leaders believe that the position with the palms up is one of great receptivity, allowing energy to enter the organism.

Once this position is attained and you feel comfortable, sit quietly for about 15 or 20 minutes. Later, when you have had more experience, you might find that half-hour sitting periods are preferable. When you meditate do not close your eyes; it becomes very easy to drift off to sleep. Keep them open and let your gaze fall a few feet in front of you. Fix on a spot but do not stare, rather, let the eyes stop there without really looking. With your eyes on this spot direct your vision inward.

What is most interesting in meditation is the state of being that can develop: a quality of clear attention and a great ability to focus and concentrate. To develop these qualities some masters assign a mantra, or group of sacred syllables, to a meditator. The meditator is instructed to concentrate on his mantra, internally; the mantra is the center of his focusing. In the Zen school, meditation begins by focusing on breathing. First, breaths are counted on the exhalation. Later, inhalations are counted, and still later, both are noted. After this has been accomplished one might be told to watch his breaths flowing in and out of his body, but not to count them. Still later, a Zen master might assign a *koan,* or problem, as the focus of meditation.

A very difficult but rewarding form of meditation is the meditation on nothing, or no-thing. This brings about an encounter with paradox. If the object of meditation is nothing and you reach this object, recognition that you have arrived at nothing will constitute something, won't it? Perhaps nothing will become no-other-thing-but-this, the latter being what is at the center of consciousness in the here-and-now. Meditation can lead to the experience of that place.

ACCESS

Section 4 of Charles Tart's *Altered States of Consciousness* contains four good articles on meditation. In the Introduction to that section (pp. 175–176) Tart lists some suggestions for further reading. To that list I would add Humphreys's *Concentration and Meditation,* Charles Luk's *Secrets of Chinese Meditation,* Kapleau's *Three Pillars of Zen,* Chogyam Trungpa's *Meditation in Action,* Maharishi Mahesh Yogi's *The Science of Being and the Art of Living* and Paul Reps's delightful *Ten Ways to Meditate.* Also see under Access for some of the RELIGIONS AND MYSTICISM entries.

"Physiological Effects of Transcendental Meditation" by R. K. Wallace appeared in *Science* (Vol. *167,* 1751–1754, 27 March 1970).

11   Prolonged observation

This is one of the easiest ways to alter consciousness without taking drugs. It requires only concentration, yourself, and an object. The basic method for turning on through prolonged observation is: STAY WITH IT!

Although visual experience is described, one can transpose this same technique to fit the other senses. Select something, say a flower. Go (with the flower) where you can relax and where you won't be disturbed or distracted. Get into a frame of mind so that you will attend only to the flower. Hold it about 6 inches in front of your eyes, or as close as necessary to bring it into sharp focus. Look at the flower. STAY WITH IT! Some people experience nothing for a couple of minutes. Try not to blink. Of course you will have to, but try to make each uninterrupted period of contact between you and the flower last as long as possible. Try to move as little as possible and STAY WITH IT!

After 5 minutes you will have noticed the changes that both the flower and the background have gone through. The boundary where the flower ends and the background begins will start to blur. The edges of surrounding objects will begin to look funny and fuzzy. With intense concentration faces might appear in the flower; movements that don't exist might be noticed. This experience is very similar to the altered perception reported by people who have taken psychedelic drugs.

You can use anything for your object. A flower is small and provides lots of background. A piece of white paper provides a large, eye-filling field which generally flows and undulates after a few moments. Other possibilities abound in your everyday environment. Two favorites are fingerprints and your own mirror image. Using another person in this exercise is also interesting. One of the curious things about this technique is the fact that it often occurs spontaneously with people who are in positions where prolonged observation is inevitable— sentry duty and the watch on a ship.

12   Problem solving

None of us looks forward to problems. They try us, tax our facilities and often frustrate us and make us uncomfortable. They make life difficult.

They also make life vital, arresting, engaging and interesting. They allow us to tap our potential. They make demands on us. Problems often require that we bring a new and unaccustomed viewpoint to a situation. It is in the experience of both the positive *and* the negative aspects of problems that we can find ways to change thought and action, the ways in which we experience the world and the ways we are. Problems provide us with the opportunity to explore fresh new ways of being.

The most important thing to remember when using problem solving as a method for altering your consciousness, is to remain open to the opportunity to experience and sense what you have not previously been aware of.

Another key to problem solving as a way to get high is persistence. By sticking with a problem, reviewing past procedures and evaluating current status, the obvious and the overlooked can become clear. This often brings out the problem's solution, and along with the solution, the feeling of insight and closure: "a-ha!"

A good example of problem solving is attempting to discover what it is about your relationship with someone that makes you dislike each other. It might be something in his personality that you dislike, whereas further reflection and insight could make it clear that what you see in him that is distasteful is something you find in yourself that you try to hide. Or it might be that when you hear the other person speak you don't like what he says. If you treat this as a problem you can enable yourself to listen more openly and perhaps hear what the other is really saying. This in turn may lead to discoveries about how you talk and what you say. These experiences can lead to new insights about other people and about you.

13   Fervent prayer

I pledge allegiance to the flag of the United States of America, and to the republic for which it stands, one nation, under God, indivisible, with liberty and justice for all.

The Pledge of Allegiance

Our Father, who art in heaven, hallowed be Thy name, Thy kingdom come, Thy will be done on earth as it is in heaven. Give us this day our daily bread and forgive us our trespasses as we forgive those who trespass against us. Lead us not into temptation and deliver us from evil. For Thine is the kingdom, the power and the glory, forever and ever. Amen.

The Lord's Prayer

Muslims praying at the Badshahi Mosque, Lahore, India

I believe in God, the Father almighty, Creator of heaven and earth, and in Jesus Christ, His only son, our Lord, who was conceived by the Virgin Mary, mother of God.

Apostle's Creed

Hear, oh Israel, the Lord our God, the Lord is one.

Jewish Sh'ma

Sentient beings are numberless; I vow to save them. Desires are inexhaustible; I vow to extinguish them. The Dharmas are boundless; I vow to master them. The Buddha-truth is unsurpassable; I vow to attain it.

Buddhist Bodhisattva's Vows

May heaven and earth swell our nourishment; the two who are father and mother, all knowing, doing wondrous work. Communicative and wholesome unto all, may heaven and earth bring unto us·gain, reward and riches.

From the Hindu Rig Veda

Praise be to Allah, Lord of the Worlds, The Beneficent, the Merciful. Owner of the Day of Judgment, Thee alone we worship; Thee alone we ask for help. Show us the straight path, The path of those whom Thou hast favored; Not the path of those who earn Thine anger nor of those who go astray.

The Koran

The Tao that can be told of is not the Eternal Tao. The names that can be named are not the eternal names. The Way of Heaven is to benefit, not to do harm. The Way of the sage is to act without striving.

From the Tao Te Ching

He who offends the gods has no one to whom he can pray.

Confucious' Analects

Fervent prayer is glowing, insistent, and passionate. Fervent prayer does not end; it burns within like fire. Make up your own prayer; find your own God. Pray over and over. Pour your prayer from your belly. Be your prayer.

Prayer conditions by repetition.
Prayer conditions by repetition.
Prayer conditions by repetition.
Prayer conditions by repetition.

ACCESS

Two papers have been written on this subject: "Friend or Traitor: Hypnosis in the Service of Religion," by M. Bowers appeared in the *International Journal of Clinical Experimental Hypnosis* in 1959. J. Runds's "Prayer and Hypnosis" was published in the same journal in 1957.

14 Long times at sea, in the desert, in the arctic

At sea the weather is obvious, it is paramount. High and low pressure rule life with pull and tug, rising and falling. The water becomes a seething paradox, one wave to another, one wave becoming another. Where do the waves go? The color of the sky is the color of water. Or is the color of water the color of the sky?

To sail around the world. To take a boat and leave land and stay only with the water. Our earth is more than three-quarters ocean and sea. Our bodies are water. We need water. We are water.

In the desert there is little water. There is wind. There is sand and heat and brush. Sometimes there is glare and sometimes gloom, and always life. Going to the desert is leaving water behind, deserting the vegetation or the concrete of our prior abode. The desert is one of the great extremes. The desert is where most of the masters go for their ultimate journey before returning to their communities. The desert is the test. When the sun is high the desert is the clear white light.

The clear white light of the arctic regions goes on for days and weeks and months. The arctic is snow and ice. White. No end in sight. Miles and miles of white in the cold. Only the wind and the sky are ever present. There is no year-round life there, save small, wingless insects and the penguin. To live in this environment is to pare down existence to the wind and cold and ice and snow and sky. To be alone. To be. Like the silent Eskimo, sitting, doing nothing in his igloo, waiting for better weather.

I don't believe that the silent Eskimo with impassive face is thinking anything. He's just not "with it" where "it" means all senses, action. . . ."

Edmund Carpenter

ACCESS

W. Gibson's *The Boat,* J. Slocum's *Sailing Alone Around the World,* and E. W. Anderson's article for the *Journal of the Royal Naval Medical Service,* "Abnormal Mental States in Survivors, with Special Reference to Collective Hallucinations" (1942), pretty much cover the experience at sea.

Jesus went to the desert to work it all out, as have many masters before and since. When I asked one of his friends what the former Gestalt therapist Claudio Naranjo was doing in Chile, studying with Oscar Ichazo, I was told that "Claudio is in the desert now for 80 days. He gets an egg and an orange every other day." A similar, but self-directed isolation experience is recounted in Tom Neale's *An Island to Myself.*

C. Byrd's book *Alone* describes an arctic experience, as does Christiane Ritter's *A Woman in the Polar Night.* Edmund Carpenter's classic study is entitled *Eskimo.*

15 Self-hypnosis

Self-hypnosis is an easy and pleasant way to alter consciousness. To induce self-hypnosis an object for the focus of your attention is needed. Anything will do; the best is a candle. Take a candle to a place where you will be comfortable and undisturbed. Light it.

You are going to hypnotize yourself by convincing yourself, through self-suggestion, that you are in a trance. Hypnotic induction also requires the selection of a key word or phrase, for use while you are hypnotizing yourself. Here are some examples:

Deeper
Now
Heavy
Further
I'm relaxed
I'm going deeper
My trance is getting deeper

To begin self-hypnosis, select a comfortable position, either sitting or lying down, and look at the candle. Don't stare at the candle for long periods of time. The purpose of the candle is to provide a centering point so that your consciousness will slip into a trance. As you look at the flame give yourself the following instructions: "I am growing sleepy. My eyelids are getting heavier and heavier. I am sinking away. I can't keep my eyes open." Accompany these instructions with full, deep breathing.

Once your eyes begin to close you are entering the beginning of the hypnotic trance. Now is the time for your key word. The word is used to deepen your trance. Stay with your key word by repeating it as often as you can.

At this stage it is important to relax. As you repeat your key word, send your consciousness to each part of your body. If you find a tight, tensed area, loosen it. Do this until you are in a completely relaxed state. This relaxation deepens and enriches your trance.

Now begin counting backward, slowly, from ten to one. As you count imagine yourself traveling downward deeper into your own self. Let your eyelids become heavy. Concentrate on the different parts of your body. Let each part become very heavy and sink, just as you yourself are sinking, into a deep, deep trance. Your limbs become heavier and you become heavier. Now lighten the different parts of your body. Let your limbs float up and away. You are floating away. Deeper and deeper, further and further, higher and higher.

To end self-hypnosis simply give yourself the instruction, "Now, I will end my trance and wake up." You will wake up feeling fine and refreshed.

You can use self-hypnosis to cope with insomnia, increase your powers of concentration, overcome your bad habits, or just to take a trip. What is most important in self-hypnosis is attitude. Skepticism, negative expectations, and tension will interfere. If you think that hypnosis will be positive, effective and helpful, and that you will be able to enter a trance easily, stay in your trance to accomplish your goals, and end your trance without discomfort, then self-hypnosis is absolutely possible.

In the realm of the mind, whatever we think is true, either is true or becomes true.

John Lilly

ACCESS

The works of Milton Erickson and Bernard Aaronson, in the *American Journal of Clinical Hypnosis,* cover this field very nicely. Tart's book, *Altered States of Consciousness,* has some interesting papers and some good suggestions for further reading. Two good popular books on this subject include *Self Hypnotism* by Leslie LeCron and *Self-Hypnosis by* Laurance Sparks.

Aaronson's paper, "The Hypnotic Induction of the Void," which was presented at the meetings of the American Society of Clinical Hypnosis in San Francisco in 1969, has also been highly praised.

16 Alterations of breathing

Our breath is our life. Air is the first food of the new-born. When we stop breathing our life ends. Breath nourishes the circulatory system and the brain, the seat of the nervous system. When we alter our breathing we alter our consciousness and our life.

Throughout our days our breathing is secondary to our daily concerns for job, family, safety. Breath is in the background. We don't pay attention to our breathing, except in an emergency. People in a burning theater will trample each other because of breathing difficulties. Weights on the chest and diaphragm and swimming under water bring about increased attention to breathing.

To begin conscious and controlled alteration of breathing requires an awareness of the "how" of breathing. Do you inhale through your nose, your mouth, or both? What about exhaling? Pay attention to your breathing for five minutes, and ignore everything but the rhythm and flow of your inhaling and exhaling, the current of your life.

How do you breathe? Is it with your shoulders, chest, ribs, back, or stomach that you breathe? What combinations do you use? When you take a deep breath, *what* do you take? Where does it go? When you inhale *what* do you get? When you exhale what do you lose? What happens in between inhaling and exhaling? Pay attention and find out.

When you breathe too much, too quickly, you lose consciousness. When you breathe too little, too long, you lose consciousness. Either of these alterations of your normal breathing changes the mixture of oxygen that goes to your brain. That mixture is of a delicate balance and to change it subtly or profoundly changes consciousness.

Close your eyes and deeply and fully inhale and exhale five times. Draw the air in through your mouth all the way down, filling your diaphragm, until the breath reaches the pit of your abdomen. When you have brought this air all the way down, pause, and then begin to let the air back up. Make sure that you exhale completely; that all of the air taken in is expired. At the completion of the expiration, pause and then begin the process all over again.

After this experiment, open your eyes and look at your world. Notice the movement, the brightening of colors, the charged atmosphere that surrounds you.

Next, sit in front of a clock or a watch with a second hand. Hold your breath for as long as you can with your eyes open. Once you know how long that is, do it again, but this time hold your breath longer. Now, try the same experiment with your eyes closed. If you are having trouble improving on your time, try watching the sweep of the second hand, or setting yourself a specific goal.

Panting, rapid intake and outbreath, and hissing also change consciousness. When you are breathing correctly you will experience your breath "breathing" you. You don't draw air into your body, nor do you push air out of your body; the air flows in and out of its own volition. In between this inhaling and exhaling are natural pauses. Healthy breathing brings about new consciousness.

The results of these breathing experiments will be an alteration of awareness.

ACCESS

Most of the source material and notes listed under Yoga (No. 145) deal with breathing as a way of altering states of consciousness. Also see "Breathing Therapy" by Magda Proskauer in Otto and Mann's *Ways of Growth*.

17 Trance

To be dazed, to be detached from your surroundings, to be possessed of your own inner state, is to be in a trance. To be absorbed in your own personal world, forsaking the reality of the world at large, is to be in a trance.

In a trance, there is no functioning, no contact. The usual attachments to our senses, our environment, our bodies and our feelings are left behind in a trance. Only inner consciousness is involved in trance.

To the outside observer those in trance appear otherworldly, possessed, occupied by something alien or foreign.

In trance, the channels of communication to the brain seem to be disconnected: information cannot get through.

Stewart Wavell

Who is it then that enters a trance?

ACCESS

The book *Trances*, by Stewart Wavell, A. Butt and N. Epton covers some interesting anthropological aspects of trance.

The word is usually associated with hypnosis, but its meaning in the West is far from clear.

18 Myths, tales and koans

Myths, tales and koans represent man's most direct attempt to encode his wisdom and make it accessible, communicable and durable.

Myths usually involve the exploits of a hero or archetypal character who undergoes interactions and transformations at the hands of a real or imaginary environment.

Tales are narrative descriptions of events, often truthful as well as fictitious, usually in the form of a story—that is, a plot with a beginning, middle, and end.

Koan is the Japanese form of the Chinese word *kung-an*, which means literally, "case," as in a legal case. In the practice of Ch'an and Zen Buddhism, koans refer to stories describing the behavior and the conversations of a Ch'an or Zen master. Here, I use the term "koan" to describe stories relating to the words and activities of various masters in religious groups with a mystical tradition, as well as in groups that have developed methods for altering consciousness. Some of these groups include Ch'an and Zen, the Sufis, and the Hasidim.

"Feng-Huang," the male-female Chinese phoenix

Myth

Herodotus tells us of the myth of a famous bird, the phoenix, known as a creature that rises from its own ashes:

This bird comes but seldom into Egypt, once in five hundred years. It is told that the phoenix comes when his father dies. His plumage is partly gold and partly red and he is most like an eagle in shape and in size.

In Chinese mythology, the phoenix is a bird of great beauty, very much like the peacock. There were two types of phoenix, male and female, *feng* and *huang*. When the phoenix chose to visit the court of an emperor, this was a sign of extreme cosmic favor. When *feng* and *huang* are together it is the symbol of everlasting love.

A Tale

Excerpted from *Andersen's Fairy Tales*, Trans. by E. Lucas and H. B. Paull—Geo. W. Jacobs & Co., Philadelphia, n.d.

The Emperor's New Clothes

Many years ago there was an Emperor who was so excessively fond of new clothes that he spent all his money on them. He had a costume for every hour in the day, and instead of saying as one does about any other King or Emperor, "He is in his council chamber," here one always said, "The Emperor is in his dressing-room."

Life was very gay in the great town where he lived; hosts of strangers came to visit it every day, and among them one day two swindlers. They gave themselves out as weavers, and said that they knew how to weave the most beautiful stuffs imaginable. Not only were the colors and patterns unusually fine, but the clothes that were made of the stuffs had the peculiar quality of becoming invisible to every person who was not fit for the office he held, or if he was impossibly dull.

"Those must be splendid clothes," thought the Emperor. "By wearing them I should be able to discover which men in my kingdom are unfitted for their posts. I shall distinguish the wise men from the fools. Yes, I certainly must order some of that stuff to be woven for me."

He paid the two swindlers a lot of money in advance, so that they might begin their work at once.

They did put up two looms and pretended to weave, but they had nothing whatever upon their shuttles. At the outset they asked for a quantity of the finest silk and the purest gold thread, all of which they put into their own bags while they worked away at the empty looms far into the night. . . .

"I will send my faithful old minister to the weavers," thought the Emperor. "He will be best able to see how the stuff looks, for he is a clever man and no one fulfills his duties better than he does!"

So the good old minister went into the room where the two swindlers sat working at the empty loom.

"Heaven preserve us!" thought the old minister, opening his eyes very wide. "Why I can't see a thing!". But he took care not to say so.

Both the swindlers begged him to be good enough to step a little nearer, and asked if he did not think it a good pattern and beautiful coloring. . . .

"Good heavens!" thought he, "is it possible that I am a fool. I have never thought so, and nobody must know it. Am I not fit for my post? It will never do to say that I cannot see the stuffs."

"Well, sir, you don't say anything about the stuff," said the one who was pretending to weave.

"Oh, it is beautiful! quite charming!" said the minister looking through his spectacles; "this pattern and these colors! I will certainly tell the Emperor that the stuff pleases me very much."

"We are delighted to hear you say so," said the swindlers, and then they named all the colors and described the peculiar pattern. The old minister paid great attention to what they said, so as to be able to repeat it when he got home to the Emperor.

Then the swindlers went on to demand more money, more silk, and more gold, to be able to proceed with the weaving; but they put it all into their own pockets—not a single strand was ever put into the loom, but they went on as before weaving at the empty loom. . . .

Now the Emperor thought he would like to see it while it was still on the loom. So, accompanied by a number of selected courtiers, among whom were the faithful officials who had already seen the imaginary stuff, he went to visit the crafty impostors, who were working away as hard as ever they could at the empty loom.

"It is magnificent!" said the honest officials. "Only see, your Majesty, what a design! What colors!" And they pointed to the empty loom, for they thought no doubt the others could see the stuff.

"What!" thought the Emperor; "I see nothing at all! This is terrible! Am I a fool? Am I not fit to be Emperor? Why, nothing worse could happen to me!"

"Oh, it is beautiful!" said the Emperor. "It has my highest approval!" and he nodded his satisfaction as he gazed at the empty loom. Nothing would induce him to say that he could not see anything. . . .

The Emperor gave each of the rogues an order of knighthood to be worn in their buttonholes and the title of "Gentlemen weavers."

The swindlers sat up the whole night, before the day on which a procession was to take place, burning sixteen candles; so that people might see how anxious they were to get the Emperor's new clothes ready. . . . At last they said: "Now the Emperor's new clothes are ready!"

The Emperor, with his grandest courtiers, went to them himself, and both swindlers raised one arm in the air, as if they were holding something, and said: "See, these are the trousers, this is the coat, here is the mantle!" and so on. "It is as light as a spider's web. One might think one had nothing on, but that is the very beauty of it!". . .

"Will your imperial majesty be graciously pleased to take off your clothes," said the impostors, "so that we may put on the new ones, along here before the great mirror."

The Emperor took off all his clothes, and the impostors pretended to give him one article of dress after the other, of the new ones which they had pretended to make. . . .

"Well, I am quite ready," said the Emperor. "Don't the clothes fit well?" and then he turned round again in front of the mirror, so that he should seem to be looking at his grand things. . . .

Then the Emperor walked along in the procession under the gorgeous canopy, and everybody in the streets and at the windows exclaimed, "How beautiful the Emperor's new clothes are! What a splendid train! And they fit to perfection!" Nobody would let it appear that he could see nothing, for then he would not be fit for his post, or else he was a fool.

None of the Emperor's clothes had been so successful before.

"But he has got nothing on," said a little child.

"Oh, listen to the innocent," said its father; and one person whispered to the other what the child had said. "He has nothing on; a child says he has nothing on!"

"But he has nothing on!" at last cried all the people.

The Emperor writhed, for he knew it was true, but he thought "the procession must go on now," so held himself stiffer than ever, and the chamberlains held up the invisible train.

KOANS

A monk once asked Chao Chou: "Does a dog have the Buddha nature?" [In Buddhism, all sentient beings are possessed of the Buddha nature.] Chao Chou replied: "Wu!" [Wu is Chinese for "no."]

Rabbi Leib, son of Sarah, the hidden zaddik [leader of the Hasidic community] who wandered over the Earth, following the course of rivers in order to redeem the souls of the living and the dead, said this:

"I did not go to the maggid [preacher] in order to hear Torah from him, but to see how he unlaces his felt shoes and laces them up again."

From Buber, Tales of Hasidim, Early Masters

One evening a Sufi dervish was passing when he heard a voice cry out from deep in a well. He looked down into the well and called out: "What is wrong?"

A voice yelled back in reply: "It is me, the grammarian. I did not know my way and in error fell into this well. And now I'm stuck."

The Sufi replied: "Do not worry, dear man. I will go immediately and bring a rope and a ladder."

As the Sufi started to leave, a voice cried up to him: "Oh, sir. Before you go, please correct your grammer. What you said before was improper in its construction."

To this the Sufi responded: "If this grammar is so essential to your well-being, then please stay right there, and I will go and learn to speak correctly."

So saying the Sufi left, and continued on his way.

Derived from Rumi and Shah.

Hsueh Feng, Wen Sui and Yen Tou were sitting together. Wen Sui pointed to a bowlful of water and said: "The moon appears in the clear water."

Hsueh Feng said: "The moon does not appear in the clear water."

Yen Tou kicked over the bowl of water.

From the Lighthouse in the Ocean of Ch'an.

ACCESS

For myths, see Robert Graves' *The Greek Myths;* Joseph Campbell's four-volume *The Masks of God,* and his *The Hero with a Thousand Faces; Bulfinch's Mythology;* and Frazer's *The Golden Bough.*

For tales, look back on the collections of the Grimm brothers; H. C. Andersen; Borges' *The Book of Imaginary Beings;* and T. H. White's *The Bestiary.*

Included under Koans are not only stories of the Ch'an and Zen masters, but also those of Sufism and Hasidim.

For Ch'an and Zen koans: *Zen Dust,* by Miura & Sasaki (also available in an abbreviated version under the title *The Zen Koan*); *Zen and Zen Classics* (Volume Four: *Mumonkan*) by R. H. Blyth; *Original Teachings of Ch'an Buddhism* by Chang Chung-Yuan; *Zen Flesh, Zen Bones* by Reps; *The Blue Cliff Records* by R. D. M. Shaw; *The Embossed Tea Kettle* by Hakuin Zenji; *The Iron Flute* by Senzaki and McCandless; *The Practice of Zen* by Chang Chen Chi; *The Golden Age of Zen* by J. C. H. Wu; *Tai Hsu* by Chou Hsiang Kuang; *Dhyana Buddhism in China* by the same author; John Blofeld's *The Zen Teaching of Huang Po* and *The Zen Teaching of Hui Hai;* and *The Lighthouse in the Ocean of Ch'an* by C. M. Chen. The Sufi tales: the recountings of Idries Shah, *The Sufis; The Way of the Sufi; Tales of the Dervishes; Wisdom of the Idiots; The Exploits of the Incomparable Mulla Nasrudin* and *The Pleasantries of the Incredible Mulla Nasrudin;* also A. J. Arberry's *Sufism.*

Martin Buber collected many stories of the Hasidim in his two-volume *Tales of the Hasidim, Early Masters* and *Later Masters.*

19 Rituals

When men did everything to please their gods, things had to be done the correct way each and every time. This was especially true of ceremonies. Rites of passage, rites of initiation, appeals for an end to a state of ill-health—all of these demanded a form for communicating with the Others. Ritual provided this form, and today still provides access to other, nonordinary states of reality. The exactness of any ritual procedure endows ritualistic action with a very unique spirit. This spirit can be felt in even the most ordinary of circumstances.*

As an experiment, designate a particular time to perform a ritual each week. Stay with this schedule for at least a month. The repetition over that long a period of time will enable the ritual to take on a spirit that will at once surprise, inform, and exhilarate you.

Ingredients might include things such as prayers, incantations, and movements. Other, more material ritual ingredients might include musical instruments, various liquids (preferably of many colors), fabrics, plants and *objets d'art*. Be imaginative and combine these things into an ordered, structured, and repeatable ceremony. This ceremony will be your ritual.

ACCESS

Most social groups, societies, and tribes have special rituals. The Amer-Indians have some really beautiful ones outlined and described in Frank Waters's two books: *Book of the Hopi* and *Masked Gods*. Haile, Oakes, and Wyman provide a detailed description of one Navajo ceremony in *Beautyway*. Frazer's *Golden Bough* provides a good starting point for introductory material.

* A familiar example of a ritual is the school graduation exercise. There are speeches, costumes and music. There are the elders bestowing power on the new initiates; there are the set and prescribed ways of behaving. Recent outbursts and walkouts by students at high school and college graduation ceremonies may have been overlooked during any other time or at any other function of the school year, but the special ritualistic atmosphere of the graduation ceremonies make these departures from expected behavior much more outrageous.

20 Chanting and mantras

Chanting is one of the most effective ways to turn on without drugs. It may take a little more time than some of the other techniques, but it always gets good results.

Chanting is a particular way of making sound with the human voice involving repetition of sound and tone. In some chants each syllable is held for an entire breath; in others a breath is taken only when needed. No matter which way you chant the main idea is to develop your breathing through your chanting. By changing your normal breathing through chanting you will be increasing the oxygen-level of the blood reaching your brain and, thereby, alter your consciousness.

A great chant for Westerners is the chanting of your own name. In his workshops on chanting, Bernard Aaronson instructs the group members to chant their own names: BER—NARD—AAR—ON—SON

Hindus, Buddhists and others chant holy syllables known as mantrum. A very holy mantra, sometimes called the sound of God, is: *OM*.

Mantrum are taken to be the sound of the universe and are chanted for the vibrational quality that they stimulate in the chanter. Chanters and singers on the streets of many American cities have recently made the Hare Krishna chant popular. The chant: *HARE KRISHNA, HARE KRISHNA, KRISHNA, KRISHNA, HARE HARE; HARE RAMA, HARE RAMA, RAMA RAMA, HARE HARE.*

There are also Western mantras. John Kennedy used to chant: *GO! GO! GO! GO! GO! GO! GO! GO!*

There is a chant used to expel evil that comes from the Gnostic tradition. The chant removes one letter with each new intonation. The "s" at the end is always hissed:
ABROXSIS
BROXSIS
ROXSIS
OXSIS
XSIS
SIS
IS
S

LIVE VERY RICHLY YOU HAPPY ONE is based on the *chakras* of Tantric Yoga. The seven *chakras* are energy centers that are located along the spine. Six of the seven centers have a mantra. The seventh and highest *chakra*, the thousand-petaled lotus at the crown of the head, has a silent mantra. The sound of each mantra in this chant is represented by the first letter of each word in the sentence: *LIVE VERY RICHLY YOU HAPPY ONE.*

This chant takes about 30 minutes. Begin by sitting on the floor in a comfortable position. Make sure that your spine and neck are straight and erect. Start chanting the first mantra: *LUM*.

Chant *LUM* for five minutes. As you chant, summon the power from the base of your spine and start it on a journey upward. Remember to take deep breaths and as you chant let the sound continue until you have let out all of your breath. As you chant you will experience the vibratory power of your voice increasing. Fill your body with your chanting.

Now, after chanting *LUM* for five minutes, go on to the next mantra: *VUM*.

Continue chanting this mantra for five minutes. This procedure is repeated for each mantra:

LUM
VUM
RUM
YUM
HUM
OM

After you chant *OM*, start five minutes of silent contemplation. The sound vibrations from the previous chanting will fill the spaces around you with energy. Work to move this energy up your spine through your neck and finally into your head. Your breathing, your vibrations and your energy will turn you on.

ACCESS

Numerous books on chanting are available. See Access for Yoga (No. 145), Buddhism (No. 152), Tibet (No. 148) and Sufism (No. 160).

To listen to chants, the following records are available:
The Music of Tibet, Tantric Rituals (H. Smith) Anthology Records (available through Big Sur Recordings) AST–4005

UNESCO Collection's *Tibet* on three records, BM 30 L 2009, 2010, & 2011

UNESCO Collection's *India* (Volume III), BM 30 L 2018

UNESCO Collection's *Turkey* (Volume I: *Music of the Mevlevi*), BM 30 L 2019

Jilala (North African Sufi chanting ceremony), on Trance Records (available through the Gotham Book Mart)

Sufi Ceremony and Rifa' Ceremony on Folkways FR 8942

Liturgy of the Dervishes on Folkways FR 8943

Mushroom Ceremony of the Mazatec Indians of Mexico on Folkways FR 8975

Music from the Morning of the World (The Balinese Gamelan) on Nonesuch H-72015

An expanded version of the Monkey chant included on the recording above is on *Golden Rain,* Nonesuch H-72028

Buddhist Chant on two records for Lyrichord LL-118

Alan Watts discusses a number of chanting techniques and demonstrates same on his two-record set, *Why Not Now* on Together Records ST-T-2R-1025

The chanting of Baba Ram Dass is available on tapes that may be purchased through Noumedia Co., P.O. Box 750, Port Chester, NY 10573

The Hare Krishna chanters may be heard on *Krishna Consciousness* on the Happening Records label. The chant is on one side with a lecture on chanting by Swami Bhaktivedanta on the other side.

21 Mudra

Mudras are symbols, hand positions created by placing the hands and fingers in certain prescribed ways which represent a variety of metaphysical states or conditions. They were developed as expressions for Hindu and Buddhist ceremonies and are often used in the religious inconography.

Mudra are used by priests at religious ceremonies. Under these circumstances mudra have a highly specialized and ritualistic function, but they can be isolated from their religious setting and used for personal expression and creativity. The use of mudra requires a high degree of discipline. They can bring about unique aesthetic experiences.

The religious uses of mudra provide some 300 separate but often highly repetitive positions for the hands and fingers. There are 14 basic positions which, when varied, yield about 40 differing forms of mudra.

First sit in a chair or cross-legged on the floor with your back straight in a quiet room. Using the illustration provided here, try out some of the mudra positions. Start with the simple, open-handed positions and gradually work your way to the more complex configurations. You will be able to experience the different ways in which mudra affect your consciousness as you let the energy generated by a specific hand position flow through your entire body.

When your right hand is open and raised up by your shoulder and your left hand is placed palm up in front of your stomach, you will feel openness and receptivity. By holding this position for extended periods you will enhance peacefulness and tranquility. Other mudra engender different consciousness experiences. In the beginning use a mirror to see that your position is correct. Hold the position for 60 seconds or so and slowly move to the next.

ACCESS

E. Dale Saunders's *Mudra* is the classic study. It is detailed and easy to read and includes copious references to supplementary material for further study. Many of the books listed under Access for Yoga (No. 145.), Tibet (No. 148.) and Buddhism (No. 152.) also include material on mudra and their use.

22   Religious conversion

To be converted, to be regenerated, to receive grace, to experience religion, to gain an assurance, are so many phrases which denote the process, gradual or sudden, by which a self hitherto divided, and consciously wrong inferior and unhappy, becomes unified and consciously right superior and happy, in consequence of its firmer hold upon religious realities. This at least is what conversion signifies in general terms, whether or not we believe that a direct divine operation is needed to bring such a moral change about. . . .

What brings such changes about is the way in which emotional excitement alters. Things hot and vital to us today are cold tomorrow. It is as if seen from the hot parts of the field that the other parts appear to us, and from these hot parts personal desire and volition make their sallies. They are, in short, the centers of our dynamic energy, whereas the cold parts leave us indifferent and passive in proportion to their coldness. . . .

Now there may be great oscillation in the emotional interest, and the hot places may shift before one almost as rapidly as the sparks that run through burnt-up paper Then we have the wavering and divided self. . . . Or the focus of excitement and heat, the point of view from which the aim is taken, may come to lie permanently within a certain system; and then, if the change be a religious one, we call it a conversion, especially if it be by crisis, or sudden. . . .

Neither an outside observer nor the Subject who undergoes the process can explain fully how particular experiences are able to change one's center of energy so decisively, or why they so often have to bide their hour to do so.

These words, from William James's *The Varieties of Religious Experience*, written during the first year of this century, still best describe religious conversion. The process sweeps everything in its way, changes the Subject and transforms all that the Subject experiences. It is, of course, impossible to summon at will.

ACCESS

In addition to William James's thorough discussion in *The Varieties of Religious Experience,* material is available in Coe's *Psychology of Religion;* Kirkpatrick's *Religion in Human Affairs,* and William Sargant's *Battle for the Mind.* Also see Anton Boisen's *The Exploration of the Inner World.*

23   Spinning (Dervish)

"Prayer has a form, a sound and a physical reality," writes Rumi, the Persian Sufi poet.

The universe is in *all* directions.

Spinning around is guaranteed to turn you on. It is easy to do and, when done correctly, as children do it, spinning is safe.

It is better to spin out of doors. Find a beautiful place where the ground is soft enough to fall on.

Stand still. Start spinning. Feel the beat of your heart. Spin around and around. Spin in a counterclockwise direction, even if you are lefthanded. Use the left foot as the pusher and the right foot as the balance. The Sufi whirling dervishes hold their arms out like wings, with the fingers of their right hands pointing up to the sky to receive energy and grace and the palms of their left hands pointing down to the earth, as a means of dispensing their divine gifts to mankind.

Turkish Sufi whirling dervishes

Use your heart to generate a mystical current, as the Sufis do when they spin for their master.

If you fall down, get back up and keep spinning. If you can't keep spinning, stop. The world will keep spinning around you.

Around and around and around.

ACCESS

For spinning consult your local child.

For Sufi dervish, the sounds have been captured on records referred to in the notes of 20, Chanting and Mudra. The performance of dervish spinning by the Mevlevi Sufi sect, formerly banned by Turkish law, is now legal and tourists can see a two-week-long ceremony in early December in Konya, Turkey. Recently, a troupe of Mevlevi visited and performed in the United States.

24 Extra-sensory perception

Extra-sensory perception (ESP) is attracting more and more interest throughout the world. In the Iron Curtain countries, especially the Soviet Union, governments are underwriting many researchers and scientists who are devising experiments to test ESP results. And here in the West, well-established scientists are delving into the strange world of para-normal phenomena.

ESP is the ability to perceive the environment without, or over and above, the limits of the senses. Most people experience ESP as a strange feeling, often like a hunch or intuition. Along with this feeling comes a knowledge, for example that the next card to be upturned from a deck will be the ace of hearts. That particular type of experience is known as precognition and is one of the easiest of the ESP phenomena to test in the laboratory. These types of tests were performed in the 1920s by J. B. and L. Rhine and their associates. They made up a new deck of cards with five suits, established the statistical probability of guessing which suit would appear at any given time, and then set about testing both normal people and those who claimed to have precognitive abilities.

Testing has continued today and now includes experiments that test for psychokinesis, or the ability to move material with mental power, out-of-body travel, ESP dream influence and the predicting of events.

You can practice ESP yourself and try to develop your own para-normal powers. Devise some of your own experiments but remember to start slowly. Don't try to move the living-room couch with your mind power as an opener. First try the card guessing. With five different cards you should be able to guess right about one out of five cards, and so on. If you seem to do much better than average, try communicating with your friends and relatives by thought power alone and then check out the results. If you have real ESP abilities contact one of the groups referred to in Access and they will submit your talents to rigid scientific testing.

ACCESS

The Parapsychology Foundation is located at 29 West 57th Street, New York, N.Y. 10019. The American Society for Psychical Research is located at 5 West 73rd Street, New York, N.Y. 10023. Dr. Stanley Krippner conducts research into ESP as well as biofeedback and other subjects as the director of the Menninger Dream Laboratory at Maimonides Medical Center in Brooklyn. Some of the results of ESP work in the Eastern European countries are chronicled in Ostrander and Schroeder's *Psychic Discoveries Behind the Iron Curtain*.

25   Visual illusions

Our brains and our eyes constantly compensate for the raw material we perceive in our environment. Our culture adds to the distortions we perceive.

A visual illusion

We see clearly into the distance when we look out on a landscape, but do not when looking down, at objects a shorter distance away, from a very high building or structure. People who live in the forest do not perceive distance at all, since there are only small clear areas in that environment.

The Zulus, who live in a "round" world—with round buildings and round doors and round everyday objects—do not perceive straight lines and their attendant illusions.

Only Westerners, brought up on movies and television, know how to watch a screen full of images by focusing directly *in front* of the screen, rather than looking *at the* screen. People not trained this way see only a portion of what occurs on the screen at any given time. Usually they are not able to integrate what they have seen into any meaningful, organized whole.

The universe is a nonsimultaneous, only partially overlapping energy-pattern event. But we see objects, not energy patterns. The earth revolves in a solar orbit, yet we see the sun "rise" in the morning and "set" in the evening; and man is yet to arrive at a satisfactory explanation of why the moon looks bigger when it rises than it does when it reaches mid-sky. All of these are illusions.

ACCESS

R. L. Gregory's two books, *Eye and Brain* and *The Intelligent Eye,* provide good background material and suggestions for follow-up and further research.

26   Auditory illusions

If seeing is not believing, neither is hearing. Our senses can be manipulated with and without our knowledge.

Perhaps the most astounding examples of auditory illusions come from Richard Warren of the University of Wisconsin. In conjunction with Richard Gregory of Great Britain, a tape that mechanically repeated a word over and over was devised. After listening to the word, which was different for each subject, each heard a word *other than* the word being played. They heard the new word emphatically, and in most cases were sure that it was part of the tape. Actually the new word was supplied by the brain. Bored with hearing the same word over and over, it created its own diversion.

Another Warren experiment replaced part of a word in a sentence with a cough, and then with a tone. Warren then played the tape to subjects and asked them which part of which word had been obscured. The sentence was: "The state governors met with their respective legi(s)latures convening in the city capital."

The "s" was replaced first by the cough, and then by the tone. None of the subjects could hear which letter had been obliterated. Some even insisted that there had been no alteration.

The future of auditory illusions is indicated by one scientist at the Bell Telephone Research Labs in New Jersey. This researcher has been able to make a step-ladder tape of tones, much like the standard "Do Re Mi, . . ." with just one difference. The tone the listener hears at the start of the tape is a higher (register) tone than the last tone on the tape. This is only distinguishable when the first and last tones are played one after another. With the normal tape sequence no subject has yet been able to perceive a difference.

Try and create your own auditory illusions. Make up a sentence that you can recite to friends, in which a letter or word is added or subtracted to a meaningful part of the sentence, much the same way as Warren did on his tape at the University of Wisconsin. See if your friends can hear the difference; ask them what they heard. Another experiment can be to reverse the order of two words in a sentence: "I'm going to dinner eat." See if your friends notice.

Some information on the research now taking place in this field is discussed by Nigel Calder in his book *The Mind of Man*. Richard and Rosalyn Warren's article "Auditory Illusions and Confusions" is the best overall description of current research. Further reading references are provided in *Scientific American, 223,* 6, pp. 30–36, December 1970.

27 Afterimages

Afterimages are the visual sensations that we take from a subject of our sight after we leave it and look elsewhere. Perhaps the most familiar of all the afterimages is the one that occurs when a flashbulb or flashgun is used for artificial lighting. After the bulb explodes, a colored image covers part or all of the visual field of those who were looking at the flash. This image usually persists for several seconds and often changes color.

Other afterimages having to do with bright light come from staring or prolonged observation. Even with a low-watt light bulb an afterimage can be created by allowing the light from the bulb to fill the visual field for a brief period of time. An interesting effect occurs when you do this, but with only one eye, keeping the other closed. After looking away, the afterimage will occur only in the open eye, whereas the eye kept closed will perceive monocularly, with normal vision. The mixture of normal vision and vision obscured by a colored afterimage is most dramatic.

There is a sect in India that spends all day looking at the sun as it moves across the sky. Most of the adherents of this sect eventually go blind. Though staring at the sun will produce afterimages, one does not recommend its practice.

Some people experience a different afterimage: the blur. This is much like the effect achieved when one moves a camera while taking a picture. The easiest way to produce these afterimages is to rapidly spin the head left, right, left, and so on.

28 Repetition

Repetition is one of the most powerful means of altering consciousness without drugs. It is part of many of the methods outlined in this book. Repetition is essential for all chanting, prolonged observation, most prayer, most hypnotic inductions, a variety of body movements, and even brain-wave feedback.

What makes repetition so effective is that whatever image, sound, or exposure is repeated is then apprehended by the observer in a new light. One is enabled to see, hear, taste, smell, feel, or otherwise experience whatever is repeated in new ways. This often leads to an alteration of consciousness.

The other aspect of repetition that makes it powerful is its "overloading" quality. It is often when things become too much for us and for our perceptual and experiential systems that we are finally ready to change. Repetition can help bring about those changes.

29 Psychological exercises

If you keep busy you won't get into trouble. While that may be generally true it usually does not apply to inventing or working on psychological exercises.

Psychological exercises are also known as brainteasers or braintwisters. A. R. Orage, who studied with Gurdjieff and Ouspensky, provides some good directions that one can start on. These are to be done subvocally in the head.

Recite Lincoln's "Gettysburg Address" while counting backward by threes; at the same time say "Peter Piper Picked a Peck of Pickled Peppers," repeatedly.

Make the above exercise more difficult by interspersing the backward number-counting in between every fourth backward-recited word of the Lincoln speech. But do remember to keep repeating Peter Piper, etc. All of this is to be done subvocally, of course.

Orage also suggests compiling lists of things associated with different parts of the earth, different letters of the alphabet, and so on.

At the same time that you are reading a book subvocally say "hello" to every inhalation and "goodbye" to every exhalation. Be careful to maintain the integrity of both tasks at once.

Let all of the letters in the alphabet be represented by a number, e.g., a = 1, b = 2, c = 3, x = 24, y = 25, z = 26; and then say something familiar like: "I do." . . . 9, 4, 15. Now try some more difficult sentences.

It's also lots of fun to invent your own psychological exercises.

ACCESS

A. R. Orage's book, *Psychological Exercises & Essays,* contains over fifty pages of simple, medium, and difficult exercises to twist your psyche. R. D. Laing's *Knots* does the same thing on another level.

30 Mathematics

Mathematics is far more interesting than its symbolic language. It is a set of penetrating and arresting ideas. The art of mathematics can be used as a technique for altering states of consciousness. This fact has not been hitherto observed, although mathematical discoverers have gained their primary intuitions of new findings through states of consciousness altered in this manner. The business of discovery is to venture from the familiar into the unfamiliar and relate the latter to the former by means of already known experience, conceptual or sensory. (To discover is at least 1000 times more difficult than to explain after discovery. The greatest discoveries are not essentially complicated, but they are always unfamiliar, and require intellectual de-conditioning to learn.)

Charles Muses in "Altering States of Consciousness by Mathematics, with Applications to Education," in Muses's The Journal for the Study of Consciousness, 3, p. 43.

What is most important when pursuing mathematics as a means of turning on, is to proceed into the unfamiliar. It is only in this realm that one will encounter the stimuli and imaginary experience necessary for changing concepts of existence. Though problem-solving can be used to turn on (see No. 12) in mathematics it is the voyage into the unknown and the use of mathematics to map the areas investigated and revealed that best contribute to states of altered consciousness.

ACCESS

The *Journal for the Study of Consciousness* regularly publishes articles by Charles Muses and others about the use of mathematics to alter consciousness. Additional material can be found in *Consciousness and Reality: The Human Pivot Point*, edited by Muses and Arthur M. Young.

31 Continuous singing

This technique has been pioneered by La Monte Young and Marian Zazeela, who practice it assiduously. Frequently they travel to India to receive instruction from their singing teacher. You can use their techniques without their extreme dedication. (Other aspects of the work of Young–Zazeela are treated in 230.)

Basically, continuous singing is singing a very exacting series of notes and tones in continuous alternating frequencies. It turns you on, much in the same way that chanting does, by altering your breathing and by the ever-present vibrations of the singing itself.

To begin continuous singing, open your mouth as if you were at the doctor's and he wanted to look at the back of your throat. The doctor might ask you to say: "aaahhh." You begin singing by not only saying "aaahhh," loudly and with force, but then turning that "aaahhh" into as melodious and continuous a song as you are capable of. Don't worry about the aesthetics of your sound in the beginning, just work on the continuity of the singing.

KEEP SINGING!!

Try variations on the tone and quality of your "aaahhh," bringing it up and down the register to the best of your ability. It will take at least twenty minutes of this singing to turn you on. If you really want to think about the potential of this technique, consider the fact that Young and Zazeela try to sing for at least six or more hours each day.

ACCESS

The teacher of Young and Zazeela, Pandit Pran Nath, has a record of his singing entitled *Earth Grove*, on the Douglas label.

32 Zen power yell

The Zen power yell is a fast way to get in touch with your own personal power and energy.

Begin the Zen power yell from a Japanese sitting position: Sit on your knees with your buttocks perched on the heels of your feet. Keep your arms at your sides.

Begin to breathe fully and deeply. Take a deep breath and then exhale. After letting out your breath say: "one." Then take another breath, exhale and say: "two." Repeat through the number five. After saying "five," as you begin to take the next breath bring your hands up, fists clenched, and cross your arms over your chest. Your left fist should be touching your right shoulder and your right fist should be touching your left shoulder.

Continue your breathing-counting cycle to "eight." After saying "eight," take a deep breath, and suddenly: BOUND UPWARD WITH ALL OF YOUR MIGHT, ROARING LIKE A LION!

Throw your arms out forcefully. In that moment you *are* powerful and ferocious.

The Zen power yell is a great way to greet the world in the morning!

33 Poetry

The most turned on language is poetry.
Read poetry aloud.

The beginning of autumn;
The sea and fields,
All one same green.

Basho

If you have form'd a Circle to go into,
Go into it yourself & see how you would do.

William Blake

Think you, of all this mighty sum
Of things forever speaking,
That nothing of itself will come,
But we must still be seeking?

William Wordsworth

> *WHO is*
Nothing. But all of it's
Everything!

Who is nothing   *Hear that!*
Meaning:
The stars sing
Because it's always all right!
So far you've
Not been near except when
You didn't know. Night's day
Was everywhere. No one is
Ever separated from every other
For then the world would die.

And the world does not die!
O Glory, Glory of the Light!

We live one life. *Message ends*

Kenneth Patchen

This snowy morning
*   That black crow*
*   I hate so much . . .*
But he's beautiful

Basho

34   Manual phosphene stimulation

Phosphenes are the "stars" we see before our eyes. We can see them whenever we want by simply rubbing our eyes. Phosphenes are subjective images that are not generated by external visual stimuli. They are produced by the structure of the eye and by the brain.

You don't have to be in the dark to see phosphenes. All you have to do is close your eyes. Spectacular phosphenes can be seen by simply turning your face toward the shower nozzle. The force of the water beating down on the eyelids stimulates a fantastic, full-color "light show."

Phosphene stimulation can be put to work any time, anywhere you can close your eyes. Make sure that your hands are clean. With eyes closed, press your fingertips lightly on your eyeballs near the inside corner of your eyes. Maintaining a steady gentle pressure and motion, rub for about five seconds. You will begin to see "stars." Light pressure creates circular forms like mandalas. More pressure will create more intricate patterns, like spider webs.

May all your eyelid movies be spectaculars.

ACCESS

Gerald Oster's article "Phosphenes," in the February, 1970 (Volume 222, Number 2) issue of *Scientific American* gives a complete review of the field, with references for further reading.

**A phosphene image
as painted by Gerald Oster**

Negative techniques

BE QUIET!

You take your language sounds for granted. The easiest way to find out how deeply you are dependent on words is to go without speaking for more than twelve hours. An easy way to turn on is to be silent for two days.

This means: No talking, no moaning, no squeaking, no sounds at all.

"[Buckminster Fuller] spent two years silent after illusory language got him in trouble, and he returned to human communication with a redesigned instrument," writes Stewart Brand in the *Whole Earth Catalog*.

You may return to communication with your own redesigned instrument but you must really *be* silent.

You might decide never to speak again. Meher Baba started a silence in 1925 that continued until he died in 1969. He often referred to the fact that all the other avatars came with a verbal message that man always ignored. Meher Baba was silent to avoid this pitfall.

ACCESS

John Cage's book *Silence*.

36 Suffering

Suffering does as much to change the life of human beings as almost anything else. Most of us do not like to suffer; those who do, seek it with a passion and explore its every contingency.

Suffering forces us to reassess our place, position, goals, aims, ways, value, worth and direction. Suffering brings about transformation. Suffering forces change.

When we are suffering mentally we are irritated and incomplete. But this suffering, this incompleteness can be the impetus to finding a new situation for ourselves. Suffering demands relief, new environments, new supports. Physical suffering is characterized by pain, and often demands that "new environment" called death.

37 Pain

Pain is any system's resistance to a stimulus. Every one has and will continue to experience pain. The intensity of the pain experienced will be modulated by the degree of resistance with which a system encounters the pain-producing stimuli.

This systemic production of pain through resistance is fully revealed during Structural Integration or Rolfing. Whenever muscles are being manipulated to the point of pain, that pain is reduced when one can open up the muscle and let the manipulation proceed.

Some people are truly turned on by pain. This is usually connected, in very complicated ways, to philosophies of self-suffering. Many people experience sexual pleasure through pain, even ecstatic pleasure. There are different types of pain: dull, sharp, quick, long-lasting. Each of these types bring different experiences. Quick, sharp pain brings about an increase in adrenalin and causes shallow breathing, whereas long, dull pain usually promotes listlessness and depression.

Initial pain brings awareness of systemic resistance. Continuous pain dulls awareness.

ACCESS

The works of the Marquis de Sade are essential. Some of his most important observations are contained in *120 Days of Sodom, Justine, Philosophy in the Bedroom* and *Juliette.*

38   Forbidden activities

KILL! KILL! KILL! is a mantra recently used in training some of the armed forces of the United States. The effectiveness of this training is achieved in part because of the thrill that one can fantasize participation in a forbidden activity. Killing is one such forbidden activity. Many soldiers go on to actually kill other human beings, many don't. Nonetheless, the training situation encourages the trainees to fantasize the experience of killing.

Earlier in evolutionary development, killing was an essential part of everyday carnivorous existence. As the evolutionary journey has progressed, social organization has segregated most killing in slaughter houses and other such institutions, thus removing it from everyday life. What remains is killing usually done by high-powered weapons and crimes of emotion (knifings and beatings). Those crimes committed with guns involve a killer who is already once removed from his prey:

The distance at which all shooting weapons take effect screens the killer against the stimulus situation which would otherwise activate his killing inhibitions. The deep, emotional layers of our personality simply do not register the fact that the crooking of the forefinger to release a shot tears the entrails of another man.
from On Aggression *by Konrad Lorenz*

ACCESS

Ed Sanders chronicles the forbidden activities of Charlie Manson and his gang in the book *The Family.*

39   Rage

We are taught to express our anger but not to express it directly. But rage, total anger, can be good for us. For example, when a man is criticized by his boss, social convention and fear of job loss demand that he not respond with what he is really feeling, anger. The result of such a situation is usually displacement: the man's wife, relative, or friend is the target for retaliation instead of the boss. Suppressing anger can be dangerous and self-destructive. As with pain, there is an anger threshold that can be tolerated without expression before a breakout is precipitated.

Most of us resist the expression of our anger because we fear our own (albeit imaginary) omnipotent destructive power. Our central catastrophic fantasy is that if we ever got really angry we'd do something terrible, something so unforgivable that we would end up in serious trouble.

A safe way to experiment with anger is to arrange to get angry at a time when you can be alone or with people you trust. Then you can try getting really angry with an inanimate object, say a pillow, so that you won't hurt it and it won't hurt you. Make believe the pillow is your boss, enemy, friend, parent, teacher, child or whoever stirs your wrath and then let the pillow have the full force of your fury. This can be a means toward both physical release and emotional catharsis. You might find your anger is more manageable than you had allowed yourself to believe.

40 Paranoia

Are you sure? Can you ever really know? I could have sworn they were talking about *you!* Wasn't that your name, just then? . . .

And so it goes, sometimes, it seems forever. Several years ago, Laura Archer Huxley brought out a very fine little book containing some simple but profound recipes for experiencing the fullness of being alive. The only problem was the title: *You Are Not The Target.*

The fact is that you *are* the target! The entire universe is a plot that is keeping you alive. Keep in mind that for every intricate scheme that you know about, someone, somewhere, is plotting something even more heinous; and the focus of the plot is you.

What was that noise? Are they whispering? Who's there?

The Dragon of Heresy from a Swiss drawing, 1521

Positive paranoia

Most paranoia concerns delusions of persecution, but positive paranoia exhibits delusions of grandeur. This kind of paranoia is often confused with telepathy and mind reading. You're driving down the highway on the 7th of July 1977, at 7:07 in the morning and you know that the car in front of you will have a license plate with sevens in it and be carrying seven passengers. And since seven is your lucky number you know that today is the day for you to realize all of your dreams. Everything that happens to you is part of a benefic plot, a grand scheme so marvelous that it's hard for you to believe it's happening to you.

41 Panic

Let it all go. Flip out. Panic. All of your catastrophic expectations just came true. There is nothing you can do about it. How can you keep calm at a moment like this? The only thing left to do is to panic: utterly and completely.

It's often the perfect way to handle a situation. If someone else is around then he becomes the helper and takes care of you. If there's cause for true panic on your part he'll enjoy taking care of you. It will keep him from panicking.

Don't indulge yourself in panic when you're alone.

42 Neurosis

Most civilized people are neurotic. Neurosis concocts special combinations of a number of experiences, including:

anxiety
fear or phobia
paranoia
suffering (without proper cause)
avoidance
inability to perceive the obvious
conflicts
obsessive-compulsive behavior
vacillation of will
nervousness

Neurosis can be treated in a variety of ways, some of which are explored in this book.

43 Psychosis

Psychosis includes schizophrenia, catatonia, hebephrenia, manic-depressive states and other conditions often referred to as madness. Society thinks of psychosis in an extremely negative way. This view protects society from the potential harm of psychotics, but does little to aid the psychotic. Often the institutionalizing of a psychotic only fixes the patient in his psychotic behavior. Recently, the theories of R. D. Laing, David Cooper, Aaron Esterson and others have suggested that madness may be the only possible adaptative response to what the psychotic believes to be an intolerable or unmanageable situation. Laing has set up an institution that he calls a *blow-out center*, where people can receive alternative treatment for psychotic experiences.

The usual treatment for psychosis is hospitalization, sedation and tranquilizing drugs. The increasing reliance on pharmacological mood manipulation often encourages a psychotic to stagnate in his illness. At Laing's center an individual is encouraged to work through feelings of madness without being drugged. Often such behavior as shouting and infantile regression is nurtured so as to allow the patient to be able to have some experience of his own sickness. By using this positive reinforcement, Laing believes that a psychotic may then be able to see his own situation with greater clarity and change his response from psychosis to other alternative forms of behavior.

Each a fuse to set you off . . . If I could turn you on, if I could drive you out of your wretched mind, if I could tell you I would let you know.
        from The Politics of Experience by R. D. Laing

ACCESS

The works of R. D. Laing, especially *The Divided Self, The Politics of Experience, Self and Others,* and *Knots* are most enlightening reading. All of the books comment on, discuss, and make suggestions about the psychotic experience.

44 Amnesia

Amnesia is the neurotic experience of losing a portion or the whole of one's memory. It is usually connected with a fright and flight process. That is, one experiences trauma, and in an attempt to block the damaging effects of the trauma, the memory of the event and possibly the events leading up to and following it are totally lost to recall. This often results in lapses of identity.

Aldous Huxley was able to produce amnesia experiences at will by inducing a light trance. This led to his experiencing selective rather than total amnesia. One example was when he induced a light trance and sat in his arm chair. The mailman came, rang Huxley's doorbell and delivered a special delivery letter. When Huxley's wife returned later, found the letter, and questioned him concerning its arrival, Huxley had no memory of what had transpired. He was able to do this in a variety of different situations. He found that when he attempted to evoke total amnesia he found himself in a deep trance and thereby curtailed in physical activities.

ACCESS

Huxley describes his experiences in Tart's book *Altered States of Consciousness*.

45 Exhaustion

To exhaust and deplete one's resources brings about altered states of consciousness. True exhaustion often causes physical collapse, hallucinations, apparitions, etc. Often present are feelings of disorientation and tension. Most people experience exhaustion because of overwork. Other ways to bring on an exhausted state are fasting and sleep deprivation.

46 Delirium of high fevers

Delirium of high fevers is a naturally occurring altered state of consciousness. Although many people run very high fevers during illnesses and still do not experience delirium, others do so at temperatures as low as 102° F.

One young boy who became delirious with scarlet fever ran a temperature in excess of 104° for almost two weeks. He began to speak to his parents as though he were wandering through a dream. He did not recognize them and he seemed to be talking about a peculiarly personal world of his own. He complained that the objects he touched, the sheets and tissues, the thermometer, hurt him and felt like pins and needles.

His sense of size was distorted. Things that he thought were small, like his toys, seemed as big as the whole room, while things that he thought of as large, like his father, seemed to him very tiny. He often responded to voices that only he could hear. Another perceptual distortion was in his experience of time. His mother would leave him alone for five minutes and he would think that she had been gone hours, while at other times, hours were kaleidoscoped into mere seconds.

Though not everyone who experiences delirium goes through visual, auditory, tactile and time-flow hallucinations, these perceptual alterations are part of many deliriums.

ACCESS

Hudson Hoagland describes his wife's delirious fever experiences in *The Voices of Time* (ed. J. T. Fraser).

47 Epileptic seizure

The convulsive brain-initiated seizures of epilepsy are one of the purest forms of possession. However, most often the victim of the seizure is not conscious or aware in any way of what is happening to him.

48   Migraine

Migraines are recurring headaches of great severity and pain. Usually they are of psychosomatic origin and are experienced in a localized area of the head. This localization takes place because migraines only occur in either the left *or* the right cerebral hemisphere.

Just prior to the onset of a migraine a specific visual pattern appears. It is often in the form of a sweeping arc or of a honeycomb design; most of the patterns formed are hexagonal.

ACCESS

See Whitman Richards's "The Fortification Illusions of Migraines," in *Scientific American*, May 1971.

49   Narcotic withdrawal

Kicking junk (withdrawing from addiction to heroin or other narcotics) is a special kind of hell. It lasts for seventy-two consecutive hours. Although drugs are required to bring about addiction, no drugs are necessary for withdrawal. In fact, it is the very absence of drugs that brings on withdrawal. Withdrawal itself is made more severe when no sedatives or pain-killers are available to ease the body pains, sweating, nausea, convulsions, and chills.

Barbiturate addiction is much more severe than heroin addiction, as is its withdrawal. Both the addiction and withdrawal are characterized by hallucinations, delirium, disorganization, and motor dysfunction.

Narcotic withdrawal, Bronx, New York

50 Demonic possession

To be possessed by the devil: to fly through the night-time sky, to feel another move your limbs, to feel the other in your mind. To know the other. Not all bad. Not all good. Demons may take you to death or to renewed life.

Most primitive societies have some possession-like contact with demonic spirits. The actual possession by these spirits comes about through a form of ritualistic cultural hypnosis. In primitive societies, the demonic spirits are often ancestors or animal spirits. The village elders often speak of these spirits, and demonic possession is often considered a privileged state.

**The Horned Dragon of Hell,
Paris, 19th Century**

ACCESS

Aldous Huxley's *The Devils of Loudun* treats the subject well. It has also been made into a movie. A. H. Neal's *Jungle Magic* and Milo Rigaud's *Secrets of Voodoo* treat other aspects of possession.

51 Self-flagellation

Self-flagellation means doing yourself in, beating yourself, trying to cause yourself pain, mutilating your body. Essentially it is a schizoid experience. One must divide to become the inflictor and the victim; the sadist and the masochist within the same man.

There are many ways to accomplish the deed: hitting, beating, whipping, biting, burning, cutting, ripping, shredding, piercing, sewing, binding, scratching, stretching, tearing, etc.

There are some positive uses of self-flagellation, the most prevalent today being the beating of the body in hot baths in order to stimulate blood circulation.

The *Penitente* group, near Sante Fe, New Mexico, incorporates self-flagellation into their religious rituals and practices. Members of the groups flagellate themselves with tree branches in order to experience religious feelings that will help to cleanse and make them acceptable to God.

ACCESS

Self-flagellation is often thought to be an indication of the close relationship between sadism and masochism. The Marquis de Sade may have been the most famous example of this. Jean Paulhan, in his introduction to de Sade's *Justine*, argues the point that de Sade was projecting himself into his masochistic heroine.

52 Fire-walking

Fire-walking and related acts such as sitting on beds of nails, walking across glass, and so forth, are usually performed in a trance.

A good example is the rite of *Anastenarides,* held each May in Northern Greece. In this rite the ecstatic fire-walkers step out onto the red-hot coals. Examination of the soles of their feet shows no burns or other markings one would expect to find on flesh that has just touched fire.

These feats of physiological self-regulation are characteristic of the ecstatic states wherein other internal and external functions are controlled. Often, observers of these phenomena are moved to participate. The results run about half and half. Half participate with no ill aftereffects; half are severely burned, cut, or otherwise injured.

ACCESS

E. S. Thomas's paper, "The Fire Walk," was published in the *Proceedings of Social Psychological Research* in 1934. George Megas of the University of Athens has done further research in this field. In Greece, in May, the festival of *Anastenarides* features public performances of fire-walking. Consult the Greek National Tourist Office for specific details. Also see *Trances* by Wavell, Butt, and Epton.

53 Fasting

Fasting can be used in both positive and negative ways. Going without eating can definitely serve the faster by purging and cleansing the body of accumulated poisons and fatty deposits. Most humans carry a good deal of usable energy around with them, energy never used until smaller food intake forces the breakdown of those deposits.

The normal period for cleansing the body is about 30 days. However, this time period varies from person to person, depending on general state of health, body type, and other factors. A cleansing fast is one during which the faster drinks some kind of nutritious liquid (i.e., fruit juice or bouillon) each day. However, infections present in the body will grow during a fast and could become dangerous. Always consult a doctor and have a *complete* physical examination before starting a fast.

The negative aspect of fasting is starvation and levels of malnutrition leading to that state. Just how long one has to fast to die depends on the individual and his state of health. At this writing, Dick Gregory, the author and comedian, has been fasting for well over a year and is still alive, making public appearances. He takes vitamin pills and liquids, mainly fruit juices.

Contrary to popular belief, a good fast can go on for many days if the faster is in comfortable, supportive surroundings, and has access to medical attention should he need it. The sensation of hunger usually departs after the first three days. It is then that a film forms over the tongue and parts of the inside of the mouth.

While fasting, alterations of a variety of sensory functions occur. Vision can be slightly impaired by susceptibility to illusions and hallucinations. A feeling of seeing things with extraordinarily enhanced color and depth also spontaneously occurs, after four days.

The sense of smell, so powerful in animals, is regained at heightened power in the fasting human being. Odors, usually relegated to background sensory experience, become paramount.

Another phenomenon experienced during long fasts is the "taste hallucination." Here the faster will vividly perceive the tastes of certain foods or spices that he has no real contact with. Many people fast with regularity and find its cleansing characteristics quite beneficial. Some, of course, fast because they have no choice.

Many societies incorporate fasting into seasonal life. A good example is the Hunza group near Pakistan. Renee Taylor discusses their techniques in her book, *Hunza Health Secrets*. A good book on the general aspects of the fast is Arnold Ehret's *Guide to Rational Fasting*.

54 Sleep deprivation

Most of us remember some disc jockey who went for several days without sleep as a publicity stunt, or a comedian running the charity telethon for days on end without a nap.

One disc jockey went without sleep for 230 hours. The record for wakefulness is 268 hours (11 days and nights), set by a California high-school student in a controlled experiment.

After about 70 hours it becomes difficult to do any normal, easy tasks without errors. After somewhere between 30 and 60 hours, depth perception becomes disturbed; after some 90 hours, hallucinations usually set in. After more than 100 hours, the alphabet and other things we "know by heart" become extremely difficult to remember clearly; after 120 hours, delirium; and 150 hours brings about the onset of total disorientation. It is in the later hours that brain waves resemble those of deep-sleep brain waves, even though the non-sleeper might still seem to be awake. Somewhere between the second and fourth day the body begins producing psychochemicals that bear structural resemblance to LSD.

Age most affects the ability to go without sleep. It does not affect the period of sleeplessness; after four days sleeplessness is hell for anyone. But young people respond better, after completing the sleepless period, than do their elders. The boy who set the 268 hour record was only 17 years old at the time. He needed just 14 hours' sleep after his ordeal, although scientists could still detect aftereffects for ten days after the completion of the project.

ACCESS

Sleep and *Insomnia*, both by Gay Gaer Luce, detail sleep deprivation and provide further references.

55 Involuntary isolation

This usually happens when nature (storms, etc.) or man-made errors (blackouts, elevator failures, etc.) conspire to trap an individual in a place he'd rather not be.

In an elevator, the walls close in after a few hours, as the feelings of claustrophobia increase. Situations like this often engender paranoid fantasies, and sometimes psychotic breakdowns.

Blinding snowstorms are often responsible for the hallucinations of trapped drivers or walkers. Men trapped in mines are also known to have experienced altered vision.

Fantasy, sleep, dreaming and sex

56 Fantasy and daydreaming

We all have fantasies and we all daydream. Our social structure does not now encourage constructive daydreaming or creative uses of fantasy and the material that fantasy produces.

An important part of the daydreaming process is the ability to let go, to go with the currents of the imagination and allow to emerge whatever will emerge. When we were caught daydreaming at school we were always criticized for not paying attention. Teachers didn't inquire into the content of daydreams. Yet the dreams we dreamt were often quite relevant to the lesson for the day.

Our daydreams and our fantasies contain many keys to our future life. On the creative side, spontaneous material that is germane to our current relationships and projects often becomes available to us in an "idle" daydream. By consciously indulging in fantasy we can tap hidden resources and release material that might not be available to us in most social situations. Daydreaming and fantasy have a great advantage in that they are always private activities. There is no way that this privacy can be invaded, short of mindreading or the as yet unknown thought police.

Fritz Perls, the formulator of Gestalt Therapy, discusses the use of fantasy as the main way to rehearse for our roles in future activities. This rehearsal can be used to avoid real action. It may produce catastrophic expectations which can freeze our ability to truly *be*.

The systematic use of fantasy in psychotherapy has been shown in the work of R. Desoille. Desoille uses a series of daydreams that he feels help to link the fantasy-creator to his or her creative collective unconscious. (The collective unconscious was postulated by C. G. Jung in his development of analytical psychology. The collective unconscious refers to a repository for universal symbols, or archetypes, that all human beings may draw upon. See Analytical Psychology, No. 95.)

Desoille gives his patients six different situations and asks them to act these situations out, internally, through their own fantasies. The series of daydreams includes:

1. The identification with the sexual symbol: the sword for the male and the ball for the female.

2. A journey to the bottom of the ocean.

3. A journey to the cave of the witch.

4. A journey to the cave of the wizard.

5. A journey to the cave of the mythical beast.

6. The reliving of the patient's own version of the sleeping beauty legend.

Fantasies and daydreams have long been rich source material for stories and tales. Writers often depend on their ability to fantasize within a given, highly structured situation. In this way a plot can be carried through an entire work of fiction.

If you have children and you read them stories, try making one up yourself. Also, ask your children to tell *you* a story. That way you will be able to see how in touch children are with their daydreams and fantasies.

ACCESS

Psychosynthesis, by Roberto Assagioli, outlines and details many specific techniques for fantasy development and discusses some of the formulations of Desoille. Jerome Singer has published a book on *Daydreaming.*

57   Remembering and reverie

Those who do not remember the past are condemned to relive it.

George Santayana

The only place we ever live, in time, is the present. Though the importance of living in the here-and-now has recently gained more acceptance, many often lose sight of what the here-and-now is made of: the fabric of our ongoing experience.

Living in the present means not just paying attention to what goes on around us, but realizing that present awareness includes memories of the past and anticipation of the future. Those who fail to live in the present (figuratively, that is; it is impossible to live elsewhere) and attempt to live in the past cannot distinguish between memory as part of present experience and memory as a retreat to a past more real than the present.

Remembering is the essence of knowing. We remember everything, but we are in touch only with selective memories. A Canadian neurophysiologist, Wilder Penfield, has electronically stimulated certain areas of the brain and has had subjects report the experience of the past as though it were happening again. The reason we do not tap our full memory-resources is mainly due to selective protective processes in our psychological make-up. It is similar to not actively experiencing all of the data our senses are receiving all of the time. This kind of overloading, like memory overloading, usually proves to be too much to handle. Certain psychedelic drugs as well as some techniques for altering consciousness without drugs stimulate greater contact with both sensory input and memory storage.

Memory is usually activated analogously. That is, when we see something it reminds us of something else which then activates a memory. This leads to the selective application of memory data to present situations. However, this type of memory use very rarely brings about changed consciousness, except for extraordinarily strong analogous responses, such as the *déjà vu* sensation. (See Déjà Vu, No. 76.)

What will help to alter consciousness is the select and complete use of all memory cues for a given situation. We very rarely take the time out to try to use our memory to completely re-create a special incident or event in our lives. Even when we do, we often neglect very important information regarding the sensory en-vironment at the time of the event, though occasionally this material presents itself spontaneously.

Pick an event about which you have strong feelings and memories. Re-create it with your memory and through the use of controlled reverie, remembering very explicit details that relate to the selected event. This means remembering all of your sensory sensations: what you saw, tasted, heard, smelled and touched at that time. Be as thorough as possible. When you picture the situation, visualize the furniture or the terrain and re-capture the feelings it brought out.

Emotional response is a tremendous key to memories. If you can recapture the feelings you had in those moments the experience will be much more realistic.

This technique can be applied to all types of experiences: good, bad, exciting, dull, tense and excruciating.

Reverie is usually an attempt to recapture the pleasures of the past.

ACCESS

Exercise 5 in *Gestalt Therapy* (by Perls, Hefferline and Goodman) deals with ways to get in touch with the forces of remembering. Tart's book *Altered States of Consciousness* includes a number of discussions of remembering during altered states of consciousness. Harmon Bro's *High Play* contain specific instructions for exercises that use reverie to produce altered states of awareness.

58 Lullabies

For most of us, lullabies are our first exposure to hypnotic techniques of altering consciousness. The use of repetition (much like mantras) and the soothing tones combine to bring about a trance state: sleep.

If a lullaby was used to lull you off to sleep in your childhood, see if it still has any of its magic power left.

ACCESS

An article in *MD* magazine, 9, 1965, pp. 177–190, details the effects of lullabies in reference to "Music and Medicine."

59 Hypnagogic phenomena (drowsiness before sleep)

Most people have experienced the hynagogic state: it is that state of limbo just before you fall asleep where you are neither awake nor asleep. This state is characterized by images, visions, conversations, mentally created events that we do not consciously generate or manipulate. They occur quite spontaneously.

Many people claim that they never experience this phase of consciousness, while others actively seek it for the free-flowing creative consciousness brought into play during this special drowsiness. Many people, including scientists, inventors, artists and others, report that they get many of their best ideas during their hypnagogic experiences.

Charles Tart has devised a relatively easy way to tap the hypnagogic phenomenon. Lie down on your back and let yourself start to drop off into the hypnagogic state prior to sleep. But keep your arm in the air by bending it at the elbow. This way, when you start to really drop into the state of sleep the muscles of the arm will totally relax causing the arm to fall. This will wake you up. Then you can start the procedure again, from the beginning. With some practice you will soon be able to remember what transpires during the hypnagogic state.

Try for yourself. Be aware of what happens to you in the hypnagogic state. It is possible that you might find some interesting images based on your experiences of the day or suddenly see your experiences in a new perspective. Or you might suddenly arrive at a solution to a problem that has been disturbing you.

ACCESS

Tart's book *Altered States of Consciousness* includes an entire section devoted to reports on hypnagogic phenomena. The two articles in that section provide further references, as does Tart's introduction to the subject.

60 Sleep

We all spend one-quarter to one-third of our entire lives in sleep. Sleep eventually dominates any kind of experience. There is no way to escape it. There is no way to live without it for more than a week or so. (See Sleep Deprivation, No. 54.)

When life becomes unendurable sleep is the escape possible for all men.

Gay Gaer Luce

Most of us know nothing of who we are and what we do when we are asleep. Considering how much attention we give to various aspects of our waking life it is astounding how we ignore the life of sleep.

What happens when we go to sleep?

ACCESS

The entire subject of sleep is covered thoroughly and readably by Gay Gaer Luce's two books, *Sleep* and *Insomnia*. Both books include copious references and complete bibliographies to aid further work in this area.

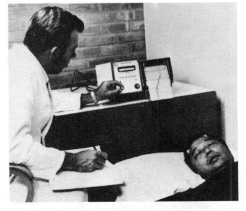

A subject in a sleep experiment, NASA

61 Dreaming

When you go to sleep you dream. There are at least five periods of dreaming that occur during each night's sleep. The dream periods are almost always characterized by rapid eye movements (REM) even though the lids remain closed.

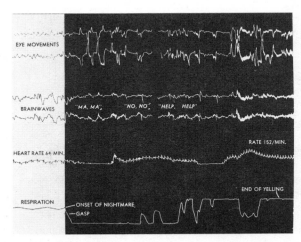

Tracings from sleep-monitoring equipment of a nightmare

More vivid than the greatest movies, dreams are great enigmas. All of us dream even if we don't remember having dreamt. When we don't remember dreaming, it usually means that we awoke from a state of non-rapid eye movement sleep (NREM). If we awaken from REM sleep we should have some memory of the act of dreaming if not of the dream itself.

Freud and others believed that dreams were a key to the past. Perls and others held that dreams were an existential message about the present. For more than 4,000 years many men have believed that dreams bear messages about the future. (An interesting side note on dreams about the future: the *Dream Registry*, a repository for the documentation of prophetic dreams, had received many dream reports that foretold disaster for the Apollo XIV flight; it was safely completed in February of 1971.)

Dreams can be so vivid that the valves of memory seem to have opened the entire life history of a person, down to the smallest details of smell and touch.

Gay Gaer Luce

Dreaming is a universally known altered state of consciousness, for we all do many things in our dreams that we might never even "dream" of attempting while awake.

The Dutch physician Frederik van Eeden wrote a study of dreaming that was published in 1913. Recently rediscovered by Charles Tart, van Eeden's paper divides dreams into nine experientially distinct types:

1. *The initial dream:* a dream that occurs just after sleep takes over from hypnagogic imagery.

2. *The pathological dream:* a dream occurring during high fever or other disturbed states.

3. *The ordinary dream.*

4. *The vivid dream:* a dream that leaves lasting impressions of a vivid nature with the dreamer.

5. *The symbolic* or *mocking dream:* dreams of an occult or "demoniacal" nature.

6. *The dream-sensations dream state:* a dream where the normal images and events do not occur, but the dreamer awakens knowing he or she has been occupied with one person, one place, etc.

7. *The lucid dream:* a dream where the dreamer is aware that he or she is dreaming, though this awareness does not interfere with the dream, but rather augments it.

8. *The demon dream:* a dream nightmare where the demon causing or perpetrating the dream action is seen clearly.

9. *The wrong waking-up dream:* a dream where the dreamer dreams that he or she has awakened, only to discover that the waking up is only part of the dream.

Tart has added another dream: *the high dream.* In the high dream the dreamer is aware that he is dreaming and is also aware that he is experiencing an altered state of consciousness, much like the kind brought on by taking psychedelics or by using certain techniques described in this book.

ACCESS

Luce's book *Body Time* provides detailed data and discussion. Tart's section on dreaming in *Altered States of Consciousness* is one of the best in the book.

62 Control of dreaming

When we sleep during a thunderstorm we might awaken from a dream where the last thing experienced was an enormous, ear-filling noise. The first thing to occupy our consciousness upon awakening will be the receding noise from a clap of thunder. What we have done in this case is to incorporate the stimulus into the dreaming experience. That stimulus controlled, to some extent, the content of the dream. A more frequently occurring experience of this type is the incorporation of the sound of an alarm clock.

Many other stimuli also control our dreaming. What we wear to bed, how it has moved about our bodies during the night, and the general condition of the bedcovers can all alter and greatly affect the content and flow of events in our dreaming. Whenever someone talks to us while we are asleep, whether to see if we are asleep, to awaken us, to annoy us, or whatever, their words are generally made part of any ongoing dream. It is interesting when the words are changed by the dream state. This means that the original sound remains but the dream turns the specific terms into something more fitted to the flow of the dream events. Often, the stimulus presented to the dreamer turns up in the dream in symbolic form. This often occurs if the dreamer hears a familiar name.

A way to control the content of dreaming is to control the stimuli that you are exposed to just before going to sleep. If you carefully examine pictures of galaxies, and think about dreaming about galaxies, chances are that you might have dreams of galaxies and stars. Another way is to induce a self-hypnotic trance and give posthypnotic instructions about dream content while still in the trance.

Experimenters have shown that by taking yourself out of social contact for at least 24 hours, you will greatly increase the amount of social intercourse that occurs during dreaming. In general, then, control of the environment prior to sleep will greatly alter the content of dreams.

An interesting experiment is to attempt to self-program the control of dreams. This would include using not only environmental controls and the programing of pre-sleep stimuli, but would also attempt to raise the level of awareness of the dreaming state. Simple pre-sleep suggestion to the effect that you, as a dreamer, will have lucid dreams (see Dreaming, No. 61), dreams where you are aware that you are dreaming, can be employed. Be careful not to program in effects which will disrupt your dreaming.

We must have a certain minimum amount of dream sleep during each sleep period in order to stay healthy.

A good way to remember and record your dream life is to give yourself the suggestion, before you go to sleep, that you will awaken when you complete a dream. Upon awakening, write down the content, symbols, and feelings of your dream on a pad that you have placed by your bedside. Another possible technique is to give yourself the pre-sleep suggestion that you will remember your dreams in the morning. Try this for at least a week. Many people are capable of doing this, providing they give themselves adequate time to absorb their own self-suggestions.

63   Dreams applied to waking life

There are various applications of dreams to the activities of waking life. I will briefly discuss two of them. Fritz Perls, in Gestalt psychotherapy, particularly liked to work with patients on their dreams:

I believe that in a dream, we have a clear existential message of what's missing in our lives, what we avoid doing and living, and we have plenty of material [in the dream] to re-assimilate and re-own the alienated parts of ourselves.

In Gestalt Therapy we don't interpret dreams. We do something much more interesting with them. Instead of analyzing and further cutting up the dream, we want to bring it back to life. And the way to bring it back to life is to re-live the dream as if it were happening now.

. . . write the dream down and make a list of all the details in the dream. Get every person, every thing, every mood, and then work on these to become each one of them. Ham it up, and really transform yourself into each of the different items.

Next, take each one of these different items, characters, and parts, and let them have encounters between them. Write a script. [Not literally, but figuratively: provide motivation and action.]

Besides using improvised psychodrama techniques à la Rashomon (with each character having his own version of the same event), Perls also used a short cut; this involved finishing what was left unfinished in the action of the dream. An example: if the dream involves a character who is about to start an action, but the dream ends before any action is initiated, Perls would have the dreamer, when working on the dream, complete the action while reliving it in the here-and-now.

Perls believed that the dream has a direct relevance to the dreamer's present life situation. He felt this is true also of repetitive dreams. Since he used all the elements of a given dream in the work on the dream, Perls could work easily with complete dreams, unfinished dreams, and even dream fragments.

Unknown to Perls until the later years of his life, was the fact that a community has existed for more than 300 years that puts many of his theories of dream work to daily, community-wide use. This group is the Senoi, a jungle tribe of the Central Range of the Malay Peninsula. The late Kilton Stewart devoted a major portion of his professional life as an anthropologist to the study of the Senoi and their work with dreams.

Stewart reports that the Senoi begin each day with the older males of the family listening to and advising on the children's dreams of the night before. When the children's dreams have been thoroughly discussed the males of the tribe gather for a council where they hear reports of the dreams of the oldest children and of the males in the community.

The Senoi believe, too, that the dream images bear messages to the dreamer about his inner world and his environment. By receiving help from the community the tribesman can learn to adapt according to the content of his dreams. His life will be changed by his ability to integrate his dream activity with his waking activity.

The Senoi encourage, in their children, the manipulation of dream feelings. When a child reports an unpleasant sensation in a dream he is socially encouraged to experience the same sensation in a positive manner in future dreams. This type of social instruction turns fearful dreams of falling into delightful dreams of soaring or flying. Positive dreams are reinforced so that in the future the dreamer can prolong them, and even bring them to fitting conclusion.

Even though Stewart's report may be overoptimistic in the degree of psychological sophistication achieved by the Senoi through this dream-integration process (he states they have not experienced war, crime, or mental illness in centuries!), it is obvious that we in the West could benefit from the adoption of some of the Senoi techniques and their social attitudes toward dreaming.

ACCESS

The material from Perls comes from his books *Gestalt Therapy Verbatim* and *In and Out the Garbage Pail*. The Kilton Stewart paper on the Senoi is now available in Tart's book, *Altered States of Consciousness*. It was originally published in *Complex* in 1951. *Complex* was a journal edited by Paul Goodman in New York City in the early 1950s when Gestalt Therapy was first developing in America. Stewart's book, now out of print, is *Pygmies and Dream Giants*. Further information on his work is available from his widow, Clara Stewart Flagg, of the Foundation for Creative Psychology, 144 East 36th Street, New York, N.Y., 10016.

64 Self-waking from dreams

Actually, this technique is part of autohypnosis and self-suggestion. We lose a good deal of content from and contact with our dreams by not being able to remember them. We can best remember dreams right after having them. This has been proved in research on sleep and dreaming. When subjects were awakened during the onset of REM sleep, more than 90 percent of them could report part or all of dreams they had just been dreaming.

One way that we can do this without being part of an experiment is to train ourselves, through simple suggestion and by means of posthypnotic suggestion, self-administered during trance, to awaken at the completion of a dream. With practice and determination, this will be successful and more dreams will be available for integration.

65   Hypnopompic phenomena (waking)

Very little is known about that dawn area of our normal sleeping cycle, the time between sleeping and waking.

A friend has reported that he is able to spend several hours of his sleeping cycle, on some days, actively experimenting with the hypnopompic state. In this experimentation he allows himself to become aware of being awake enough to manipulate his state of consciousness, but not so much as to destroy his ability to resume a state of sleep wherein dreams could develop. In this way he is able to experience very vivid dreams.

His semicontrol of the hypnopompic state allows him to remember many of these vivid dreams. It also enables him, on occasion, to awaken from a dream, hypnopompically perceive that the dream is incomplete or unfinished, return to the sleep state, and re-enter the dream. He is not always able to use hypnopompic awareness to control his dreaming, but he reports that the shifting back and forth between dreaming-sleep, hypnopompic awareness, and waking often brings about feelings of having had a very complete night's sleep.

66   Sun-bathing

Sun-bathing offers the unique opportunity to experience and manipulate a variety of states of consciousness while still being a social, even public animal.

Sun-bathing allows hypnagogic and hypnopompic phenomena to develop at a variety of different intervals, depending on how much time one spends. The added physical changes brought on by exposure to the sun—dehydration, excessive sweating, phosphene stimulation (when the sun is directly in line with the closed eyes), and the fatigue brought on by exposure—all of these elements make sun-bathing potentially a fine time for playing with altered states of consciousness.

After some exposure to the sun the skin begins to dry out and feels tight and tingling. At the same time certain areas of the body—the armpits, the groin, the face, the scalp—begin to give off perspiration. The free flow of these bodily juices is almost like a consciousness "lubricant" when combined with the feeling of heat on the genitals. Sun-bathing is exciting.

67 Floating

The floating experience is very similar to the sun-bathing experience. The extra element is, of course, the water you are floating on. Such contact with the water can totally alter the tactile, olfactory, and auditory self-perceived environment.

Especially in salt water, where floating can be done easily and for long periods of time, the sound of the lapping waves, the odor of the salt air, and the all-enveloping feelings of the surrounding water combine to create very special feelings.

Add to these factors the sun, the slipping into and out of various states of sleep, dream, and hypnagogic and hypnopompic awareness, and you have another instance where turning on can be achieved in a very social situation.

The undulating water laps at your body as the tide pulls the sea back and forth, in and out. The sea massages your body with its coolness as the sun warms both the air and your body. Your buoyancy carries you off into a personal, erotic state of consciousness.

68 Sex

Sex is the means of altering consciousness that almost everyone has had the pleasure of knowing. Different people have different sexual pleasures, different tastes, different fantasies that will sexually turn them on. Each of us has the right to enjoy sex.

Sexual fantasizing is an excellent technique for finding out what turns you on. You can fantasize about anything sexual that makes you feel good, no matter how outrageous that might seem. Indulge your wildest fantasies, and know that just thinking something, no matter how realistic your fantasy might be, cannot hurt you, in and of itself. And a good fantasy has the potential to excite you, to turn you on to new, personal sexual potentials.

And to fulfill your sexual potential you will have to allow yourself to discover your own sexual depth. Maybe most of the time you are shy, quiet and passive, but part of you yearns to be more aggressive, stimulating, exuberant and alive. Perhaps you have never experienced your own sexual gentleness or caring. All of these roles, and many more are open and available to you. Experiment with yourself. Try everything out. See how you feel. Be sexy with yourself . . . be sexy with another. Be sexy.

ACCESS

Even though their evasively pedantic language makes them difficult to read, both books by Masters and Johnson are excellent collections of data on sex. *Human Sexual Response* and *Human Sexual Inadequacy* are pioneer works that open up new ground after Kinsey's *Sexual Behavior in the Human Male* and *Sexual Behavior in the Human Female*. One of the best explanations of their work, and one that is also interesting for its own ideas is *Sex Energy* by R. deRopp. W. Reich's *The Function of the Orgasm* is excellent and is readably expanded upon by Alexander Lowen's *Love and Orgasm*.

69 Orgasm

The human sexual orgasm can be the most ecstatic, most exciting experience in life, and certainly is a time-honored way to alter consciousness and leave this world.

Wilhelm Reich was the first to systematically and scientifically examine the human sexual orgasm. His work has recently been carried on by his followers, Alexander Lowen and Stanley Keleman. Reich felt that: "The severity of any kind of psychic disturbance is in direct relation to the severity of the disturbance of genitality." He postulated that a patient's emotional problems were directly related to their ability to achieve full genital response, or orgasm.

Reich's work also defined two types of orgasm: genital orgasm and full body orgasm. Genital orgasm results from a build-up of energy resulting from the stimulation to the glans penis or the clitoris. When this energy builds up to a certain point, the orgasm occurs.

But there is the possibility of a fuller, more complete, more satisfying orgasmic experience. This is the full body orgasm. Keleman describes this for the male:

". . . the orgasm can also be triggered from inside, from the pelvic cavity, and if you allow the excitement to run back in the penis . . . and re-excite and flood the whole body, then the whole body is capable of discharging, not just the penis."

In building to full orgasm, sensations of excitement fill your body, you begin to rhythmically move your pelvis, and then you lose control and no longer consciously direct your actions. Your pelvis begins to move forward and back. You can feel the sexual energy flowing freely through your body. You are charging and discharging. You are purged and completed, spent and fulfilled at one and the same time.

What frightens many people about a full body orgasm is the loss of control, the letting go. Many women who seek a cure for frigidity in psychotherapy report the same fear: if they have a full orgasm they will lose control and lose their grip on reality. When control is surrendered your body takes over, takes charge. It is this experience of letting go and being completed by orgasm that enables us to taste what the ecstatics, mystics and shamans have been reporting for centuries.

ACCESS

Wilhelm Reich's study of the dynamics of human sexual orgasm are contained in his *The Function of the Orgasm*. Part of the same work is summarized and extracted in *Wilhelm Reich: Selected Writings*. Alexander Lowen writes about orgasm in his *Love and Orgasm* and *Pleasure*. The Stanley Keleman quote comes from his *Sexuality, Self & Survival*.

70   Nudity

We are born into this world without clothes. Immediately after birth our bodies are clothed, whether environmental conditions demand clothing or not. From then on, our social conditions require that we wear clothing and pay inordinate attention to its style, selection, and maintenance.

After childhood, even the most naive investigation of the unclothed body is frowned upon, and considered to be embarrassing and wrong.

Take time to examine your own body carefully, inside and out. Use mirrors. Look carefully and pay attention to minutiae. Examine your *entire* body, being careful not to overlook anything. Overcome your embarrassment and let your curiosity guide you. Be satisfied.

Walk around your house or apartment nude. Be aware of yourself as a being, without clothes, one who is fully prepared for life. Sense your body and move so that you can feel how your naked body functions free of clothing.

71   Prolonged masturbation

Prolonged masturbation, or masturbation accompanied by strong emotional content, highly charged fantasies and the like can produce altered states of consciousness. This state is very similar to certain trance states, including those induced through hypnosis.

If, after the orgasm (and a small rest), a man continues self-stimulation, he will begin to feel certain changes in his consciousness. Some of these can be due to the fatigue brought on by the exertion of continuing masturbation beyond the energy-releasing orgasm. Others have to do with the inner changes of physio-chemistry brought about by the increase in adrenalin and other hormonal secretions.

In the female, the changes may be more subtle. The fact that no seminal ejaculation occurs means more energy may be available to the (female) system. Multiple orgasms are possible and delightful.

For either men or women the altered state of consciousness produced through prolonged masturbation requires a dedication to purpose over and above feelings of exhaustion or the waning erotic interest in the by-now satisfied sexual urge.

Prepare an erotic setting; take the phone off the hook, dim the lights or light a candle. After orgasm when interest would normally flag, evoke erotic fantasies and images.

For some, fantasies and the promise of an altered state of consciousness will be enough motivation to go on beyond exhaustion and orgasmic satisfaction. Others may use techniques such as pornographic pictures or literature or perhaps some sexual implement, like a dildo.

The ability to relax, let go and experience the erotic feelings still present within you, even after a series of orgasms, is difficult but most rewarding. Drive on and find glory.

ACCESS

To my knowledge the only essay that deals with this phenomenon is R. E. L. Masters' "Sexual Self-Stimulation and Altered States of Consciousness," which appears in a volume that Masters edited, entitled *Sexual Self-Stimulation*.

72 Orgiastic or corybantic dancing

Dance until you drop. Dance as sex, as animal, as energy. Dance until the "you" is lost. Dance and spin and jump and be. Dance to abandon. Dance to orgasm.

Dancing allows you to feel all of the parts of your body as they unite and come together and stretch in all directions. Dancing lets you express inner feelings and feel inner expressions as with no other type of movement.

Dancing by yourself will give you insight into the many ways that you may manifest your being. The only partner that you will have to satisfy will be your own projections, your own feelings. You will be allowed to do things you might never dare reveal to a partner. It will be your dance.

Everyday life

73 Zen morning laugh

This technique was taught to me by Alan Watts, who learned it from a Japanese Zen master in California. The Zen master does this every morning as a form of meditation. He indicates that it accomplishes something similar to rigorous *zazen* without the aching legs that usually attend several hours of sitting.

The gist of the technique is to arise each morning and assume a standing position. Put your hands on the back part of your hips, with your palms faced upward. Now, begin to laugh. Keep laughing. Let your laughter feed off itself and propel itself through your body and out. Laugh fully and completely, for a few minutes. When it feels comfortable, stop laughing.

This is a great way to start the day. After a Zen morning laugh you're ready for anything.

ACCESS

The Alan Watts record referred to in the notes for Chanting and Mantras, No. 20, "Why Not Now," has a detailed description and demonstration of this technique on Side 2 of Record No. 2.

74 Impressions are food

When we feel hungry we satisfy this need by seeking nourishment: food. We eat and fulfill the need for several hours.

But edible food is not the only type of nourishment our selves seek. We also seek the nourishment of impressions, stimulation, excitement.

We don't think of the seeking and receiving of impressions as being the same process as that involved in satisfying food hunger. But in many ways the processes are similar.

Experiments with both animals and children have shown that those exposed to more impressions, more stimulation and more attention are the ones who make a healthy adaptation to the environment and develop their senses. Infants who are deprived of attention, impressions, and stimulation are often deficient in natural growth. Some become retarded in their development.

Boredom is an unlikely but instructive example. Boredom begins with the manifestation of restlessness. After a while the restlessness might be translated into nervous energy or into idiot's play (twiddling thumbs, etc.). By the time the experience of ennui has set in one could be driven to distraction. And that is the point, *to be driven*. And to have that drive results in distraction. By this I mean that impressions and stimulation can then be sought out and replace, or feed, the needs earlier experienced as boredom.

If, when you feel bored, you can stay with the experience without trying to change it; if you can really feel your boredom, you will see what a hungry state it is.

75 Sensory reminiscence

Sensory reminiscence is very close to what I described when I spoke of true remembering (see Remembering and Reverie, No. 57). I call attention to it again because we have opportunities to put sensory reminiscence to work every day, with powerful results.

We are constantly referring to our past experiences to help us sort out and make sense of current sensations and events. But we most often stop short of really *experiencing* some of the keen elements of our past experience.

A good place to start is with bacon. Can you remember it right now? Can you see it as it lies in the pan, cold? Can you see it as the heat begins to curl the edges of each strip? Can you smell the heavy odor as the smoke from the bacon rises out of the pan, permeating the entire kitchen? Perhaps you can think of some other predominant, unmistakable memories. What about being alone in a field? If it was a pretty day there are all sorts of sensory data to go back to, to make into a collage for present appreciation.

These trips into our past experience can help to make our senses keener and more precise for the present and the future. It is only when we learn to truly put something to use that it will work for us and show us how to live and how we do live.

76 Déjà vu

Déjà vu is a French term; the literal translation is *already seen*. But it is not quite as simple as having seen something before.

In *déjà vu* what is involved is not just a sensory reminiscence but an entire complex of attitude and experience. *Déjà vu* is being swept up in the feeling that it is the second time around for this particular sequence of life. The feeling is that somewhere, sometime, somehow one has precisely experienced what is happening, and knows what is going to happen next.

What accompanies this feeling is the nagging sensation of not being quite able to tell where, when, or how this past experience was lived. But the feeling of having already lived through it is strong and persistent.

Déjà vu cannot be brought on at will, but it is an experience well worth waiting for.

77 Seeking

Freedom is and must always be at the beginning: it is not an end, a goal to be achieved. One can never be free in the future. Future freedom has no reality, it is only an idea. Reality is what is.

Krishnamurti

Seeking a way of being

It is the intangible that we seek most deeply. For many, seeking is all that is worth doing. Seeking becomes an occupation in itself. Sometimes seekers are convinced that seeking is The Way.

In the course of seeking, the seeker may happen upon someone who claims to have found. The seeker may be temporarily impressed, but soon he will resume his search, his life of The Way. The one who has spoken of finding speaks from ignorance, so the true seeker thinks. And his search goes on.

But seeking in itself can also be a revelatory experience. It can be a search for understanding, for values, teachers, helpers, new ways to *be*.

What is sought after in all cases is the self. The end of the search comes when the parts of the self not known to the self are revealed.

78 Forgetting

If we agree that the only constant of life is change, we must loosen our hold on all that is precious to us. If we are to bend and change with the times we must let go. Letting go is the most difficult thing we ever have to do, and an important part of letting go is learning how to forget.

To learn to forget one has to dispense with all excess baggage. Forgetting is letting things take their proper place; forgetting is learning how to abandon the small voice with the ready-made instructions; forgetting is knowing that something new lies ahead; forgetting is moving, flowing.

The ability to resign, to let go of obsolete responses, of exhausted relationships and of tasks beyond one's potential is an essential part of the wisdom of living.

Fritz Perls.

79　Creativity

Creativity is something new, something fresh, something that arises out of the absence of preconceived ideas. Intuition—ideas that spring from the untapped, unpredictable parts of the self—results in creativity. To observe the unexpected, the unknown, and then use what one finds there in a new, unique way: that is creativity.

The process of creativity is an experience of ongoing attitudes, sets, shifts and changes that shape our way of relating to our environment. A great part of this process is perspective. When one has perspective one has a good overview of a situation or event; one can see clearly the emerging patterns in their various manifestations and configurations. With this perspective comes the ability to let the whole being consider a situation without hindrance and operate within the situation without premature conceptions.

Creativity is the ability to bring *something* into existence from *nothing*. That is, from chaos comes a meaningful, organized whole.

80　Profound esthetic experience

Esthetics is the branch of philosophy that deals with what is beautiful. Most often we think of it in relation to the fine arts. For many, "profound esthetic experience" sounds far away and generally inaccessible. But not so.

"Wood" by Gary Azon

The model of the beautiful is nature, whether it be the world around us or the world within. Looking at a natural landscape can evoke a profound esthetic experience. So can focusing on a colorful, truly magnificent phosphene. What counts is awareness and openness.

ACCESS

E. A. Gombrich's *Art and Illusion,* as well as the works of Bernard Berenson and Rudolf Arnheim, provide good material for consideration and instruction.

81 Peak experience

Peak experiences are those highlights of our lives that give us awareness and insight into a deeper level of existence.

The peak experience is the event that changes our way of viewing reality. Peak experiences are similar to the transcendent awareness described by mystics and others who have undergone religious experiences. What makes the peak experience unique and different from the mystic and/or religious experience is its secular naturalistic nature.

Peak experiences do not require the presence of the supernatural. They are characterized by the spontaneous awareness of some or all of the following points:

unity
nonjudgmental perception
detachment and objectivity
ego-transcendence
self-trust
ends rather than means
time/space disorientation
receptivity
transcendence of dichotomies
strong self-identity
strong sense of "free will"
humility and surrender

Peak experiences often occur during such diverse activities as making love, climbing mountains, experiencing or creating works of art, sailing, giving birth, reading, looking at a landscape, and listening.

For some people peak experiences can remain in the memory as a reference point, making further peak experiences more accessible.

ACCESS

The works of Abe Maslow are reviewed under the Access section of No. 113. Paul Bindrim's article "Facilitating Peak Experiences" appears in Otto and Mann's *Ways of Growth* and describes methods for realizing peak experiences. The discussion of the points frequently experienced with peak experiences is from Appendix A of Maslow's *Religions, Values, and Peak-Experiences*.

82 Movement

Although we may imagine "being at peace" in terms of stillness and serenity, the only constant is change.

Change is movement: being in action. To move is to be. Movement is our expression. Even when we are apparently still, we move; our insides pump and churn and strain and process.

Awareness of movement can come about through the absence of movement, through stillness. Feel the desire to push, to pull, to initiate. Know how to start, but be still. Move inside and feel movement inwardly before you do it.

Now move! Burst forth! Go out, be the world. But know what you move, how you move.

A good exercise is to move every part of the body, both as isolated parts and together with other parts; all sorts of ways you haven't tried before. Move your scalp, ears, eyes, lids, forehead, cheeks, jaw, neck, shoulders, back, spine, abdomen, arms, wrists, hands, fingers, elbows, pelvis, hips, thighs, knees, ankles, feet and toes.

Move slowly, softly, sweetly, seriously, madly, happily, fleetingly; all of the ways you are.

83 Postures

Stop reading and go and stand on your head for five minutes or do a shoulder stand. This is an excellent way to get high.

Postures are body gestures, positions sometimes natural, sometimes contrived, into which we can arrange our bodies. Postures help us to become our bodies, to become our selves.

Postures

Postures, body positions and physical actions which bring about awareness include:

stretching	turning
holding	hunkering (*a crouch with the*
twisting	*buttocks as near to*
expanding	*the floor as possible*)
contracting	raising the limbs
knotting (*intertwining the limbs*)	pushing
sitting	pulling
standing	tapping
lying	lifting
crouching	slapping
touching	shaking

84 Tensing

Relax. That's the first thing to do when tensing. Tensing is the deliberate, conscious play of the musculature. There are many methods that will teach you how to relax; what is fundamental is to learn how you don't relax.

You can try it now by sitting down in a chair with your back straight. Put your right hand on the back of your neck so that you can feel the different muscles there. Relax. While still touching and feeling your neck with your hand slowly raise your left leg off the ground, bringing your knee as close to your chest as possible, without altering your position.

Could you feel the muscles in your neck tense and shift as you raised your leg? Could you experience how you use muscles that are not directly connected with the action you are carrying out?

While still sitting, totally relax as much as possible. Now, deliberately tense the muscles in your right forearm by making a very tight fist. Continue to increase the tension until your arm begins to quiver and shake. Then relax. Repeat this process two more times until you can experience the dynamics of your tension/relaxation cycles. Try the same procedure with other sets of muscles.

ACCESS

Edmund Jacobson's *Progressive Relaxation* is a classic and is still an authoritative text in this area. Also see Bernard Gunther's *Sense Relaxation*.

85 Jumping up and down

I am not really qualified to talk about this method. Only certain masters know its full potential. When wrongfully employed, JUAD (Jumping Up And Down) can bring about severe mental aberration and radical psychic transformations.

To begin with, you should be standing. It is much better to practice JUAD out of doors, where, if you fall you will not be seriously injured.

Ball both hands up into fists, and keep your hands this way throughout the JUAD. Then begin to crouch down, bending the torso and the knees. Some find that it helps to bend the arms at the elbows. When you are almost in a full crouch, use the power of your legs to propel your body upward. The aim is actually to leave the ground and soar high into the air. Try to land flat on your feet. Don't stop. Repeat the above procedure, trying to go higher and higher each time.

Keep going higher. If JUAD is done properly you'll never come down.

If a real JUAD master is required, find one who is under eight years old.

86 Running

Running is a fine way to alter consciousness. It is accessible and can be great fun. However, before beginning serious running or any other vigorous exercises, it is advisable to get a check-up from a doctor.

When you start running, begin slowly, build up your confidence, endurance, ability, and speed and eventually you will be able to run distances you never imagined. Running gets you high in the same way as many other techniques offered here: by altering your breathing. When you run you change your breathing and the amount of oxygen reaching your brain. This in turn alters consciousness. Running also changes the speed of your heart and this too, can alter consciousness.

The difference between running and jogging is speed. When you jog you move along at what might be the equivalent of a horse's trot. When you run then you're cantering. When you sprint you're into your own version of the gallop. Running and sprinting cause your heart to beat much faster than normal, jogging does not. The long-distance runners in the Andes mountains in South America have been tested and shown to have slower than average heartbeat and pulse. This is because when they are running their hearts speed up but then after they have stopped running their hearts slow down to a level lower than before they had begun running. This is not true for someone who runs once a month or even once a week, but applies only to those who run every day.

Real running requires both effort and practice. If you are going to run a mile you should do so in under 8 minutes. You can run 5 miles at a somewhat slower pace and achieve the same results: an altered state of consciousness.

ACCESS

Cooper's *The New Aerobics* gives detailed information on how fast to run, for how long, and what running will do to your heart and circulatory system.

87 Gymnastics

Doing somersaults, handsprings, and various flips and dives can alter consciousness. Working out with rings, parallel bars, saw horse, and rope will do the same thing, and allow you to develop personal coordination and grace. These need to be done properly so that you do not injure yourself.

Gymnastics are similar to running in that they really make your heart and your lungs work hard.

Gymnastics on the horizontal bar

88 Mountaineering

Whether you have sought out a local mountain or are climbing in the Himalayas with full pack, gear, special equipment and Sherpa guides, mountaineering can be a fantastic adventure. It requires not only physical endurance and fortitude but also skill, and keen attention and awareness.

What makes mountaineering a means to alter consciousness is a combination of factors. First there are the surroundings. The natural elevation of mountain summits over the surrounding land affords the climber magnificent views and vistas, as well as new environmental perspectives. By climbing high you are also changing the oxygen composition of the air you are breathing. The higher above sea level you are the less oxygen there is in the air you breathe. The effort required to climb most mountains will change your breathing pattern and your heartbeat. These in turn will change the oxygen mixture of blood reaching your brain and make you high.

Rockclimbing

Another factor affecting mountaineers is the negatively ionized air high above sea level. Most urban environments abound in positively ionized air. (See No. 235.)

By climbing mountains you are facing a challenge. Successful completion of the challenge, the endurance of hardships along the way, and the exercise of your skills can provide unique sensations. The trip down can be equally exciting and exhilarating.

Alan Blackshaw's *Mountaineering* is a good one-volume treatment of the subject; it includes a bibliography and a list of films. The mountain climb as a metaphor for the metaphysical quest is presented in René Daumal's *Mount Analogue,* now being made into a movie called "The Holy Mountain" by Alexandro Jodorowsky.

89 Survival tests

Members of many primitive, preliterate tribes used to use survival tests to initiate young boys into the adult life of the community. The survival test allowed the boy to act as an adult for the first time, to prove himself to his fellow men, and to show what he had learned from his upbringing in the community.

Contemporary versions of the survival test exist in the U.S. military, especially in the Rangers, and in groups like Outward Bound. The Rangers and other branches of the services have been known to test the graduates of their training by parachuting them into desert, jungle, or forest areas, miles from civilization, with only their parachutes and the clothes on their back. Most of the young men make it back to civilization and some report altered consciousness as a result of lack of food, intensity of effort, isolation and exhilaration.

90 Futures

. . . [This] book sets out to change the reader in a subtle yet significant sense. . . . successful coping with rapid change will require most of us to adopt a new stance toward the future, a new sensitive awareness of the role it plays in the present. This book is designed to increase the future consciousness of its reader. The degree to which the reader, after finishing the book, finds himself thinking about, speculating about, or trying to anticipate future events, will provide one measure of its effectiveness.

Alvin Toffler wrote the above in his introduction to his book, *Future Shock*. Future consciousness, which, needless to say, is an altered state of consciousness, is no longer a game or occupation; it is now a necessity.

The future of the past is in the future
The future of the present is in the past
The future of the future is in the present
John McHale

I am vitally interested in the future. After all, I'll be spending the rest of my life there.
Charles Kettering, World Future Society

ACCESS

There are several hundred new books and articles dealing with the future every year. Three good texts to begin an inquiry would be John McHale's *The Future of the Future*, Arthur Clarke's *Profiles of the Future*, and M. J. Dunstan and P. W. Garlan's *Worlds in the Making*. *The Futurist* is a bimonthly periodical that covers the whole field. It also has a book service.

91 Voluntary social withdrawal

Often it becomes necessary, after one has spent a long time seeking essential and personal universals, to enter into a new phase where integrative processes resulting from the alteration of consciousness are allowed to coalesce. This integrative process can often be furthered in an isolated situation. The length of time spent in voluntary social withdrawal must vary according to the individual and need not be a full retreat from social spheres. It may be an afternoon alone in an apartment, a walk alone in the woods, or two years alone on an island.

There is the danger that social withdrawal will prove seductively attractive, and one will be tempted to drop out permanently. When this happens it is usually because illusion has superseded the sense of reality. Dropping out can be used creatively to assimilate new data about one's culture, but staying dropped out usually means lapsing into rationalizations, believing that one is superior to society at large.

Voluntary social withdrawal allows a new phase of aware consciousness to develop. When this temporary withdrawal is combined with cultural assimilation (see 92), and the individual is able to maintain the insights and universals of previous altered states of consciousness and develop the ability to transcend cultural patterns, then the final stage of maturational integration begins: the individual is involved in and turned on by what happens every day (see 93).

92 Cultural assimilation

Cultural assimilation is important for transcendence. If you don't know your own culture it becomes very difficult to rise above it, to see through the cultural manipulations that keep us in a state of stagnation.

If changes from outside your culture are to be brought to bear with authority and meaning, a firm grounding and understanding of your own cultural manifestations are required. Being able to experience your culture fully indicates a readiness for new insights and developments.

Altered states of consciousness bring new awareness, and often bring insights that seem to tap a universal core of species experience, a collective unconscious. If archetypes and life-patterns are perceived and contacted, then a fusing of one's experiences will be necessary in order to introduce these insights into the culture. Without knowledge of the culture one will be thought a crackpot. For example, a student may tell his parents that they and he are really God, that we are all one. But since they have no background in relating to this idea, they will probably be hostile to it. The student's approach, proceeding without clues indicating receptivity, indicates his cultural insensitivity. Cultural assimilation helps one to bring it all home in subtle and meaningful ways.

Re-culturation contributes to re-integration and happens whenever the individual has assimilated his own culture; it then becomes a step toward the next re-birth.

> A. Reza Arasteh

Free men obey the rules which they themselves have made.

> Alfred North Whitehead

93 Everyday experience

If the doors of perception were cleansed every thing would appear to man as it is, infinite.

> William Blake

The "supreme reason" does not lie in the domain of mystical visions of any kind.

> Suzuki Daisetz

A monk asked Ummon, "What is the Buddha?" "It is a shit-wiping stick," replied Ummon.

> Case XXI of the Mumonkan

Joshu asked Nansen, "What is the Way?" Nansen answered, "Your ordinary mind—that is the Way." Joshu said, "Does it go in any particular direction?" Nansen replied, "The more you seek after it, the more it runs away." Joshu: "Then how can you know it is the Way?" Nansen: "The Way does not belong to knowing or not knowing. Knowing is illusion. Not knowing is lack of discrimination. When you get to this unperplexed Way, it is like the vastness of space, an unfathomable void, so how can it be this or that, yes or no?" Upon this Joshu came to a sudden realization.

> Case XIX of the Mumonkan

"I do not ask you about last month, or about next month. I ask you to say something about here and now." None of the monks responded to this, so Ummon said, "Every Day is a good Day."

> Case VI of the Hekiganroku

A monk asked, "What is my own self?"
"Have you finished your rice gruel (breakfast)?" asked the Master (Joshu).
"Yes, I have finished it," replied the monk.
"Then go and wash your dishes," said the Master.

> From The Transmission of the Lamp, Chuan 10

If you understand, things are such as they are;
If you do not understand, things are such as they are—

> Gensha

Before enlightenment, chop wood, carry water;
After enlightenment, chop wood, carry water.

> Zen Dust

This is it. There's nothing hidden at all. Nothing special. *Tada* (*only* this, *just* this, nothing but). The final alteration of consciousness is the perception of things as they are. To perceive the world without excess, without fetters. To be in the moment.

When you eat, *just* eat. When you sleep, *just* sleep. You are: *just* be.

PART TWO

HELP FROM OTHERS

Therapies and miscellaneous

In this section are included brief descriptions of a number of psychotherapies. Chosen are those psychotherapeutic techniques which attempt to change or alter the individual's perception of himself and his world. The methods covered are those which have proved especially successful, either as models or schools of thought assimilated by the culture. When psychotherapy is successful it effects an altered state of consciousness.

94 Psychoanalysis

Sigmund Freud, as is well known, developed a system of therapy aimed at the cure of mental and nervous disorders; it is known as psychoanalysis. Only the bare bones are presented here. There is more literature on psychoanalysis than on any other form of psychotherapy.

Freud developed his system working with Josef Breuer on the treatment of hysterics through hypnotic techniques. After some experimentation, Freud began to formulate general theories of the structure of the mind and therapies based on these theories.

He described the mind as divided into the *unconscious* (seat of repressed material) and the *conscious* (the part that is in contact with the environment). Both parts are energized by the *libido,* or life force, which he characterized as being primarily sexual in nature.

The unconscious is ruled by the *id,* the original animal-like portion of the mind or self. Out of the id develops the *ego,* which attempts to deal with the external world while still helping to satisfy the baser needs and drives of the id. But the ego is also serving a second master, the conscience, which Freud referred to as the *super ego.* It is the super ego that internalizes parental prohibitions. The super ego is a perfectionist.

Generally, the patient in psychoanalysis says whatever enters his mind while lying on a couch where he cannot see the analyst (the psychoanalytic practitioner) sitting behind him, listening and taking notes. The talking is linked to Freud's theories of catharsis: by verbally expressing the nature and source of his problems, the patient will be able to recontact repressed feelings and drives. Some of this newly contacted energy becomes available for healthy living. The patient expresses whatever comes to mind, letting his associations come freely and allowing the repressed material to guide his talking.

Another important aspect of psychoanalysis is the theory of transference. Transference occurs when the patient transfers strong emotional feeling, such as love and hate, from the person he actually loves or hates to the psychoanalyst. The importance of transference is that it gives the patient an opportunity to solve many problems by proxy—that is, by allowing the analyst to emotionally "stand in" for the real object of love or hate.

Freud pictured man as being highly complex: as living in reality and operating under rational principles and yet also living in fantasies and dreams, operating under conflict and confusion. The mature individual can cope with these inconsistencies and ambivalences. His very complexity is one major root of his maturity.

Freud had many disciples who went on to form their own schools of psychological thought. Reich, Rank, and Jung, among others, will be considered separately. Alfred Adler, another follower, believed that Freud did not deal properly with the importance of feelings of inferiority. He also placed high value on the social relationship between the therapist and the patient. This is also evident in the interpersonal theories of personality developed by Harry Stack Sullivan. Erik Erikson brings much social behavior to bear on psychoanalytic theory. Both Adler and Wilhelm Stekel believed that Freud emphasized the past too heavily in psychoanalysis. Sandor Ferenczi, though never truly breaking with Freud, attempted many alterations of psychoanalytic technique. Guided by his roots in psychoanalysis, Erich Fromm has moved from the theoretical considerations of psychoanalytic practice to the philosophical implications of human experience.

ACCESS

The Modern Library edition of *The Basic Writings of Sigmund Freud* coupled with Jones's *The Life and Work of Sigmund Freud* will provide a good introduction to the field of psychoanalysis.

95 Analytical psychology

Carl Gustav Jung is easily the most extraordinary scholarly talent to emerge from the psychoanalytic group. Though the basis of his psychological theories and practice centered around analytical psychology, Jung's interest ranged literally from alchemy to Zen Buddhism.

Many believe that his most important role in contemporary psychology was his interest in and acceptance of Eastern ways of thought and wisdom. His basically open intellectual stance allowed him to draw material from a variety of sources. He was thereby in a position to integrate the psycho-philosophical truths expressed in Oriental religio-psycho-philosophical systems into his decidedly Western *Weltanschauung*.

After breaking with Freud, Jung went on to build a system of psychology based on a desexualized libido. In addition, Jung sought to interpret behavior rather than discover its causes.

Jung felt that he had observed the existence of certain *archetypes,* or universals, that stemmed from the creative forces of a *collective unconscious* shared and tapped by all mankind. In addition to this deeper human contact, Jung divided personality into *persona,* social mask, and *ego,* the conscious and unconscious part of the personality responsible for personal behavior.

Throughout his collective works one sees the influence of and interest in a variety of areas including the study of the phenomena of the self, the development of culture, flying saucers, Taoist yoga, Tibetan Buddhism, religion and spiritual needs, dreams, symbols, Taoist and Western alchemy, Zen, art and literature.

ACCESS

Jung's collected works have been published in 18 volumes by the Bollingen Foundation. His autobiography, *Memories, Dreams, Reflections* is both enlightening and entertaining. Selections of his thought have been edited by his associate Jolande Jacobi under the title *Psychological Reflections. Man and His Symbols,* a volume of papers edited by Jung and beautifully designed by Aldus Books in London, may be the best introduction to Jung's ideas.

Of all the theoretical developments of Wilhelm Reich, character analysis has had the most profound influence on contemporary developments in psychotherapy. Today there are many therapists who call themselves Reichians, others who are known as neo-Reichians, and still other groups that have developed out of the ideas of bio-energetic therapy, which is a direct offshoot of Reich's work with character and the human body.

Reich made the character the center of his clinical observations. First, Reich would analyze a patient's character. This was done as a prelude for orthodox Freudian psychoanalysis. Reich felt that character and its somatic manifestations, which he referred to as *character armor* or body armor, were important resistances that the patient used to guard against the unveiling of his unconscious processes.

Reich's real importance came with the attention that he paid to the body of the patient. He was the first of the psychoanalytic school to pay attention to the patient's posture, especially as an expression of personal character. Reich felt that the patient's physical stance expressed, unconsciously, defenses against the analytic process. He would make the patient aware of these defenses and the resultant character armor, and he would analyze the sources of the resistant character formation.

Reich always believed that a true sign of a patient's health was the ability to achieve a full orgasm. He devoted a great deal of his work and attention to the manner in which the patient experienced orgasm and in the investigation of orgasmic potency.

In addition to character analysis, Reich spent many years working on the discovery, analysis, and description of what he called orgone energy. Orgone energy was Reich's term for a general life energy or cosmic energy. Reich believed that orgone energy affected all life and also controlled such complex processes as weather and planetary radiation.

Part of Reichian therapy was devoted to having the patient sit in an orgone energy accumulator or orgone box. These boxes varied in construction, some being merely wooden boxes thoroughly lined with metal foil, while others possessed linings of a steel-wool kind of insulation. Reich theorized that orgone energy, if understood, would provide answers for many of mankind's most pressing and bewildering problems, including cancer and war. His research was interrupted by the U.S. Food and Drug Administration. He was brought to trial and refused to defend himself. He was convicted of contempt and died later in a Federal prison. The FDA had all of his books confiscated, and the orgone boxes and other machines connected with Reich's work destroyed. Though most classical analysts respect his work on character, it is only in the last five years that Reich's work as a whole has come under serious consideration. Hopefully, his more controversial theories will be tested under rigorous scientific controls and evaluated fairly and without hysteria.

ACCESS

Character Analysis is the title of Reich's book on the description of his psychoanalytic method. A good introduction to his later work is to be found in *Wilhelm Reich: Selected Writings*, which includes a bibliography.

97 Will therapy

Will therapy is the psychoanalytic development of one of Freud's students, Otto Rank. Though Rank remained faithful to Freud and orthodox psychoanalytic theory for many years, he finally made a break that forced him to leave "Freud's Vienna" for Paris and New York.

One of Rank's major differences with Freud was in the term of treatment required. Rank came to believe that short-term therapy was just as effective as protracted treatment.

Rank believed that the major fact of life was the trauma of birth (also the title of one of his more important books). He thought this traumatic experience paralyzed the will of the adult patient. In treatment he would analyze the birth trauma and then help the patient to free the will. Rank saw the will as a positive force that enabled the patient to grow toward total independence.

ACCESS

The work of Otto Rank is available in *The Myth of the Birth of the Hero* and *Will Therapy and Truth and Reality*.

98 Self-analysis

Self-analysis is associated with the work of Karen Horney, one of those who provided psychoanalytic theory with aspects of social psychology. Whereas Freud's theories are based on a biological or instinctive premise, Horney believed that cultural factors were far more important in shaping man's behavior.

Horney's primary concept is oriented around the anxiety of the child, ". . . isolated and helpless in a potentially hostile world." The anxiety is generally produced by anything that disturbs the security of the child in relation to his parents. It motivates the child to develop strategies to cope with his feelings of helplessness. It is these strategies and manipulations which are the hallmarks of the neurotic personality. The neurotic believes that his manipulations are in his own best interest, but due to the neurosis, anxious strategies interfere and needs are aggravated by dependencies. For example, the need for personal admiration is aggravated and disrupted by the need to manipulate other's behavior for self-gain.

Horney saw that people move in three directions with respect to the other people they encounter in life: one, toward people, e.g., love; two, away from people, e.g., independence; and three, against people, e.g., the exercise of power. The healthy person manages to integrate these attitudes, while the neurotic distorts the position of one or more of these stances.

Horney tried to help patients become free of an idealized self-image, to experience the real self (in the present) rather than the hoped for (and nonexistent) ideal self. By self-analysis Horney meant for the patient to be able to experience and analyze his own resistances to his real self, not for him to do analytic work without the analyst.

ACCESS

Karen Horney's work includes two excellent and expository volumes: *Self-Analysis* and *The Neurotic Personality of Our Times*.

99   Logotherapy

Logotherapy was developed by the existential analyst Victor Frankl. The name is taken from the Greek *logo,* translated as "meaning and spirit."

When asked to give a one sentence definition of logotherapy, Frankl replied: "In logotherapy the patient sits on a chair and hears things he finds unpleasant to hear."

Frankl contends that since man is the only animal who seeks meaning, since man is the only animal who worries, this meaning is the source of the very spirit of the human condition. In logotherapy he attempts to help the patient discover his (the patient's) own "will to meaning."

A logotherapist will lead the patient to what Frankl believes to be the major stumbling block in all human development: lack of meaning. When life has no purpose the patient will be unable to function in a world where values have no connection with his own personality. The task of logotherapy is to help the patient experience for himself his own personal meaning of life.

Frankl derived a great many of his psychological insights from experiences he had in a German concentration camp during World War II. In the camp, Frankl regularly saw people die from lack of hope. Frankl came to correlate positive, active consciousness with mental health and, conversely, mental passivity with mental illness. This mental passivity he saw was characterized by a feeling of nothingness, which he came to call the existential vacuum. After leaving the camp and entering private practice, Frankl saw many patients exhibiting neurotic symptoms that paralleled those that he had seen in the camp. Complaints detailed feelings of nothingness and lack of meaning to life. By confronting his patients with their emptiness and urging them to take personal responsibility for their condition, he was able to help patients develop and recognize strong meaning in life. This led to more will and eventually to health.

ACCESS

Frankl's logotherapy is set forth and expanded upon in two of his works: *The Doctor and the Soul: An Introduction to Logotherapy* and *Man's Search for Meaning.*

100   Daseinsanalyse

Daseinsanalyse is the existential psychoanalytic system developed by Ludwig Binswanger. *Da* means there; *sein* means being; thus, daseinsanalyse means, literally, "being there." It is often referred to as "being-in-the-world."

This therapeutic approach is inextricably woven with philosophical concepts and theories. The assumptions begin with "there" being taken as a *personal* "there." Since man can become aware of his "being-there" he can become responsible for his being. His being then goes from "being-in-itself" to an extension: "being-for-itself."

Besides the classical psychoanalysis of Freud, another influence on Binswanger is the "I–Thou" philosophical postulation of Martin Buber.* From this, Binswanger extrapolated the *dual* and *plural* modes of existence. The dual mode refers to the intimacy and closeness of Buber's I–Thou, whereas the plural refers to the social existence of one and others.

Daseinsanalyse is essentially a philosophy in psychotherapeutic action. As such, it lacks many of the neoscientific underpinnings of contemporary psychotherapies and is rooted too much in psychotherapeutic discipline (with its allegiance to Freudian psychoanalysis) to be a true philosophy.

ACCESS

This particular form of existential psychoanalysis is presented in Binswanger's *Being-In-The-World* and in the volume on existential psychology edited by Rollo May entitled *Existence.* The latter book covers other developments in this area.

---

* Buber posited two types of individual experiences of things other than himself: *I–Thou* and *I–It.* By emphasizing the I–Thou, Binswanger seeks to define relationships from one individual to another individual, rather than from the individual to a thing. The incorporation of this philosophical vantage point enabled Binswanger to try and experience the patient's world as if he were viewing it through the patient's eyes, rather than imposing his own value systems on the patient.

101 Psychodrama

Psychodrama is a system developed by J. L. Moreno as an adjunct and expression of his sociometric analysis. It is a technique used in group psychotherapy and has powerful and far-reaching applications.

Moreno points out that the word "drama" comes from the transliteration of a Greek word that really means "action" or "things done." He sees psychodrama as a technique for reaching the truth through dramatic means, by acting out one's feelings. Moreno defines five necessary instruments for psychodrama.

1. The stage: a safe environment for psychological action.
2. The subject or actor: this is the man or woman who chooses to be on the stage to present his or her interior and personal world through the psychodramatic technique.
3. The director (usually the therapist): he or she fulfills three basic roles: the producer, the counselor, and the analyst. It is the responsibility of the director to be aware of clues from the subject and to turn those clues (to the subject's inner dynamics) into dramatic action. The director may attack the subject or support the subject, depending on what is necessary in the course of dramatic action.
4. The staff of auxiliary egos: these staff members have their function in playing out the untold roles of the actor. They must serve his needs as well as supplement his acting and his behavior.
5. The audience: this group has a dual purpose. By presenting public opinion the audience can attempt to help the subject. By being itself, it can gain help by observing what occurs on the stage. It is the responsibility of the director to guide the audience as well as the subject.

The process of bringing feelings to the surface through psychodrama can lead to new emotional insights.

ACCESS

J. L. Moreno's work is reviewed in his book *Who Shall Survive?*, which includes a complete bibliography. *Psychodrama* provides specific details on the dramatic technique.

102 Transactional psychology

Transactional psychology is the development of Adelbert Ames, Jr. (The Ames demonstrations in perception will be examined in 204.) It has its roots in vision and in the general phenomenology of perceptual processes.

The basis of transactional psychology lies in the idea that our perceptions are learned responses rather than responses elicited entirely by the stimuli that provoke them. These learned reactions are acquired through our interactions and *transactions* with our environment. The transactional psychologist believes that we all build up a repertoire of expectations based on our past perceptual experiences. We bring to each new perceptual situation a script of probabilities for what is about to occur. And it is this script that greatly determines our future perceptual experiences.

The most interesting aspect is that knowledge of a situation does not change that situation. Even if we know in advance that what we are about to experience is an illusion, we cannot stop ourselves from being taken in by the illusion, be it visual, auditory, or otherwise. We may even distort other functions of the situation in order to stay with our prior conceptions.

The Ames monocular distorted room shown in 204 is a prime example. Even though we know that the room is distorted, and not its contents, our prior expectations about rooms color our perceptual experience. When we look into the room we *see* the contents as being distorted, not the room.

The most radical departure from generally accepted beliefs that we have demonstrated scientifically is that man will be more successful in carrying out his purposes if in concrete situations he bases his selection of alternative courses of action on value-judgements and not on logical intellectual mental processes.

Adelbert Ames, Jr.

ACCESS

The philosophical groundwork and results of this approach can be found in *The Morning Notes of Adelbert Ames, Jr.* F. P. Kilpatrick edited *Explorations in Transactional Psychology,* which provides a good overview.

103 Attitude psychology

Attitude psychology, developed by Nina Bull, is based on a specific and simple principle of body-mind relationship. This relationship illuminates the fact that a specific motor attitude prepares any emotional occurrence. This motor attitude will then color the feelings and expressions of the emotional response. Bull applies this theory (of the influence of prior motor attitude on behavior) to all feeling states. She includes not only emotions but frustration, depression and goal orientation.

To test her system, Bull devised experiments that would monitor the physiologic responses of subjects under hypnosis as they experienced the emotional states of disgust, fear, anger, depression, triumph and joy. Bull reasoned that although these emotional states are popularly understood, no experiments had ever verified one-to-one correspondence between patterns of behavior (including motor response) and the experience of feeling specific emotions.

The subjects were given prehypnotic suggestions and instructions to act out emotional feelings in a natural way. Then they were hypnotized and wired so that their physiological responses could be monitored. What these tests confirmed was that there was a preparatory motor response prior to the feeling of the emotion. That is, the subjects' bodies set themselves up for the emotional feelings before the subjects experienced the feelings. Be aware of how your tensions and physical responses telegraph the emotions you are about to experience.

ACCESS

Nina Bull published a book and a monograph which present the theory and experiments behind attitude psychology. The book is *The Body and Its Mind* which explores the later developments of the monograph, *The Attitude Theory of Emotion*, which has recently been republished in book form.

104 Rational psychotherapy

Rational psychotherapy, also known as rational-emotive psychotherapy, holds that man's emotions are caused and controlled by thinking. It is the development of Albert Ellis, who holds that someone experiencing positive emotions is reinforcing those feelings, causing them with thoughts like "this is good." "This is bad" would tend to cause negative emotional experience. These phrases are usually subvocal and often not part of awareness.

The aim of the therapy is to help the patient understand and realize what internalized sentences are now the basis of the patient's thoughts. Once this is discovered, the patient is encouraged to substitute more positive, more rational, and more realistic supportive sentences. It is believed that this sentence substitution will help the patient to change his own behavior.

In this respect rational psychotherapy is like many of the "positive-thinking" philosophies. Ellis encourages his patients to realize that they control their own destinies by the way they deal with problems and the way they talk to themselves.

Our patients . . . frequently remark: "I can't stand it when things go wrong."

. . . we quickly interrupt: "What do you mean you can't stand it? It doesn't really exist—is just a figment of your imagination. What you really mean to say is: 'I can't stand myself when things go wrong—because I falsely tell myself that things shouldn't go wrong, or that I'm no good for letting them go wrong. But if I stopped telling myself this nonsense, then I could fairly easily stand—though never perhaps like—the frustrations of the world and could respect myself for being able to accept these frustrations.' "

Albert Ellis

ACCESS

Ellis's initial statement of theory was presented in his book *How to Live With a Neurotic*. Also consult *A Guide to Rational Living* and *Reason and Emotion in Psychotherapy* for later changes in viewpoint. The quote above is from *A Guide to Rational Living*.

105 Eidetic psychotherapy

Eidetic Psychotherapy is a system of psychoanalysis developed by Akter Ahsen. Ahsen also calls his system eidetic or objective analysis. Eidetic psychotherapy is based on the classical theoretical conceptions of Freud. But unlike Freud, who felt that visual imagery was an incomplete state of consciousness, Ahsen follows D. H. Lawrence: "Man thought and still thinks in images." The word eidetic is used by Ahsen to mean:

. . . a clear image, usually visual, which is so vivid that it is practically seen as being externally perceived. It is a life-like image which, if attended to, completely absorbs the individual to the exclusion of everything else.

By combining traditions of Western psychology and psychoanalysis, mythology (with special attention to the Greek and Hindu myths), and religion and Oriental philosophy, Ahsen has devised a system of treatment that he claims leads to a meaningful form of phenomenological consciousness. Starting with the basic procedures of the standard psychoanalytic interview, Ahsen encourages his patients to present images which they find to be eidetic, either from dream material or from free association. By relating the images brought forth to established mythology, Ahsen helps point the patient toward a better understanding of himself based on the meaning of the images within the context of the patient's own life. Unlike classical psychoanalytic treatment, which can extend over five or more years of analytic interviews four times a week, Ahsen's therapy can complete treatment with interviews two times a week for three to six months.

ACCESS

Ahsen published *Eidetic Psychotherapy* in Lahore, Pakistan. *Basic Concepts in Eidetic Psychotherapy* comes closer to making a full presentation. Two new works round out the presentation of this analytical approach. *Eidetic Analysis* has three chapters by Ahsen, one of which compares his methods with Gestalt Therapy, Zen, and Yoga. *Eidetic Behavior: A Manual of Objective Psychoanalysis* is Ahsen's complete statement of his therapeutic theories.

106 Synectics

Synectics, a management creativity technique, was developed by William J. J. Gordon. The theory is based on making an observational investigation into the nature and process of creative activity.

The word "synectics" comes from the Greek and refers to the bringing together of diverse elements, elements that seem unrelated. Gordon proposes bringing groups together to solve problems in a creative manner. This involves first stating the problems and then moving on to their solutions.

The major aim of synectics is for people to become aware of the psychological processes by which they operate, especially with reference to the way in which they approach problems. Gordon also shows that in creativity it is the emotional rather than the intellectual, and the irrational rather than the rational elements that most help to bring success to problem-stating and problem-solving situations.

Synectics is specifically designed for enhancing creativity in business groups, but its techniques can easily be applied to other groups. A great deal of attention is devoted to the place of the creative group in the outside world.

ACCESS

William J. J. Gordon has published an introductory guide to his management methods called *Synectics*. Synectics, Inc. is located in Cambridge, Mass.

107 Synanon

Synanon is the name of a halfway house for narcotics addicts. It has also come to refer to a method of group psychotherapy that was developed at Synanon by its founder, Charles Dederich. Dederich was never a narcotics addict, but was at one time an alcoholic.

The basic premise of Synanon therapy is for addicts to gather together in a group to share their problems and help each other. The one who is most valuable in helping the addict get off drugs is the ex-addict. Abraham Maslow has described the Synanon therapeutic approach as "no-crap therapy." It has also been classified as an "attack" therapy.

When the addicts meet together in a group, the addict who is in the spotlight is generally attacked by the others present. At Synanon this is to keep people from hiding behind various street junkie strategies and "hustles." Groups often "gang up" and devastate whoever is on the spot, in an attempt to break down all of his defense systems. Many who go through the Synanon process do not go back to being junkies; but many stay at Synanon rather than return to the outside, non-junkie world.

The name Synanon derived from Dederich's inability to say either symposium or seminar.

ACCESS

Yablonsky's *Synanon: The Tunnel Back* is the best introduction to the group and the method. Synanon is also treated in a chapter of Ruitenbeek's *The New Group Therapies*. Synanon has groups throughout the United States.

108 General semantics

General Semantics was recognized and formulated by Alfred Korzybski. Korzybski is best known for his work on words as symbols, their usage and their meanings. Much of this work involved examinations of symbols and their relationships to the things that they symbolize. These studies led to his analysis of the influence of symbols on behavior.

Alfred Korzybski

Korzybski found that human beings have a unique property that arises from their manipulation of symbols: time-binding. Time-binding indicates the preservation of memories and the recording of experiences for the use of subsequent generations. This time-binding is usually accomplished through the use of language.

Language is a verbal map of a nonverbal territory. But language carries with it culturally acquired powers that influence the user of language to mistake the map for the territory it attempts to describe. This is similar to mistaking the name and advertising credo of Kool cigarettes with the hot reality of cigarette smoke, mistaking the symbol for the thing symbolized. Language acts as a projection device, carrying the personal values of the language-user out into the territory (objects, persons, relationships, etc.) and giving the impression of modifying the territory. This impression is illusory.

The map is not a map, but a mapping of the mapper mapping both himself and the territory.
                              J. S. Bois in Breeds of Men

Korzybski believed that the scientific method of careful, accurate observation, logical structuring of concepts and an experimental view of experience could help to bring increased awareness to the nature of human thought, perception and the use of symbol systems, such as language.

ACCESS

See Access for No. 8, Semantic Awareness.

109   Ampernistics

Ampernistics is a system for learning how to learn. It was developed by Harold Thompson, recently connected with L. Ron Hubbard's Church of Scientology in England (see No. 172).

Ampernistics attempts to teach people the difference between symbols and the things that they represent, and then show them how to manipulate those symbols. Thompson has developed a number of teaching implements for use in the ampernistics system. All are now in the process of being readied for Patent Pending status in the United States.

One is a set of cards with different symbols on each card. The student is shown the card by a monitor and gives a response, much as in a Rorschach test, which the monitor then interprets. As far as I could discover, some of the system is similar to "auditing" in Scientology (see No. 172). Once the machines are patented, perhaps Thompson will publish information fully explaining ampernistics.

110　Final integration

The term *final integration* is associated here with the theories of A. Reza Arasteh. Primarily a teacher and writer, Arasteh combines the theories of Western psychology with Eastern philosophical and spiritual teachings. He pays special attention to Sufi material familiar from his native Iran.

Arasteh points out that many industrial cultures make the dangerous and mistaken assumption that the individual has solved all problems of personal identity during adolescence. The identity crisis of adolescence is only a prelude to further identity crises where the questions of "Who am I?" and "Who are you?" must be answered. Arasteh feels that a solution to these adult identity problems can be achieved by a final integration in the adult personality.

A final integration necessitates a number of experiences, such as: new degrees of awareness, both internal and environmental; an anxious search for the truth, both personal and social; an existential moratorium, a period of time for maturation where one leaves oneself open and flexible to new views and experiences; intentional alienation from one's social role, or dropping out; an experience of liberation or transcendence where one's life gains meaning; and the experience of strong meaningful figures in one's life after returning to one's social group.

ACCESS

Arasteh's work is well presented in two books. *Rumi the Persian: Rebirth in Creativity and Love* examines the integrative process in thirteenth-century Persia through the study of a great Sufi poet and mystic. *Final Integration in the Adult Personality* is a clear-cut theoretical presentation of Arasteh's insights into the integrative process and its social applications through psychotherapy.

111　Thanatological awareness

Everyone who ever existed, everyone who exists now, will die. This fact is very difficult to stay with, to make truly real. There are many ways to rationalize death and to rob its eventuality of "realness."

Richard Alpert (Baba Ram Dass), when he was involved with psychedelics, suggested that a thanatology center be set up so that people could take psychedelics and learn about death. Though that might have been an interesting development, it is not altogether necessary to go to a center to learn about death. Most of us have known someone who is now dead, and most have lost someone close: parent, spouse, friend, or child.

The experience of the death of another can reveal new horizons to the living. Often, we think of the death of a relative or someone close solely as a negative experience. Death can be experienced in a very positive way. (This is not to discount the necessity for sadness and mourning over the dead; grief is a healthy emotion, in context.) The death of someone close can bring about a new view of life, a re-experiencing of life's very preciousness. Life can often be seen more clearly, and with new eyes, in the face of death.

Another positive aspect can come from the shock of impending death. Often people who are told that death is imminent totally change their attitudes toward life and their way of living.

And now she would have peace. And where there was peace and love, there too would be joy and the river of the colored lights was carrying her toward the white light of pure being, which is the source of all things and the reconciliation of all opposites in unity. . . . When the breathing ceased . . . it was without any struggle.
　　Aldous Huxley describing the death of his first wife

Both the Egyptians and the Tibetans made elaborate preparations for death. The Egyptians made sure that the individual about to die would be well-versed in how to behave in the next world and would have all of the tools needed there.

The Tibetans treated dying as an art; a great deal of their wisdom has been preserved in the *Tibetan Book of the Dead.*

. . . the Art of Dying is quite as important as the Art of

Living (or of Coming into Birth), of which it is the complement and summation.
                    W. Y. Evans-Wentz, the Tibetan Book of the Dead

ACCESS

The Huxley quotation comes from the magnificent volume of his letters edited by Grover Smith. Consult the *Egyptian Book of the Dead* and W. Y. Evans-Wentz's rendering of *The Tibetan Book of the Dead.*

112   Gestalt therapy

Gestalt therapy was developed by Frederick S. (Fritz) Perls. Some believe it to be the most noteworthy clinical application of psychology/philosophy since Freud.

The development of Gestalt therapy can be traced through seven major influences, all of which Perls brought to bear as he constantly changed, revised and strengthened his clinical approach. These influences are:

1. Phenomenology and existentialism: Gestalt therapy is deeply rooted in phenomenological investigation. What Perls did was to turn from the existential question back to the phenomenological tool of the awareness continuum.
2. Gestalt psychology: Perls's work with the brain-injured, and with the great Gestalt psychologist Kurt Goldstein, did much to impress him with the pragmatic nature of Gestalt formulations and with the theory of the self-actualizing organism.
3. Psychoanalysis: Perls spent most of his life fighting the shadow of Freud's powerful theories. Perls's analysis by Horney, and later by Reich, plus interest in the work of Rank, helped to guide and shape his own therapy.
4. Reich: In the work on the body Reich used in his character analysis, Perls found the unification that he had previously intuited was missing in psychoanalytic method.
5. Holism: While in South Africa, Perls had contact with the holistic theory of evolution of Jan Smuts. This helped to expand his view of the individual/organism-in-the-world.
6. General Semantics: Korzybski's work called attention to the all-important verbal level of the patient's world. Semantics aided the general phenomenological approach that Perls had already adopted.
7. Taoism/Zen Buddhism: these pragmatic mystical religions from the East enabled Perls to understand and complete the picture of the healthy Western man. From this picture emerged Man in relation to his true nature: freely being-in-the-world.

The early development of Gestalt therapy started with the organism and its striving to complete its current unfinished situation in order to maintain organismic balance: homeostasis. Perls paid special attention to the connection between hunger and aggression, discussing and theoretically examining the child's initial contact with food, the subsequent destructuring of the food, and the final digestion of nourishment achieved through this process which he considers a form of healthy aggression.

Also present in the early work was the insistence on staying with the present, the here-and-now situation. Perls worked with projection (the patient's attempt to project on to others his own feelings), introjection (the patient's attempt to make something outside of him his own, often by "swallowing whole"), and retroflection (what the outside world bends back to the patient after he has directed it outward). From these insights and examinations came the realization that neurosis is a system of avoidance used by the patient to try to maintain some balance, often between his personal feelings and what he perceives as the world's (society's) dicta. Perls used as treatment a therapy based on concentration and awareness of the ongoing situation.

In Gestalt therapy, the therapist acts as a sensitive frustrater. He directs the patient to become aware of his own attempts to manipulate the situation and to then take responsibility for his behavior. In essence, the workings of Gestalt therapy allow the patient to become self-therapist once he is aware.

Fritz Perls

To Perls, the rhythm of human emotion was determined by the organism's ebb and flow of contact and withdrawal. For most patients the withdrawal is related to feelings of anxiety which merely represent controlled and de-pressed (lack of breathing and diaphragmatic expansion) excitement. In order to help the patient become aware of these processes in action the therapist encourages feeling the whole self, the organism-as-a-whole. Perls often said: "You have to lose your mind to come to your senses."

By mind, he meant the computer-like subvocal *thinker* that most patients experience as their own consciousness, while ignoring messages and impressions from the sensory and intuitive areas of the organism. To make contact, Perls devised a number of exercises to help the patient develop a sensitivity to the awareness continuum, to feel the urge to remain in control, and avoid letting

go, to experience neurosis as the avoidance of seeing the obvious, and to acknowledge experientially that all guilt is really resentment.

Perls used the Top Dog/Under Dog technique to bring about integration. Since Gestalt therapy does not use interpretative means, Perls felt that the I–Thou encounter could better make contact with the integrative forces. The Top Dog is the part of the self who is always saying "should" and who is always correct: "You should have called your mother. You know she'll be angry with you now. You've been a bad boy."

The Under Dog is the alternate self who confronts Top Dog: Under Dog is apologetic, manipulative and usually the winner in any contest of the self: "I know I should have called; I'm sorry. I didn't mean to forget. I'll call tomorrow."

These "shoulds" represent the perfectionistic demands the patient makes upon himself as he splits into different pieces to better manipulate his self-image. These dialogues bring the patient in contact with all his selves and with his use of fantasy to rehearse for imagined future situations and encounters. These splits in the self usually enable the patient to find comfortable ways of manipulating, maintaining a *status quo*. Often the manipulation is used to avoid phobic attitudes and dreaded experiences.

Perls said that neurosis exists on five levels or in five layers. The first layer is the *phony* layer, the place where the patient tries to play games, live out roles and be what he is not. The second layer is the *phobic* layer.

When the patient becomes aware of his phony behavior he begins to make contact with the fears that he uses to maintain roles or poses. This is the level of experience of catastrophic expectations that keep the patient from action and may bring him to the third layer. The third layer is what Perls called the *impasse,* what is known in Russian psychology as the "sick point." The negative experience of the impasse is one of inability and lack of support. The positive experience of the impasse is similar to the experience of the void, especially the creative, or fertile void of Eastern philosophies and religions. The fourth stage is the *implosive* layer where such emotions as fear, grief, and despair are experienced as a prelude to action. The fifth layer is the *explosive* layer. This is when the patient is in contact with new energies made available through "explosions." These can be of anger, grief, sexual orgasm, and joy.

Perls also described three *shits:*

Chicken shit: The cliché talk of "hello, how are you, I'm fine, oh how nice." Most of this talk avoids real, meaningful contact.

Bull shit: Lies, exaggerations, stories, etc. "I'm the greatest (lover, talker, etc.) that ever lived." "I told him off."

Elephant shit: Theories, grand schemes, and explanations: ". . . the transcendental apperception which, through the essential mediation of the pure imagination, must be joined to pure intuition. . . ."

The aim of Gestalt therapy is to help the patient become an integrated, responsible, mature, whole organism-in-the-world. Gestalt therapy attempts to help the patient discover how he can make more of his true potential available to his everyday behavior and action. Perls often used the approach to dreams I have described in No. 63 as an integrative procedure to help the patient contact more of his real self-experience and more of his potential.

Part of the development of potential has to do with the patient's acceptance of what he is. Perls used to give the example of the elephant who wanted to be a rose bush and the rose bush that wanted to be an elephant:

Until each resigns to being what they are, both will lead unhappy lives of inferiority. The self-actualizer accepts the possible. The one who wants to actualize a concept attempts the impossible.

Perls defined maturity (in true "elephant-shit" fashion) as the transition from environmental support to self-support. When the patient can produce his own support for his own ventures and world actions he is then operating as a mature and self-actualized organism. How to do it:

Don't make a perfectionistic program out of it (integration), that you should chew up every bit of what you are eating, that you should make a pause between the different bites so that you can complete one situation before you start the other; to change every noun and it into an I. Don't torture yourself with these demands, but realize that this is the basis of our existence and discover that this is how it is. It is how it should be and it should be how it is.

The crazy person says, "I am Abraham Lincoln," and the neurotic says, "I wish I were Abraham Lincoln," and the healthy person says, "I am I, and you are you."

Fritz Perls

ACCESS

The theoretical, practical, and experimental work of Gestalt therapy is available in Perls's books: *Ego, Hunger and Aggression* (the beginnings); *Gestalt Therapy* with Ralph Hefferline and Paul Goodman (the middle period); *Gestalt Therapy Verbatim* (the later work); and *In and Out the Garbage Pail* (an autobiography and history of the therapy). A fine collection of papers on Gestalt therapy is Fagan and Shepherd's *Gestalt Therapy Now.* Films and video tapes of Perls in action are available from The Mediasync Corporation, Box 486, Del Mar, California. Other films are available through Encyclopedia Britannica Films. Audio tapes are available through Big Sur Recordings.

Barry Steven's book *Don't Push the River* (which was Perls's working title for the manuscript that appeared as *Garbage Pail*) is a record of her experiences at the Gestalt community or kibbutz on Lake Cowichan, British Columbia, Canada.

113 Maslovian psychology

Maslovian psychology encompasses the work of Abraham Maslow, who was basically a theoretical psychologist in that he did not develop a specific course of treatment for neurosis or psychosis. In fact, his most important contribution to the psychological sciences was his recognition that psychology was lacking a most important perspective, a perspective that had made most previous psychological contributions one-sided.

Maslow noted that all psychology was based on psychopathology, or the behavior and processes of sick people. Maslow decided that a new psychology was necessary, a psychology based on healthy people. He called these people self-actualizers (a term first used by the Gestalt psychologist Kurt Goldstein, with whom Maslow studied and worked).

A major aspect of the lives of these healthy people was their propensity to have what Maslow called peak experiences. Peak experiences are experiences of wonder, awe, ecstacy, altered consciousness, universal oneness, revelation, or transcendental states of being. (See No. 80.) With his studies of self-actualizers and their peak experiences, Maslow was able to help direct the attention of the psychological world toward developing methods of becoming healthy. This led to the development of Third Force or Humanistic Psychology (as opposed to the behavioristic or psychoanalytic models).

At the time of his death in 1970, Maslow was helping bring to birth the creation of a new psychology: ". . . a still higher Fourth Psychology, transpersonal, transhuman, centered in the cosmos rather than in human needs and interests. . . ."

ACCESS

The work in this field by Abraham Maslow begins with *Motivation and Personality* (originally published in 1954; new edition Fall 1971); finds full development in *Toward a Psychology of Being;* and is further developed in *Religions, Values, and Peak-Experiences,* plus numerous articles published in *The Journal of Humanistic Psychology* and *The Journal of Transpersonal Psychology.*

Colin Wilson gives a detailed account of Maslow and Maslovian Psychology in *New Pathways in Psychology: Maslow & the Post-Freudian Revolution.*

Abraham Maslow, 1966

114 Sensory training

Sensory training refers to the work of Charlotte Selver and Charles V. W. Brooks. Their work, in turn, is based upon the formulations of Elsa Gindler and Heinrich Jacoby. Sensory training involves the re-education of the senses. Today, with so much going on in the environment, we are often sensorily overloaded. In order to cope we shut down our sensory equipment so that we receive a minimum amount of sensory input. This is an attempt to cut out the noises, the blaring colors of advertisements, and the conditions brought on by urban overcrowding.

The idea of sensory training is to bring people back to their senses so that they may appreciate all of the wonderful sensations available to them.

Selver and Brooks start by having people lie on the floor. The attempt is then made to help individuals return to original perceptions. Distinction betweeen inside and outside (the floor touches me; I touch the floor); right and wrong; watching and looking; thinking and experiencing are relearned.

After this, a process often called inner awakening, has progressed, the work on balancing begins. Again natural positions and activities, lying, sitting, standing and walking, are used for relearning experiences. These involve sensing the differences between habit and coordination; noting the constants of change and flux; and awakening to the entire environment.

We find ourselves being more one with the world where we formerly had to cross barriers. Thoughts and ideas "come" in lucidity instead of being produced. We don't have to try to express ourselves (as the word so vividly depicts), but utterances become just part of the natural functioning. Experiences can be allowed to be more fully received and to mature in us.

Selver and Brooks

ACCESS

Some references for this work are given in the Access material for No. 3. A good description of a Selver workshop is included in *Turning On* by Rasa Gustaitis.

115 Sensory awareness

Sensory awareness here designates the work of Bernard Gunther. Gunther studied with and was influenced by a number of teachers, including Ida Rolf, Oscar Janiger, Fritz Perls, Charlotte Selver, Jacques Hondorus, and Richard Hittleman. He has developed techniques which attempt to re-establish contact with sensory experience, to quiet compulsive and habitual thought, to end chronic tension, and to help free trapped potential and awareness.

His techniques include tapping, slapping, stretching, dancing, crawling, shaking, breathing, lifting, looking, listening, smelling, tasting, touching, and massage. Some of the more unusual exercises he prescribes are the blind shower, the silent meal, washing the hands with salt, and the sense to walk.

Gunther describes two of these exercises:

Blind Shower; Step in the shower and close your eyes. Shampoo your hair. Soap your whole body. Rinse and dry yourself completely before you open your eyes.

Silent Meal; Share a meal with someone or with a group without talking. Listen to sounds; smell, taste, touch, see, feel. Eat some of the meal with your eyes closed. Variations: (1) Eat part or the whole meal with your hands. (2) Serve one dish, like ice cream or yogurt, that must be eaten without utensils or the use of the hands.

Sensory awareness training

Gunther's book *Sense Relaxation* has already been referred to. An article of his, "Sensory Awakening and Relaxation" is included in Otto and Mann's *Ways of Growth*. Two of his new books describing sensory awareness are *What To Do Until The Messiah Comes* and *How The West Is One.*

116   Bio-energetics

Bio-energetics is a continuation of the character-analysis and body-armor work of Wilhelm Reich. This extension has been pursued mostly by Alexander Lowen and John Pierrakos.

Bio-energetics deals with the person as body. It stresses the fact that we *are* our bodies; we do not *have* bodies. It deals with body on a number of levels including shape, flexibility, rigidity, blocks, and total body form and expression.

We have no real existence apart from our bodies. What goes on in our minds is, basically, a reflection of what goes on in our bodies.

Alexander Lowen

Bio-energetics seeks to reintegrate man with five very recognizable realizations. The first is to re-establish the individual's identification with his body. The second is the recognition of the pleasure principle as the basis for conscious experience. The third is to accept, to *be* one's feelings. The fourth is to know that all awareness is subjective awareness. This allows for objectivity when the subjectiveness of consciousness is acknowledged. The fifth is humility. Humility is the recognition of ultimate powerlessness in the cosmos. It knows that neither humbleness nor arrogance is the answer, but that realization of the uniqueness of individuality leads to true grounding in reality.

Lowen has devised a number of postures and exercises which he feels help the individual on a path of natural healing. These include the two body bows, stretching backward and bending over forward; arching the back over a stool; and the hyperextensionized body circle. The above are all passive positions. Lowen follows these with a number of active movements. The passive positions help the individual experience the body and the areas of tension. They add dynamics and help liberate new energy.

The first active position is striking: females strike a bed with a tennis racket, males with their fists. In the second active movement the individual kicks the bed while lying on his or her back. The bed may be kicked with legs bent or extended. Flailing of the arms may accompany the kicking.

These exercises and postures enable the organism to breathe and then translate that breathing into action.

ACCESS

The principal exposition of bio-energetic theory is in two of Lowen's books, *The Betrayal of the Body* (which includes detailed descriptions of the bio-energetic exercises) and *Pleasure*.

117   Grounding and energy

The term "grounding" is used here to describe the work of Stanley Keleman. Keleman reunifies man with his animal origin so that he will then be able to be his body, to experience the flow of energy through the body, and to experience being grounded. Keleman says:

To me, grounding means being anchored in our physical-psychic growth processes: expanding, contracting (contact, withdrawal), charging, discharging.

. . . The opposite of grounding is flight, or interference with our human essence; its products (our common ailments) are fear, rage, frustration and dissatisfaction. Separation from the biological ground results in anguish and despair instead of the great potential for vitality, love, contact and growth with which we have been endowed.

Seeing the human animal as an energy system, Keleman recognizes three ways in which the organism accepts, transforms, and redistributes, different forms of energy, through discharge. First, the energy that moves from the head toward the earth. Interference releases unsureness, doubt and anxiety. Second, the build-up and discharge of tension on the part of the organism: expansion and contraction. Interference here produces frustration, anger, and despair. Finally, there is sexual energy centered in the lower section of the body. Interference produces immobility and panic.

Grounding enables the patient to become aware of tensions, blocks, splits, and interferences and thus deepens world contact and available energy. While increasing feeling, it helps him learn to live with the heightened awareness.

Keleman states that there are three layers to the individual. The first is the peripheral, or social layer which involves the musculature. The second is the middle or antisocial layer, with blocked anger, rage, and fear which involves deep-muscle patterns and vegetative organs. The third is the core layer, with deep feelings of aliveness, love, and knowing (without overstressed cognition), and with connections to our cosmos.

In his therapy and workshops with groups, Keleman uses repetition tapes. (See No. 47.) He sees these tapes as a time-kaleidoscoped system of negative programing; he uses his tapes to de-program. They are capable of letting the group hear everyday demands and commands ("Don't do that") many thousands of times in several hours. As we grow up we hear these commands that many times only in a number of years. He plays these tapes while the group members have increased energetic charges. These charges are created through the use of the exercises devised by Lowen (No. 116). What then occurs is that the organism responds by lifting out old memories and new possibilities and the individuals take possession of their bodies. This technique changes the psychological and physiological status of the individual.

While this is occurring Keleman often uses a tape with a positive universal program ("You and I are one"). To another track on the tape, he often adds music which he feels supplies the equivalent of background neural noise (e.g., Terry Riley's *In C*, Columbia Records MS 7178) and then has the group lie or sit in a circle, holding hands or putting their feet together. This leads to a variety of cosmic experiences, including visions, hallucinations, out-of-body experiences and mythic journeys.

Keleman finds that the intensity of these techniques increases with the size of the group.

ACCESS

Keleman has not published a book outlining his theories and practice. This information was drawn from a personal communication and two pamphlets. One, entitled "The Body Groups and Consciousness" (though the title page has the title as "The Body, Energy, and Groups") is available through the growth center, Kairos. The other, "Bio-Energetic Concepts of Grounding" was published by Lodestar Press, Box 31003, San Francisco, California 94131. *Sexuality, Self and Survival* has been produced from edited audio tapes of several Keleman workshops.

118 Psychomotor therapy

Psychomotor therapy refers to the techniques of psychotherapy and movement developed by Albert Pesso. It is a nonverbal technique teaching patients to be aware of their emotions and the expression of emotional impulses.

Pesso works with groups, and his technique revolves around a group that can come together regularly under the guidance of a therapist trained in psychomotor therapy. The work of the group proceeds through three stages. In the first stage, the group is presented with sensitization of motor impulses. This is achieved through learning how to stand and through such exercises as proper stance (a "species stance" where the oscillating body aligns and realigns itself with the field of gravity), raising the arms in the stance, a torso twist, and basic walks.

The second stage deals with the enactment of specific emotional situations. The group acts as "accommodators" by giving the expected and appropriate response to the individual's enactment.

In the third stage, the emotions and their functional expressions are polarized into positive and negative configurations. This too is achieved through group responses. The bad figures (played by group members) represent the bad aspects of real life and often provide the opportunity for cathartic release. The positive figures (also played by group members) represent the desired goals, the ideals of real life, and facilitate the replacement of frustrating and often harmful experiences.

Pesso has been a professional dancer, a teacher of dance, and a choreographer.

ACCESS

Pesso has published a book that outlines his methods and describes group procedures, *Movement in Psychotherapy*.

119 Psychosynthesis

Psychosynthesis is a system developed over more than half a century by Roberto Assagioli. It is concerned with the separate and separative elements of the psyche. It postulates that there is an unchanging "I-consciousness." Unlike physical-emotional-biological-mental states which change constantly and consistently, this "I-consciousness" is a persistent central core of the self.

In order to reach this unifying center of the self, Assagioli has developed methods for self-identification awareness, strengthening the will, and visualization. All of these revolve around imaginative evocations. These are certain key phrases, similar to hypnotic inductions, that are repeated and experienced. Symbols, colors, programed daydreams, and a variety of other techniques are used in this treatment.

Assagioli and his associates have developed and described over forty separate techniques of psychosynthesis. Following is a description of the technique of visualization:

First, imagine the setting, which is a classroom with a blackboard, grey or dull black. Then imagine that in the middle of the blackboard appears a figure; let us say the number 5, as if written with white chalk, fairly large and well defined. Then keep it vividly before your inner eye, so to speak; that is, keep the image of the five vivid and steady in the field of your conscious attention. Then on the right of the five visualize the figure two.

So, now you have two figures, a five and a two, making fifty-two. Dwell for a while on the visualization of this number, then after a little while, imagine the appearance of a four at the right side of the two.

Now you have three figures, written in white chalk, five, two, four—making the number five hundred and twenty-four. Dwell for a while on this number.

Continue adding other figures until you are unable to hold together the visualization of the number resulting from those figures.

ACCESS

A book named for the method, *Psychosynthesis,* outlines Roberto Assagioli's principles and techniques. It also includes a bibliography of his publications. The Psychosynthesis Research Foundation is located at 527 Lexington Avenue, New York, N.Y. 10017.

120 Client-centered therapy

Client-centered therapy was one of the first American attempts at an existential, humanistic psychology. The approach was developed by Carl Rogers. Rogers constantly and consistently centered the therapy around the experience of the patient by offering him a phenomenological feedback of what he had just described to the therapist.

An example through dialogue will illustrate:

Patient: My wife made me so mad this morning.
Therapist: You're angry with your wife for something she did.
Patient: Yes, she forgot to take my shirts to the laundry. She did it deliberately because I ignored her.
Therapist: I see. Your wife forgot your shirts on purpose, to punish you for not paying proper attention to her.

In this way the patient is exposed to how he is reporting his experience, and thereby can gain insight into his own behavior.

ACCESS

Rogers's books, *Counseling and Psychotherapy* and *Client-Centered Therapy,* spell out the basics of his approach. His later work is described in his *On Becoming a Person, Freedom to Learn,* and *Person to Person* by Rogers and Barry Stevens.

A film, "Three Approaches to Psychotherapy" devotes time to three psychotherapeutic interviews with the same female patient. Rogers, Albert Ellis (Rational Psychotherapy), and Fritz Perls (Gestalt Therapy) shows their techniques. Available from Psychological Films, 205 W. 20th St., Santa Ana, California.

121 Encounter

The word "encounter" was first used in relation to group therapy by Moreno (see No. 101) in 1912. But it is only in the last two decades that encounter groups have gained wide popularity.

Briefly, encounter signifies the attempt by a group, with a leader or without, to meet (existentially) and experience each other as real individuals, without masks, roles, or protective games. This means that many will have to drop their defenses in the group experience. They will have to stand naked before the group, with all of their faults and deficiencies on display. For some individuals this means an opportunity to find new strengths, to use potentials untapped in the workaday world, to find and/or to give support, and to experience crisis and growth in a safe environment.

Encounter presents a safe environment in which to experiment with taking chances, to try out involvement, feeling, and the expression of emotions. With this experience can come the development of facilities for trusting.

By trying out these experiences in the safety of the encounter group, by taking chances where support is forthcoming, it is hoped that the individual will gain self-assurance and be able to extend his strengths into the world at large.

ACCESS

Encounter technique is described in several essays in H. Otto and J. Mann's *Ways of Growth*, in Ruitenbeek's *The New Group Therapies*, and in Schutz's *Joy*. A basic text showing the origins of this method is Bradford, Gibb, and Benne's *T-Group Theory and Laboratory Method*.

An encounter group

122 Marathon

Marathon was devised by George R. Bach as an extension of the encounter process. It is a very simple procedure. A group meets in an encounter situation, but instead of breaking up after 3, 6, or 8 hours, they continue to stay together, exploring in a variety of different ways, for as long as 14 hours. Sometimes groups will stay together for a full 24 hours. The usual schedule is to meet for 14 hours, part to sleep, meet again for another 14 hours, and disband.

Staying with a group for a long period of time, where human interaction is as direct, spontaneous, open, and honest as is possible, can be taxing on defense systems after only an hour or two. After 10 hours most defenses have been stripped away.

ACCESS

Ruitenbeek's chapter, "The Encounter Marathon," is one of the best in his book, *The New Group Therapies;* the book also has many references to other articles. Another of his books, *Group Therapy Today*, reprints some important comment on marathon, including a paper by its founder, Bach.

123 Potentials

The term "potentials" refers here to the work in psychotherapeutic processes developed by Herbert Otto. Otto has used a number of systems to bring people into better contact with the potentials they possess but do not use. This includes his system of sensory restimulation, which is similar to the type of work done by Selver, Brooks, and Gunther. He advocates that sensory awakening experiments be done not for "kicks" but for what he refers to as *affirmation*. He has also developed techniques for increasing the awareness of family potentials and strengths. One of these is the inventory technique. Here the family gathers and takes an inventory of its specific strengths and weaknesses as a group. Members of the family support the person reporting and help to make him or her aware of things overlooked. Assignments can be given in order to follow up material that is uncovered during the inventory, with an agreement to meet again for reassessment.

Potentials group

Another method used is the "strength bombardment" technique. One family member is selected and the others "bombard" him or her with verbal reports of the individual's strengths and assets in relation to the family. Another technique developed by Otto is the Minerva experience. Otto describes the Minerva experience as a positive, creative past experience with which are associated deep emotional feelings. These experiences alter and affect the way the individual grows and develops potentials. By uncovering and recalling these experiences, the individual can tap old *and* new sources of psychic energy. The Minerva experience may also free creative potential that is applicable to current life situations.

ACCESS

Two books edited by Otto, *Explorations in Human Potentialities* and *Ways of Growth* (with John Mann as coeditor), contain a number of his papers. The *Explorations* book gives references for further reading.

124 Art therapy

A few hours alone, or with friends, and a box of paints, pens, crayons, or finger paints can be one of the simplest and most interesting techniques for altering consciousness.

In Art theory the object is to provide the patient with a nonverbal technique for freeing his feelings through a medium of self-expression. In addition, it can often allow hidden talent to be exposed. In a group, if all the members are engaged in the production of a single work, it may be even easier for the individual to expose his inner feelings. Art therapy can be used to treat blocks and unresolved problems as well as problems of identity and creativity.

Janie Rhine has pioneered in the combination of Gestalt therapy and Art therapy. She introduces some of her groups by having each member do something with a selected medium, e.g., clay, chalks, finger paint, and so on. What is stressed, once the art works are in process, is that you are the work of art that you create; the work is an extension of your self.

Another exercise involves breaking a group down into subgroups of five (a nucleus, and North, South, East, and West). These five are told that they are the only people left on the planet and are then urged to design and create their own community, in models.

Experiments such as these make Art therapy a vehicle for nonverbal self-discovery and consciousness enhancement.

125 Reconciliation

"Reconciliation" is the name given to the theories of Franklin J. Shaw. Here I will describe those theories and briefly discuss the emerging work of one of Shaw's followers, Sidney Jourard.

Shaw believed that aside from either heredity or environment, man's affirmation is a powerful psychological molding and shaping process. Man's capacity for self-fulfillment receives much of Shaw's attention. He felt that reconciliation was the means whereby man could merge the opposing forces of his own inner turmoil and those contradictions thrust upon him by society and biological uniqueness. Commenting on Shaw, Jourard (and Overlade) said: "[He] dedicated himself to the enterprise of liberating man from the 'determiners' of his [man's] existence, by working a kind of 'judo' upon those determiners."

Jourard has sought to find new ways for man to become a direct, open and "transparent" human being. The major thrust of his therapeutic and philosophical inquiries has been directed at helping man find unique ways of allowing himself to be who he really is, for all others to see, touch, feel, and experience.

If I, from time to time, suspend my concept of myself, and "tune in" on my being; if I meditate, or reflect on my experience, then I must re-form my self-concept. I will believe myself to be different. I will act differently. I am different. Moments of meditation are the times (rare in our culture) when we try to let the changing flux of our being disclose itself to us. . . . In meditation we also let the world disclose more of its changing being to us, and we may find ourselves experiencing more of the variety in the world.

The experience of surprise is also a sign of one's readiness to grow. Amazement and wonder signify that one's concept of self and of the world and of other people are "loose," ready to be re-formed. The "know-it-all," the "cool" one, has pledged himself never to be surprised.
Sidney Jourard

ACCESS

Reconciliation, edited by Jourard and Dan Overlade, presents the work of Shaw. Jourard's own work includes *The Transparent Self.*

126 Family therapy

Family therapy is practiced by any number of therapists. Probably the best known is Virginia Satir who calls her approach "conjoint family therapy." In conjoint family therapy she stresses the various aspects of communication—verbal, nonverbal, and sensory, as well as the problems of having close but free relationships. In her workshops she synthesizes a variety of techniques including sensory awakening, encounter, and role-playing to strengthen perception and awareness of family abilities.

She has also established what she calls "well-family" clinics throughout the United States to stress and aid in the fostering of positive family functioning. Often, new thinking and rethinking of family roles, rules, and relationships is referred to as "thinking about the unthinkable," since the very core and structure of family ties can be threatened by exposure and examination. But most often, the family that can expose its inner cares, order, and workings to thorough evaluation benefits through the development of more flexibility and interchange between the different family members.

ACCESS

Satir has established a work outlining her theories and practice entitled *Conjoint Family Therapy*. Audio tapes of her workshops are available from Big Sur Recordings.

127 Self-therapy

Self-therapy was developed by Muriel Schiffman as a collection of techniques to be used for personal growth. These methods are designed to be implemented and explored with the individual acting as his or her own therapist.

Schiffman is concerned with the recognition of the value of bad experiences, or the therapeutic nature of suffering. But this value lies in the awareness of the bad games that one is playing with one's self. Recognition of inappropriate actions and responses, thinking out loud, writing as an expressive means to inner feelings, and contact with one's own idealized self-image are methods that she describes in her self-therapy system.

ACCESS

Schiffman has outlined her ideas and suggestions in her book, *Self-Therapy*. Her later book, *Gestalt Self-Therapy*, integrates Gestalt techniques with her earlier work.

128 Nude therapy

Nude therapy is therapy that is conducted with patients and often the therapist wearing no clothing. I use the term here also to cover developments in the field of nude sensitivity training. Extensive work in both of these areas has been pioneered by Paul Bindrim. Many people are frightened by the possibility of spending time with a group of strangers where no one is wearing any clothing.

One of the questions that always comes up concerning this is the possibility of sexual activity. Bindrim says that the longer groups spend together in the nude, the less self-conscious people feel about being looked at and visually explored, and about doing their own visual explorations. Bindrim has also noted that body contact in nude therapy groups, especially marathon groups, becomes more and more spontaneous and less sexually oriented as the group continues and time goes on.

The advantages of nude therapy have been summed up by Alexander Lowen:

. . . nakedness is the great leveler of social distinctions for it reduces all persons to the common bodily or animal level on which they came into the world. Nudity strips the individual of his ego pretensions and, sometimes, of his ego defenses. . . . Nudity removes all privacy and reduces all pride.

ACCESS

Ruitenbeek's *The New Group Therapies* devotes a chapter to nude group therapies. This chapter includes quotations from and references to papers by Bindrim and Alexander Lowen on the use of nudity in psychotherapy.

129 Dance therapy

Dance therapy was originally formulated by Marian Chace as a means for dealing with catatonic veterans who were hospitalized following World War II. Her initial discovery was that these patients could be temporarily lifted out of their catatonic state by starting to dance. If they could be enticed to dance they were then encouraged to form a circle. When they danced and started to move their pelvic regions, their eyes would begin to come back into focus.

As a result of the dancing many of the patients began wanting to get well and would, for the first time, become amenable to help from the psychiatric staff.

Later, Chace trained dancers to do dance therapy in mental hospitals, and before her death she was able to open up nearly every psychiatric hospital to dance, where before there had been none.

Dance therapy is very similar to movement in therapy. The aim is to help the individual find a means of self-expression and of integrating movement.

Generally, dance therapy takes two forms. Some groups operate around a series of set movements which are practiced until they can be executed to the satisfaction of both patient and therapist; they may be individual movements or a programed sequence.

The second type of dance therapy group emphasizes free-form discovery. Different types of music are played and the patient is encouraged to try out spontaneous expression of body position and varied movements that fit the music, the environment, and the patient's feelings and ongoing experience. The aim is toward self-awareness through the discovery of personal spontaneity and style.

What can be particularly exciting in Dance therapy is the discovery of some new form of self-expression. Often the leader will request that the dance form be used to express the emotions between group members.

What we do dancing is often more honest and direct than what we do verbally in day-to-day contact.

130 Theater games

Theater Games are a result of the application of the principles of psychodrama (See No. 30) to therapeutic and political situations. Street theater, guerilla theater, The Committee on the West Coast and La MaMa E.T.C. on the East Coast are examples of the political aspects of theater games in action.

The therapeutic approach to theater games was pioneered by Viola Spolin. She describes a number of strategies in the form of theatrical "games" that groups can play together. Some examples:

One member of the group assumes a position on the floor. The other members of the group are told to link up to him, one by one, to form a machine, with moving, working parts.

Three members of a group are picked to tell a story. But none of them knows what the story is, how it begins, proceeds, or ends. The story is determined by the three improvising with each other.

The whole group is told to tell a story. Each member tells part of the story and the person next to him has to pick up where he stops, even if it is in mid-sentence without a pause of more than three seconds.

ACCESS

Improvisations for the Theatre by Viola Spolin is the main work in the field. In it she makes reference to other writers.

131 Primal therapy

Primal therapy was developed by Arthur Janov. Janov claims that the primal therapy technique is not only the cure for neurosis and psychosis but for a variety of other ailments:

I believe our discovery [primaling] is the end of mental disease, and probably the cure of all other disease. I do not say that lightly. And I am sick of [others] taking it sensationally. There is nothing sensational about it. We have the answer, that's all there is to it.

Primal therapy, or primaling, starts when the prospective patient is accepted by the primal therapist on the basis of a handwritten autobiographical account. No personal interview is conducted. Next comes a thorough medical examination to insure that the patient is physically sound enough to withstand the rigors of primaling. After the medical examination the patient is isolated for 24 to 48 hours. Any contact with outsiders, media (including reading material), drugs (including tobacco and alcohol) are prohibited. This isolation lowers the patient's defenses. The patient then begins a three-week period where he is the only patient seen by the therapist. The course of therapy might well be called "pain encounter." The patient is told to relive his life, and goes back into his past to recount all of his painful experiences, often including a fantasy re-experiencing of childbirth itself. Janov claims that through this contact with pain, the primal pains will eventually appear. With the primal pains come the primal screams for "mommy" and "daddy."

Individual treatment with a therapist, who might spend as long as 12 hours each day with a patient, lasts for 3 weeks. Then the patient moves on to group primal experience, 3-hour sessions which take place twice a week and can go on for several months. Twenty to fifty or so patients make up the group. At the completion of the group experience the patient is "cured."

Unlike other therapies, which fluctuate in cost, primal therapy charges run $1650 for the 3-week intensive, isolated primaling, and $20 for each group session.

ACCESS

Primal Therapy is the name of Janov's first book, detailing his therapeutic approach and procedures. The quote is from an article, "The Primal Doctor" by Jerry Hopkins, which appeared in *Rolling Stone* (February 18, 1971). Janov's latest published books are entitled *The Anatomy of Mental Illness*, and *The Primal Revolution*.

132 Multiple psychotherapy

Multiple psychotherapy was devised by Richard Miller and Larry Bromberg. The basis of the technique is quite simple: more than one therapist is always present during the therapy sessions. This offers a new dynamic to a group psychotherapy experience because some of the attention of the group toward integrating behavior is focused on the relationships between the therapists as well as the way the individual therapists deal with the patients and with the group as a whole.

133 Behavior therapy

Behavior therapy was developed by psychiatrists and psychologists in Great Britain. The theory maintains that neurosis is truly only the symptom or observable behavior of the patient. By treating the symptom—that is, by helping the patient unlearn old types of behavior responsible for the symptom, and by helping him develop new ways of adapting—the neurosis is cured.

Behavior therapy holds that a series of hierarchies of anxiety is built up by the patient. To deal with these psychological structures, two basic techniques are used by the therapists.

In the first technique the patient learns to relax by tensing each part of the musculature separately. After holding the tense position for some time he completely relaxes the area just tensed. The entire body is worked on in this way with the therapist determining when relaxation is achieved. Following this instruction the patient is usually capable of achieving a form of total body relaxation.

In the second technique the patient is encouraged to fantasize a scene that relates in some way to his self-described symptoms. When the therapist senses that the patient is experiencing anxiety, he encourages him to develop the fantasy, and then instructs him to relax totally. After relaxation is achieved the patient returns to the fantasy. Eventually anxiety is reduced.

Behavior therapy also uses other methods, including aversion therapy (punishment during exposure to symbols of the neurotic behavior), operant conditioning of both the positive and the negative type, and rewarding of assertive behavior.

Operant conditioning, formulated by B. F. Skinner, has two basic premises: one, to reward correct behavior by positive reinforcement, and two, the instruction of desirable behavior patterns in small slow steps. Assertive behavior is usually rewarded by verbal approval and reinforcement from the therapist. The types of negative conditioning used range from verbal threats and castigation to the use of certain forms of electric shock.

ACCESS

The primary text in this field is *Behavior Therapy Techniques* by J. Wolpe and A. A. Lazarus. A good introduction to the technique is available in Beech's *Changing Man's Behavior*. It has a bibliography with almost 150 entries for further reading.

Rolfing, or structural integration, takes its name from Ida Rolf, who developed this system of deep-muscle manipulation and realignment. In rolfing the practitioner focuses on the client's body and the physical manifestations of the body's relationship to gravity and the environment. A rolfer analyzes the interplay of structure, movement, energy and tension in the way the client lives in the environment and helps the client to free his body for new ways of working with gravity.

Rolfing teaches that the client's body is a mirror of past experience and will display the damage resulting from emotional experience as well as physical trauma. Experiences from early childhood are often reflected in the posture and carriage of the adult.

Your body reacts to a variety of stimuli with tension, rigidity and resistance. These reactions eventually bring about a habitual muscle position because the muscle sheaths, or fascia, lock and control muscle movement and tone. Once the fascia become rigidified, it is almost impossible to change muscle position at will. All the mothers in the world telling Johnny to stand up straight won't help. Johnny can temporarily pull his shoulders back, but he's already fixed into contracting his diaphragm as a habitual response to situations of anxiety and stress.

The rolfer works with the client by reaching in and realigning the muscle fascia so that body structure may be reintegrated, with special attention paid to gravity and the client's contact with and grounding to the earth.

Rolfers claim that work on a client can be completed after as little as ten hours of structural integration work. The result is new freedom in posture, alignment, muscle tone and usage. This can be accompanied by a reduction of tension.

A frequent complaint associated with rolfing is that the procedures cause great pain. In the beginning this is so. The manipulation of the muscle fascia is painful, but when the hands are removed the pain subsides.

An adjunct to rolfing, involving a series of exercises that an individual who has been rolfed can do at home, is called "structural patterning," and was developed by Judith Aston in association with Ida Rolf.

ACCESS

Ida Rolf has published a booklet called "Structural Integra- tion." It costs $1.00 and is available from her at 11 Riverside Drive, New York, N.Y. 10023. A journal devoted to rolfing appears quarterly. The *Bulletin of Structural Integration* is located at 16756 Marquez Avenue, Pacific Palisades, California 90272. Sam Keen described his own rolfing experience in the article "My New Carnality," published in *Psychology Today,* Vol. 4, No. 5, October 1970.

135   Alexander technique

The Alexander technique is named after its developer and founder, F. Matthias Alexander. The technique provides a method of awareness training that enables the individual to experience the way his muscular and skeletal systems are used, both during movement and at rest. Once this becomes part of conscious awareness, an Alexander technique teacher can then show the patient how to choose more appropriate ways to use his body.

The Alexander teacher helps the patient to come to this new awareness by a series of movements, exercises, and by the "laying on of hands." An example will illustrate this. You are with an Alexander technique teacher, lying on your back on a massage table. The teacher softly but firmly places his hand under your neck and directs you to raise your right leg, bending it at the knee as you do so. When you raise your leg you can feel the muscles in your neck tighten and contract against the teacher's hand, demonstrating how you use your neck muscles to "help" your leg muscles. If you can learn to become aware of this unnecessary neck tension you can go on to learn how to correct it.

ACCESS

F. M. Alexander's writings have been collected by Maisel under the title *The Resurrection of the Body*. The American Alexander Center is located at 227 Central Park West, New York, N.Y. 10024. An article, "The Alexander Technique" by Ilana Rubenfeld and Edward Rosenfeld, appears in *Workshops of the Mind*, edited by Bernard Aaronson.

136   Breathing therapy

Breathing therapy is learning how to breathe as one did when an infant. It is practiced by Magda Proskauer and others. The breathing pattern of an individual is an expression of his inner being, in the same way that the posture and physical set represent his personal dynamics. Breathing is a bridge from the conscious to the unconscious.

Our breathing throughout the day is without rhythmic regularity: it becomes rapid when we are angry, stops when we are scared, chokes us when we feel grief, and so forth. Proskauer believes that self-corrective procedures in breathing follow awareness of the way we breathe. She also has indicated what real breathing is:

Normally, when at rest, one breathes more with the diaphragm, like the abdominal breathing of the infant. Complete chest breathing, where the ribs expand and lift, occurs only at times of maximum effort. It usually starts the moment we pull ourselves together for action, or if we focus our attention toward outer events. . . . To put it in oversimplified terms: abdominal breathing goes with sleep, rest, inertia, letting things happen. Where it is disturbed, the inner life is disturbed; one is driven, unreceptive, and lives too intentionally.

ACCESS

An article by Proskauer, "Breathing Therapy," describes the theoretical basis for her work. It was published in Otto and Mann's *Ways of Growth*.

137 Autogenic training

Autogenic training, also known as autogenic therapy, was developed by J. H. Schultz. Autogenic training is a combination of psychotherapy and psychophysiological exercises. The emphasis is on combining mental and physical functioning.

Autogenic training includes two sets of exercises, standard and meditative. The six standard exercises are to be executed in a quiet place, with low lights, loose clothing, in either a sitting, reclining, or horizontal position, with the eyes closed.

The first standard exercise is designed to affect the neuromuscular system. A key phrase is "My right (left) arm is heavy." The heaviness is indicative of true relaxation. The second exercise deals with the vasomotor system. The phrase is "My arm is warm." This can cause the expansion of blood vessels in the desired area. The third exercise deals with the heart. The key phrase is "Heart beat calm and regular." The fourth exercise concerns the respiratory system. The key phrase is "It breathes me." This can produce relaxed, natural breathing. The fifth exercise applies to the central nervous system. The key phrase is "My solar plexus is warm." This can bring calming. The sixth exercise concerns the cranial region. The key phrase is "My forehead is cool."

These exercises are to be attended to with *passive*, rather than intensive or fixed, concentration. When first doing the exercises 30 seconds to a minute is sufficient. After several months the time can be extended to over a half-hour.

The meditative exercises are for advanced autogenic students. The therapist usually tests to be sure that the standard exercises can be maintained without effort for more than a half-hour.

The meditative exercises are tried and practiced over a period of months. The patient meditates on:

spontaneous phenomena
spontaneous colors
colors at will
imaginative objects
imaginative abstracts (freedom, truth, etc.)
feelings (emotions)
interrogations of the unconscious

ACCESS

J. Schultz and W. Luthe have already published 2 standard texts: *Autogenic Training* and *Autogenic Therapy*. Further information and a summary of the work is included in Luthe's article in the C. Tart book *Altered States of Consciousness*. The article and the books give references for further reading. A review of some of the exercises is included in R. S. deRopp's *The Master Game*.

138 Massage

Massage is the rubbing or kneading of the body. It helps to relax the muscles and generally stimulates circulation. As in Marshall McLuhan, *The Medium Is* (also) *the Massage*. A massage is a pleasure to give as well as to receive.

There are specific massage techniques, and many states license professional masseurs. Below are some general considerations prepared by Bernie Gunther for the art of massage.

Ask the person to be massaged to take a hot bath or shower first; it will add to his pleasure. Use ⅔ cup vegetable oil and ⅓ cup baby oil, then add something that smells good, such as oil of clove or almond extract. Try to maintain continuous touch, if only softly. The person being massaged will help you discover specifically how to touch when rubbing. Always try to rub toward the heart.

Stroke in circles on the neck, and then down from the head. Stroke up and down the arms and around the shoulders. Stroke and knead up and down the legs and thighs. Stroke up the stomach and down the sides. Stroke up in circles, then down in circles on the back. Lift the head gently, and corkscrew the fingers and toes.

George Downing gives the following suggestions in his *Massage Book:*

Try stroking with the balls of the thumbs
moving the fingertips with deep pressure in tiny circles
kneading
raking
stroking with the heels of the hand
stroking with the undersides of closed fists
drumming with the fingertips
making large sweeps and circles with the undersides of the forearms

When you are being massaged, feel it. Don't talk—just be with the touch. When the massage is over, lie still and enjoy the sensations.

ACCESS

A fine, simple guide to massage is the one by Bernard Gunther available in pamphlet form from Esalen Institute. It is called "Keep in Touch with Massage." A textbook on the subject, with many illustrations, is Beard and Wood's *Massage: Principles and Techniques.* In *The Last Whole Earth Catalog,* Stewart Brand has nice words for George Downing's *The Massage Book.*

139 Hypnosis

Self-hypnosis is mentioned in No. 15, where instruction is given on hypnotic induction. However, many professionally trained hypnotists hypnotize others for purposes of relaxation, psychotherapy, restoration and cure, psychic exploration and experience, and for such frontier investigations as time distortion.

Ronald Schor defines hypnosis as follows:

Hypnosis is a complex of two fundamental processees. The first is the construction of a special, temporary orientation to a small range of preoccupations and the second is the relative fading of the generalized reality-orientation into nonfunctional unawareness.

Hypnosis can be used (and has been by Bernard Aaronson, et al.) to change color perception, spatial orientation, perception of locale, experience of heat, and even to produce mystical states. Many subjects have achieved astounding results through the use of Aaronson's hypnotic induction of the void experience.

ACCESS

See the access material for No. 15. For another view of hypnosis see T. X. Barber's *Hypnosis: A Scientific Approach* and *LSD, Marihuana, Yoga and Hypnosis.*

140   Kinesics

Kinesics, also known as body language, is an elaborate attempt to read the way in which we arrange our bodies in response to the variety of situations and environments that we experience during our waking hours. The main work on body-motion communication and its meanings has been done by Ray L. Birdwhistell.

Birdwhistell has developed a notational system, which he calls kinegraphs, that divides the body into eight different sections:

1. total head
2. face
3. trunk and shoulders
4. shoulder, arm, and wrist
5. hand and finger activity
6. hip, upper leg, lower leg, and ankle
7. foot behavior
8. neck

KINEGRAPHS

Sc ≥   Scalp forward

⌣ ⌣   Brow moderately furrowed

\ /   Medial brow contraction:
               light asymmetry

⊗ ⊗   Eyes open, in focus

△ ʒ   Nose at zero position (at rest)

< ℓℓ >   Lips with corners of mouth
               pulled slightly to each side

∪   Chin in light tension

Kinegraphs, the notational system of Kinesics

To give an example of the descriptors of this system I will list the ten indicated positions for the neck:

1. anterior projection
2. posterior projection
3. right lateral projection
4. left lateral projection
5. neck tense
6. neck sag
7. swallowing
8. adam's apple jump
9. neck twist right
10. neck twist left

When this system, or systems like it, are mastered, then the nonverbal systems that most Westerners are committed to using in all social contexts become real communications rather than hidden movements of dubious meaning.

The next time you are speaking with someone and you notice him moving away from you, crossing his legs, folding his arms over his chest and generally retreating, examine what you're saying that is driving him away.

ACCESS

Ray Birdwhistell's work, *Kinesics and Context,* is scholarly and has an excellent bibliography. Fast's *Body Language* is a popular presentation that lacks depth but reads easily. Some of the best material in this field can be found in Edward Hall's works, *The Silent Language* and *The Hidden Dimension.*

141   Laban movement

Laban movement is based on the insights and work of Rudolf Laban, and is also known as effort-shape analysis. The method stresses inner experience of movement above theory about it. Through awareness of inner states during movement, the subject can learn functional actions as well as emotionally expressive postures and gestures.

Laban developed a comprehensive system of notation for the positions of the human body. This system is often employed to "write" choreography, in much the way that music is written. Beyond delineating the individual positions of a dancer's body, it may be used to record an entire dance piece, including the complex interactions of any number of dancers dancing at the same time.

Laban notation can increase your awareness of how you use your body and what you experience during specific movements. In this sense the Laban system may become not only a map of movement, but of feeling.

ACCESS

Laban's work has been carried on by his student, Irmgard Bartenieff. Further information is available from the Dance Notation Bureau School which is located at 8 East 12th Street, New York, N.Y. 10003. Laban's book is called *The Mastery of Movement*.

142   Bates method

The Bates method, named after its developer, W. H. Bates, is a system for improving vision so that glasses need not be worn. Bates prescribed exercises for helping to strengthen and relax the eyes. However his aim is also to re-educate the process of seeing. When we see all things anew our entire experience of life changes. As we change the quality of our sensory processing we change the quality of our consciousness.

One of these exercises is called "palming." The object is to provide rest and relaxation for the eyes by closing them. When the lids are closed light can still penetrate. Bates suggests that the way to keep light from reaching the eyes is by placing the palms over the eyes, with the fingers being crossed on the forehead. This shuts out the light and allows the eyes to rest. The hands cover the eyes but do not touch them.

After resting the eyes, shift from side to side and swing around, clockwise and counter-clockwise. Do this with the eyes closed for about 30 seconds each exercise. Palm the eyes before and after for rest and relaxation.

Another technique that Bates advocated was to look at a black surface so that one can *see* the black. This is also restful and relaxing to the eyes, especially when no attempt is made to see by holding or fixating. Just allow the black to calmly fill the field of vision.

ACCESS

The Bates book, *Better Eyesight Without Glasses,* has been reissued after many years of being out of print. An even better treatment is Aldous Huxley's long out of print *The Art of Seeing.* The book is in many libraries and describes Huxley's struggle with impending blindness and the use of the Bates techniques. There are many references to Bates and his method in the *Letters of Aldous Huxley.*

143 Compressed time

Compressed time has to do with investigations, now under way, that are examining the subjective experience of time. These experiments attempt to instruct and train individuals to manipulate, slow down, and speed up their experience of time.

Robert Masters and Jean Houston refer to their work in this area as accelerated mental process (AMP). They point out that we all experience AMP conditions: when we have a dream that seems to take hours and actually passes in seconds or minutes; during periods of emotional duress when one's whole life is experienced in a matter of seconds; and in other altered states of consciousness.

Masters and Houston use methods pioneered by Milton Erickson and Linn Cooper in hypnotic time-distortion. They induce a trance in their subjects and instruct them that they are now free to increase the amount of experience that would usually be possible during normal clock time. Their subjects have included composers, dramatists, priests, and artists. The subjects have returned from trance having had experiences of many hours, even days, in a matter of minutes.

In June, 1969, Stewart Brand led a compressed-time workshop at the Esalen Institute. I quote the program description:

Multiply time by ½2. An hour passes every 5 minutes. It's meal time every half-hour or so. Night is brief and oddly restful. Altogether it's an unboring, unhurried experience in which more (and different) accomplishments are possible than in normal time. The evening will be paced by clocks, sounds, lights, meals, and social cues to contain the events of a weekend.

This controlled environmental situation was uniquely effective. Brand said that people reported later that it had taken more than 24 hours after the workshop to adjust to normal clock time.

ACCESS

The pioneering work in this field was done by Linn Cooper and Milton Erickson. Consult their book, *Time Distortion in Hypnosis*. Masters and Houston will publish a paper, "Subjective Realities," in the *Yale Scientific Review* (in press) and more details of their work will become available in their forthcoming book, *New Ways of Being*.

144 Golf

Ecstatic experience and adventure lurk in the queerest of places. Michael Murphy, founder of Esalen Institute, stopped off in Scotland many years ago on his way to India. While in Scotland he played some golf and had, as a result, some of the richest mystical experiences of his life.

Murphy's mystical, mythical master of golf, Shivas Irons, initiated him into a system where golf symbolizes the true spiritual potentialities of the human soul. Golf is seen as the transcendental journey, not so much as a venture to get somewhere as a mythical circumnavigation of inner space. The components of the journey, those that lead to spiritual reunification, include a study of the whiteness of the ball, the mystery of the golf cup and the cup as a metaphor for the doorways in ordinary life, the art of replacing the divot, and the study of true gravity as produced by the backswing.

Speaking of Shivas Irons's ideal, Murphy concludes:

His ideal would have us know this Body and this Dance, would have us live in it while playing golf and singing ballads and talking to our friends; yes, and even while we are trying to pass it on to others.

ACCESS

Michael Murphy has described his experiences of and thoughts on golf in his book *Golf in the Kingdom*. Arnold Haultain's 1908 classic, *The Mystery Golf*, was reprinted in 1965. Also see articles and books by golfer Bob Toski.

Religions and mysticism

145   Yoga

Hindu religion, philosophy, and psychology are at the root of many developments that have reached us in the twentieth century. Hinduism brings man toward ultimate unity with the godhead, the Atman. Yoga is a *means* of achieving this unity.

If I were asked under what sky the human mind . . . has most deeply pondered over the greatest problems of life, and has found solution of some of them which well deserve the attention even of those who have studied Plato and Kant—I should point to India.
                                                      Huston Smith

There are many Yogas: Hatha, Jnana, Bhakti, Karma, Raja, Mantra, Laya, Shiva, Swara, Gyani. (Other forms of Yoga, including Agni, Kundalini, and Taoist will be discussed separately.)

The four main Yoga forms are all Hatha Yogas, the physical Yoga form popular for its variety of postures (asanas). There is Jnana Yoga which seeks knowledge of the godhead through intellectual knowledge; Bhakti Yoga, the Yoga of emotion, which seeks the godhead through the outpouring of love; Karma Yoga, the Yoga of work. Karma Yoga is usually realized through either the path of knowledge, Jnana Yoga, or through the path of love, Bhakti Yoga. The fourth way is Raja Yoga which is the path of psychological experimentation. It is in Raja Yoga that the asanas are practiced. It is also here that one hears of the astounding physiological self-control accomplished by its practitioners. Such feats as walking on coals, sitting on nails, regulating body temperature in adverse climates, and live burial can be claimed by the Raja Yogi.

There are eight steps in the pursuit of Yoga. They are

"The Lion," a yoga asana, or pose

generally divided into *outer* and *inner* phases. They include:

1. Abstinences (nonviolence, truth, no theft, chastity, and nonpossession)
2. Observances (purity, contentment, austerity, self-development, and constant thought of divinity)
3. The postures, positions, or asanas (The asanas are based on the placement of bodily centers. There can be, according to Yogic teaching, 84 × 1,000 potential positions for the centers. The 84 fundamentals are often reduced to 21 major postures.)
4. Control of the breath (Pranayama)
5. Removing the mind from concern with external objects (Pratyahara)
6. Concentration (Dharana)
7. Contemplation (Dhyana)
8. Ecstasy, bliss, or identification (Samadhi)

Different teachers, or gurus, emphasize different combinations of the above for the attainment of unity.

The West has attracted many Yoga teachers, who in turn have attracted large groups of followers. One group in particular has achieved widespread popularity. Heard in the streets of most American cities, it is known as the Hare Krishna chanters. Belonging to a group known as Krishna Consciousness and led by a guru, Swami Bhaktivedanta, they believe that union with the godhead can be achieved through repeated chanting.

HARE KRISHNA, HARE KRISHNA, HARE HARE, KRISHNA KRISHNA; HARE RAMA, HARE RAMA, HARE HARE, RAMA RAMA

This is the mantra that is chanted and sung repeatedly in the streets. In addition to chanting, they study the *Bhagavad Gita*, a sacred Hindu text.

ACCESS

Essential books for the study of Yoga and Hinduism include *The Upanishads, The Bhagavad-Gita;* DeBary's *Sources of Indian Tradition;* Zimmer's *Philosophies of India* and *Myths and Symbols in Indian Art and Civilization; Hindu Polytheism* and *Yoga: The Method of Re-Integration* by Alain Danielou; *Light on Yoga* by Iyengar; *Fundamentals of Yoga* by Ramamurti Mishra; Vithaldas's *The Yoga System of Health and Relief from Tension;* Satchidananda's *Integral Hatha Yoga;* Ramacharaka's *Hatha Yoga* and *Raja Yoga;* and Chaudhuri's *Integral Yoga.*

Yoga Centers in New York: Vedanta Society, 34 W. 71 St., 10023; Ramakrishna-Vivekananda Center, 17 E. 94th St., 10028; Yoga Institute, 50 E. 81 St., 10028; Integral Yoga, 500 West End Avenue, 10024.

The Huston Smith quotation is from his book: *The Religions of Man.*

146   Transcendental meditation

Of all the many forms and variations of the Yoga movement to become popular in the United States, none has achieved such widespread devotion as the Transcendental Meditation movement led by Maharishi Mahesh Yogi. Transcendental Meditation, known to its followers as TM, claims to bring peace and happiness without struggle. The basic TM method involves assigning a personal mantra, or holy syllable, to the meditator. The meditator is instructed in simple meditation techniques and is told to sit in meditation, meditating on his mantra, 40 minutes each day, 20 minutes in the morning and 20 minutes in the evening. It is better to sit before meals so that the body will not be busy with the digestive processes during the meditation period.

Maharishi Mahesh Yogi, founder and leader of Transcendental Meditation

During these meditation periods the focus is the personal mantra. Whenever his attention wanders the meditator gently brings his mind back to concentrate on his mantra. The aim is to develop a smooth, relaxed style of meditation.

There have been many claims for the effectiveness of TM. In this regard, a number of TM meditators have served as subjects for experiments that measured their brain-wave patterns, heart beat, respiration rate and other physiological indicators while they were practicing TM. The results of these experiments, showing what are thought to be beneficial changes in these indicators, have been published in leading scientific journals.

Though the initial publicity surrounding Maharishi has subsided, the movement has gained steadily in popularity. There are now TM groups in most major cities throughout the world. These groups maintain centers where interested individuals may be initiated into TM and given their personal mantra. The centers often have special rooms, or areas, set aside for meditation by TM members.

ACCESS

The results of the physiological studies of TM meditators were published in *Science, 167,* pp. 1751–1754, 27 March 1970. The article "Physiological Effects of Transcendental Meditation," by R. K. Wallace, describes decreases in heart rate and oxygen consumption, increase in skin resistance and persistency of alpha EEG rhythm. *The Science of Being and the Art of Living,* by Maharishi Mahesh Yogi, describes his personal development and the establishment of the TM movement. The TM movement is treated in a chapter of *The New Religions* by Jacob Needleman.

147 Agni yoga

Agni Yoga is fire Yoga, or fire union. There are two kinds of Agni Yoga now prevalent. One is the teaching brought back from the Himalayas by the Russian painter, Nicholas Roerich, and his wife. The Roerichs investigated central Asia, particularly Tibet and the Himalayan mountains. From this journey came their interpretation of Agni Yoga based on the Buddha of the future, Maitreya. The Roerich version of Agni Yoga draws on a variety of teachings present in the Vedantic schools of Hinduism and in the Mahayana Buddhist sects.

Their practice consists of paying special attention to diet, which they call astrochemistry, and meditation, to bring about the calm that eases the strains of reincarnation.

Recently, Ralph Metzner and others have called attention to another Agni Yoga teaching known as actualism. This teaching is related to the initial works of Madame Blavatsky, Alice Bailey, and Maurice Nicoll. It now centers around the work and experimentation of Russell Paul Schofield. Actualism purports to present the actual design of man as a cosmic being. It differs from other systems in that it aims to make the unconscious conscious by means of new methods that, according to Metzner:

> . . . *eliminate the images and mechanisms obstructing and deviating energy flow through the various structures and functions of the personality systems.*

Actualism posits three kinds of food: physical food, including the solids and liquids and gases that we eat, drink and breathe; psychological food, including perceptions, feelings, thoughts, and attitudes; and energy food, which comes from life—light-channeled energy. Actualism's third law of energy states: "Obstructions to energy flow cause discomfort, if mild, or pain and dis-ease, if strong."

The exercises of actualism are based on the principle that the individual will think, allow, and observe. An energy exercise involves thinking about a point of white light located some 6 inches above the center of the head. Once recognized through thinking, allowing, and observing, the light is thought of as opening up and pouring a shower of white-light energy over the entire body. It is advised that this exercise be done every day for a few minutes. Another use of this exercise is to focus the white light on the points in the body-energy system where blockage is experienced. These exercises are all done while sitting comfortably, straight-backed, in a chair, legs uncrossed, feet flat on the ground, hands on legs. A variation is to assume this position but place the right palm over the solar plexus and the left palm over the heart. While in this position the white-light exercises are repeated.

ACCESS

A series of Agni Yoga books are available through the Agni Yoga Society, Inc. at 319 W. 107 St., New York, N.Y. 10025. These include most of the works written by Madame Roerich. The work of Russell Paul Schofield is reviewed, as is actualism in general, in Ralph Metzner's *Maps of Consciousness*. Metzner makes reference to a forthcoming text by Schofield on actualism: *The Actual Design of Cosmic Man*. Schofield's poetry has been published under the title *Imprint Unmistakable*.

148   Tibet

When one talks about Tibet one thinks not only of the country, but of a state of mind, a mysticism generated by both the physical and the psychic heights. In Tibet there exists, or did exist (we do not know the full extent of changes brought about by Chinese rule there), Tibetan Lamaism, Tibetan Buddhism, Tibetan Yoga, Tantric Yoga, and Kundalini Yoga.

A number of Tibetan religious and mystical teachers called "tulkus" have recently settled in the West. The teachings they bring with them are arduous and thorough. Tibetan Buddhist philosophy is based on compassion and the accumulation of merit. In order to accumulate merit the initiate works on the Bhum-nda, or the exercise of 100,000. This is a series of exercises or meditations; each must be performed 100,000 times. There are five such exercises, the first of which is a prostration.

The hands are held with the palms close together but not touching. Holding the hands this way, they are then raised over the head, brought down in front of the throat, and then in front of the heart. The prostration is completed by touching the ground, with five simultaneous points of contact: the palms, the knees, and the forehead. While this bow is being executed a series of complex concentrations is also being executed, as well as an involved visualization and the repetition of a mantra.

The Tibetan initiate in Tibet will complete 100,000 of these bows in one month's time. When studying in the West, with emigré Tibetan masters, up to three months is usually allotted for completion of this first bhumi. The second bhumi is a series of 100,000 visualizations. The third bhumi is the recitation of the One-Hundred Syllable Mantra 100,000 times, as part of a meditation procedure. The fourth bhumi is the visualization of the mandala of the entire universe in miniature. The fifth bhumi is the recitation of the meditation of the Universe. After this, the initiate meditates for 3 years, 3 months, and 3 days.

It was in Tibet that Tantric study and Kundalini Yoga came to its flowering. The tantras teach that there are seven energy systems in the body. These systems, or centers, are known as chakras (cakras). Chakra means wheel. There are seven such centers postulated:

1. The root chakra, muladhara, at the base of the spine
2. The spleen chakra, svadhishthana
3. The navel or umbilical chakra, mani pura, at the navel or over the solar plexus

4. The heart chakra, anahata
5. The throat or laryngeal chakra, vishuddha, located at the front of the throat
6. The frontal or brow chakra, ajna, located just above and between the eyebrows
7. The crown chakra, or the thousand-petaled lotus, sahasrara, located on the top of the head

The Kundalini is thought of as a serpent (called by Art Kleps "an electric boa constrictor") that lies coiled at the root chakra. In meditation it begins to uncoil, releasing the energy of each chakra center as it ascends through the body.

The Tibetan Wheel of the Law

ACCESS

Jacob Needleman's *The New Religions* has a very good chapter devoted to "Tibet in America." The anthropologist Turnbull has written, with Norbu, an excellent guide to the country. Evans-Wentz's great works are all essential. Other fine books include Chogyam Trangpa's *Born in Tibet* and *Meditation in Action; Peaks and Lamas* by Mario Pallis; *Initiations and Initiates in Tibet* by A. David-Neel; Guenther's *Tibetan Buddhism without Mystification;* and Lama Govinda's *Foundations of Tibetan Mysticism.*

Books on Tantric Buddhism include the works of Sir John Woodroffe; *Introduction to Tantric Buddhism* by John Blofeld; A. Bharati's *The Tantric Tradition;* C. W. Leadbeater's monograph, *The Chakras;* and Omar Garrison's *Tantra: The Yoga of Sex.*

Tibetan Buddhist groups now exist in New York, Vermont, Colorado, Berkeley, Paris, Switzerland, England, and Scotland, as well as many other cities.

149 Tantric sex

Tantric sex is a form of yoga; the only yoga that deals with human sexuality. Tantric sex is a means for channeling the sexual energy that is manifested in every man and woman. The rituals and instructions that form the core of tantric sex seek to release that sexual energy through the use of physical techniques, prayers, mudras (gestures) and chanting mantra (holy syllables and words).

The most important of the physical techniques is the practice of controlled breathing. The tantric masters give their disciples careful instructions; the breath flowing through the right nostril is masculine, hot and electrical. The breath that flows through the left nostril is feminine, cool and magnetic. The disciples learn to control their breathing so that they can make their breath flow through either nostril at will.

A typical sexual ritual is the Panchatattva or secret ritual. Usually this is performed by a husband or wife. To begin the guru selects the proper mandala (a magical, circular meditation image) for the rite and this mandala is drawn on the floor where the ceremony is to take place. The guru also gives the man and woman specific mantrum to recite, both silently and out loud. The ceremony takes place in the evening in a dark room with many ritual elements such as candles, glasses, decanters, trays and incense. Small portions of meat, fish, rice and seeds are set in readiness. Alcohol is sometimes served as a prelude but is not required. The man and woman take a ritual bath to cleanse and purify themselves physically and spiritually. The man enters the room, empties his lungs and begins a breathing ritual to equalize the air in his body. Twelve times he inhales for a count of seven, holds the breath for a count of one, and exhales for a count of seven. On the thirteenth breath of the cycle he directs his energy to a spot between his phallus and his anus. As he holds his breath he helps to stimulate this area by contracting the muscles of his sphincter, releasing energy throughout his body. During this energy release he concentrates and meditates on the cosmic union between cosmic consciousness and cosmic energy. After this breathing cycle is completed the woman enters the room and the man chants several mantra. Then some of the food is eaten and several prayers are intoned.

At this time the two partners go to the bed. The woman disrobes and sits, upright, at the side of the bed. The man stands in front of her and admires her, while saying certain mantras, as specified by their guru. He touches her heart, head, eyes, throat, ear lobes, breasts, arms, navel, thighs, knees, feet and yoni (vagina). The man then disrobes and they lie on the bed together, the woman on her back, the man on his left side, facing her. He makes sure that his breath is emanating from his right nostril as she raises her legs and brings her knees to her chest. He moves his head and chest away bringing his phallus in touch with her genitals. She then brings her legs down and he moves his right leg between her legs. He then enters her, but not deeply.

The partners then lie together, relaxed and motionless, for 32 minutes, visualizing the flow of energy between them. At some time during the last four minutes a rush of energy occurs. In order to avoid ejaculation the man holds his breath, curls his tongue backwards in his mouth, and tightens his anal sphincter. After the 32 minutes (providing the man has not ejaculated) the energy is reversed and flows inward rather than outward from the partners. A sense of relief and joy is usually experienced at this time. If the man does ejaculate before the energy reversal the ceremony can be started again.

In the Eastern traditions of Tantric sex there is no orgasm but many Westerners practice variations of the Tantric procedures that include orgasm. Usually this orgasm is of a different nature than is usually experienced in the West. This is a relaxed, open and flowing orgasm. By relaxing rather than tensing at the moment of most intense pleasure the participants can discover an entirely new way to experience the sexual and loving union.

ACCESS

The most explicit description of Tantric sex can be found in Omar Garrison's *Tantra: The Yoga of Sex.* Other treatments are in the works of Sir John Woodruffe (pen name: Arthur Avalon), especially *The Serpent Power.* Another, more Western, treatment of this material is to be found in *Sex and Yoga* by Nancy Phelan and Michael Volin.

150   Taoism

Taoism is a way of thought derived mainly from the teachings of two Chinese masters, Lao-Tzu and Chuang Tzu. Academic arguments rage over whether the collected works that appear under these two names are from two minds or many. The answer is not important here.

Tao means "Way" (as well as many other things). It is the Way of Life, the Way of Truth. The major work attributed to Lao-Tzu is the Tao Teh Ching. No other book except the Bible has been translated into English more times than the Tao Teh Ching.

Traveling the Taoist way is a nonordinary reality, a special experience. Arthur Waley quotes the Taoist Master Hu-chiu Tzu: "The greatest traveler does not know where he is going." Buckminster Fuller says: "When I'm really working, I don't know where I am in the Universe."

Once Chuang Chou dreamt he was a butterfly, a butterfly flitting and fluttering around, happy with himself and doing as he pleased. He didn't know he was Chuang Chou. Suddenly he woke up and there he was, solid and unmistakable Chuang Chou. But he didn't know if he was Chuang Chou who had dreamt he was a butterfly, or a butterfly dreaming he was Chuang Chou.
  From Chuang Tzu *(Burton Watson's translation)*

Bend and you will be whole.
Curl and you will be straight.
Keep empty and you will be filled.
Grow old and you will be renewed.

Have little and you will gain.
Have much and you will be confused.

Here is the Way of Heaven:
When you have done your work, retire!

  From Lao Tzu's Tao Teh Ching *(John Wu's translation)*

In the Taoist tradition there is also a form of Yoga which is interconnected with Taoist alchemy. Taoist alchemy is quite straightforward. Unlike Western alchemy, which claims to concern itself with the transmutation of base metals into gold but actually offers esoteric data and formulae on the transformation of the psychological and philosophical *matter* of man, Chinese alchemy aims at nothing less than immortality. And the practice is concerned with, among other factors, the sexual processes.

The way the alchemy and the Yogic practice proceed is

by instructing men to keep from ejaculating semen, which was thought in China to be the life essence and generative force. Once immortality was achieved, the man could then look forward to an earth life free from all illness. After this life comes the great emptiness in which he will appear in order to help others along the noble way.

Other Taoist texts that have survived aim at the liberation of consciousness through the control of breath, much like Hatha Yoga, and through the circulation of light in the practitioner, much like Agni Yoga.

ACCESS

The major texts of Taoism are the collected writings attributed to Lao Tzu under the title *Tao Teh Ching*. The main translation is by Arthur Waley, *The Way and Its Power*. A good modern translation is by J. C. H. Wu, *Tao Teh Ching*. The works of *Chuang Tzu* are in a fine translation by Burton Watson.

Creel's *What is Taoism?*, Welch's *Taoism*, and Waley's section on Chuang Tzu in his *Three Ways of Thought in Ancient China* all make good commentary on the Way and its development.

Taoist alchemy is presented in the original forms in Lu K'uan Yu's (Charles Luk) *Taoist Yoga*. A less sexual treatment of material from a similar source is *The Secret of The Golden Flower*, translated and explained by Richard Wilhelm and with additional commentary by C. G. Jung.

The *I Ching*, a basic Taoist text, is considered in No. 190.

151   Confucianism

The works of Confucius, Mencius, and Hsün Tzu form the basis of the ancient Chinese way of social organization that is known as Confucianism. Though now out of favor with the political organization of China's Communist Party, Confucianism, and its ability to find a true place for all men in society, was responsible for China's long history as a united nation-state.

Confucianism as a means of enlightenment has been considered by Huston Smith. Commenting on possible means of planetary organization for the future, Smith suggests incorporating the essentially Western skill of making technology work, the essentially Eastern skill of investigating the Self and the self, and the essentially Chinese (Confucian) skill of organizing men into groups. He writes:

I believe that the Confucian concept of jen, *which translates literally as tribesmen, freemen, or equal men, is the one social concept that might find success in helping us orient ourselves toward planetary retribalization. In Confucius's time,* jen *stood for cultivating human relationships, developing interpersonal faculties and abilities, and upholding human rights, often requiring the sublimation of one's own personality. Confucius said:* Jen *should never be abandoned even though one goes off to live with the barbarians.*

ACCESS

The essential works of Confucian thought have been gathered together by Chai and Chai under the title *The Humanist Way in Ancient China*. *The Analects of Confucius* have been translated by Arthur Waley. The works of Mencius have been translated by D. C. Lau, treated by Waley in his *Three Ways of Thought in Ancient China*, and analyzed for meaning by I. A. Richards in *Mencius on the Mind*.

The *I Ching*, a basic Confucian text, is considered in No. 190.

Ezra Pound's translation of the *Classic Anthology* has appeared under the title *The Confucian Odes*.

The quote from Huston Smith appeared in the *Center Diary* (17) March–April, 1967.

152 Buddhism

Buddhism as a religion, a philosophy, and a psychology comes from the historical character of the Buddha, Siddhartha Gautama of Sakyas, near Benares in India. The name Buddha means one who knows, one who is awake. Buddha woke up by sitting under the now famous bodhi tree and coming to his enlightenment. He formulated the Middle Way, a way between asceticism and indulgence.

Buddhism as a religion grew out of a background of Hinduism and was, in many ways, a rebellion against the Hindu practices of the time. Eventually, Buddhism divided into two sects, Hinayana and Mahayana, Lesser and Greater vehicles, little and big rafts. What follows is a discussion of the part of Mahayana Buddhism which seeks what the Buddha sought: to awake, to know. That sect is known in China (where it began) as Ch'an and in Japan and most of the twentieth-century world as Zen Buddhism.

Buddha, lacquered bronze, Siam, 16th Century

The meeting of Indian dhyana (contemplation) practices with the Chinese Taoist Way yielded Ch'an (the Chinese word for meditation; Zen in Japanese).

Zen is the essence of Christianity, of Buddhism, of culture, of all that is good in the daily life of ordinary people. But that does not mean that we are not going to smash it flat if we get the slightest opportunity.
R. H. Blyth

The main practice of Zen and the basis for the Zen now alive in the West is dhyana or meditation, which in Zen is known by the Japanese word *zazen*, sitting.

Communication in Zen is through the koan (Japanese for the Chinese *kung-an*—general case, or case establishing some legal precedent). Koans are the records of the enlightenment of the masters. Koans are cases, records, writings which illuminate by example or description.

D. T. Suzuki, who was almost singlehandedly responsible for most of the interest in Zen in English-speaking countries, always enjoyed describing Zen with the Four Statements:

A special transmission outside the Scripture;
No dependence on words or letters;
Direct pointing at the Mind of man;
Seeing into one's Nature and the
*   attainment of Buddhahood.*

Some koans:

Kui Cheng said: Do not try to conjecture about Buddha Dharma [Truth] by employing this bodily mind of yours. Where can you start to put it into words? Is there a Dharma to which you can draw near? from which you can withdraw? Is there a Dharma which is the same as you? that is different than you? Why are you creating all these difficulties for yourself?

A monk asked Chao Chou: What is the mystery of mysteries? Chao Chou asked: How long have you been in the mystery? The monk answered: A long time. Chao Chou responded: If you had not met me you probably would have been killed by the mystery.

A monk asked Shih Pei: What is myself? Shih Pei replied: What you do with yourself.

Often koans refer to Bodhidharma coming from the West (India). Bodhidharma brought dhyana from India to China where it took root as Ch'an. The monk asking a master what the purpose of this journey was, like all other monk's questions to masters in koans, is asking: what's it all about?

A monk asked Ching Chu: What is the purpose of Bodidharma coming from the West? Chin Chu said: A slab of stone in mid-air. The monk bowed and thanked the Master. Ching Chu asked: Do you understand? The monk replied: No. Chin Chu said: It is fortunate that you do not understand. If you do, it will break your head.

A monk asked Chao Chou: Does the Master go to Hell? Chao Chou replied: Yes. The monk asked: Why? Chou Chou answered: If I don't, who is going to teach you?

A nun came to Chao Chou and asked about the secret teaching. Chao Chou felt her vagina. The nun said: Does the Master have this? Chao Chou said: I do not have this, but you have it.

A monk asked Chu Tun about the Tao. The Master said: Do you think that you differ from the others. If a person can realize this, he then is one who has attained the Tao. He should feel that there is nothing different between himself and others in all matters even as [ordinary as] wearing clothes and eating meals. He has no mind to deceive. If he says "I've got it! I understand!" Don't have anything to do with him!

A monk asked Chih Chin: What is the continuous flow of eternal reality? Chih Chin replied: It is like a mirror that forever shines. The monk asked: Anything over and above that? Chih Chin responded: Break the mirror and come to see me.

Huston Smith has observed:

A group of Zen masters, gathered for conversation, have a great time declaring that there is no such thing as Buddhism or Enlightenment or anything even remotely resembling Nirvana. They set traps for one another trying to trick someone into an assertion that might imply, even remotely, that such words refer to the real things. Artfully they always elude the shrewdly concealed traps and pitfalls, whereupon the entire company bursts into glorious, room-shaking laughter, for the merest hint that these things exist would have revealed that they are not the true masters of their doctrine.

And finally, here is Blyth again:

. . . Zen tells us that the world is saved as it is. The ordinary man is the Buddha, time is eternity, here is everywhere. But this is only "so" if we know it is so. In the history of Zen, each monk as he becomes enlightened gloats over it almost indecently, just as the Buddha himself did, but how about all the poor unenlightened chaps, or those who died five minutes before they became enlightened? No, No! The universe must suffer, in being what it is, and we must suffer with it. Above all, the universe is a paradox, and we must laugh with and at it.

ACCESS

A good introduction to Buddhism can be found in the book of that name by Christmas Humphreys. The basic text of Hinayana Buddhism is *The Dhammapada*, which has been translated by Irving Babbitt. Some fundamental texts retell Ch'an and Zen koans (See No. 18). A fine work that deals with Ch'an and its development through modern times is

Charles Luk's three-volume *Ch'an and Zen Teaching.* The transmission of Japanese Zen (and with it the Ch'an tradition) was accomplished almost singlehandedly by D. T. Suzuki. All of his works on Zen are excellent. A one-volume sampling of Suzuki is available under the title *The Essentials of Zen Buddhism,* edited by Bernard Phillips.

A History of Zen Buddhism, by H. Dumoulin, is adequate. R. H. Blyth supplements this (*see below*). An excellent comprehensive anthology is Nancy Wilson Ross's *The World of Zen.* Two modern approaches to Zen are revealed in Kapleau's *Three Pillars of Zen.* Kapleau is director of the Zen Meditation Center of Rochester, New York. Shunryu Suzuki, better known as Suzuki-Roshi, the master at Zen Mountain Center, Tassajara, California (treated fully in Needleman's *The New Religions*), has published a book of his talks, *Zen Mind, Beginner's Mind.*

The most joyful of all the Zen writers and writers on Zen is the late R. H. Blyth. His *Zen in English Literature and Oriental Classics* is exactly what the title says and most fulfilling. His finest work on Zen was cut short by his death. *Zen and Zen Classics* is a five-volume work. Three volumes treat the history of Zen and Ch'an with Blyth spirit, the fourth volume is a supreme rendering of the Mumonkan collection of koans, and the fifth volume is made up of essays.

153 Tea

The Tea Ceremony, also known as Cha-no-yu in Japanese, is an expression of Buddhistic consciousness. There are very specific and rigid rules to the serving of tea. These regulations guide the setting, the building, the implements, the participants, the sequence of the ceremony, and the tea itself. To be spontaneous within this rigidity, to let perfection *happen* despite all these prescriptions—this is Cha-no-yu.

What is most outstanding about the tea ceremony is its serenity and its beauty. Beauty surrounds the tea house, in the gardens and ponds. The architecture of the tea house represents another kind of beauty. The lamp, the furnace to heat the tea, the board that is used to support the kettle stand, the kettle stand itself, the kettle, the kettle hanger, and the jars where the leaf tea is kept are all made by craftsmen and masters with the utmost care and aesthetic consideration.

All of this beauty has but one aim: to open the mind, the body, the senses.

ACCESS

Two classics exist on the art of tea. One, *The Book of Tea*, by Okakura, is an essay and an appreciation. The other, A. L. Sadler's *Cha-No-Yu*, is the most complete work in English on the Tea Ceremony.

Cha-No-Yu, the Tea ceremony

154 Haiku

Haiku is a form of poetry which is written in seventeen syllables. Each poem contains a word that refers to the season described in the haiku. The following haiku are by the three greatest haiku poets of Japan. (All translations are by R. H. Blyth)

Spreading a straw mat in the field
I sat and gazed
At the plum blossoms.

Basho

It is deep autumn;
My neighbour—
How does he live?

Buson

The autumn storm;
A prostitute shack,
At 24 cents a time.

Issa

Many Westerners have attempted to write haiku. Some have succeeded.

In a railroad yard,
bound for a world with flowers,
butterfly and I.

James Hackett

In my medicine cabinet
the winter flies
died of old age.

Jack Kerouac

ACCESS

R. H. Blyth has written the finest books on haiku in the English language. Harold Henderson was the first to make translations; they all rhyme, which misses the point. Blyth has two multivolumed works which cover haiku and make it clear: *Haiku*, in four volumes: *Eastern Culture, Spring, Summer–Autumn, Autumn–Winter;* and *A History of Haiku*, in two volumes.

James Hackett has published *The Way of Haiku*. Jack Kerouac's haiku were remembered by Allen Ginsberg in an interview published in *The Paris Review*, No. 37, Spring 1966.

155 Kyodo

Japanese fencing, kyodo or kendo

Kyodo, also called Kendo, is Zen archery—"artless" art, an effortless exercise. The aim is not the target, the target is the archer. Herrigel describes his master:

He placed, or 'nocked," an arrow on the string, drew the bow so far that I was afraid it would not stand up to the strain of embracing the All, and loosed the arrow. All this looked not only very beautiful but quite effortless.

The aim of kyodo practice is to become oneself. When loosing the arrow only that activity will be taking place. In many ways kyodo is similar to sitting zazen. When one is a master of Kyodo, the arrow, the bow, the target, the archer, the present moment, and the universe know no separation, no boundaries. All are one.

ACCESS

Herrigel's account of his bout with kyodo is in his *Zen in the Art of Archery* now published with another of his essays, *The Method of Zen,* in one volume entitled *Zen.* A new book, called *Zen Archery,* is large and includes illustrations.

156 T'ai Chi Ch'uan

T'ai chi ch'uan is also known by the names: Tai chi, and Chinese boxing. It is moving meditation combining deep breathing with a series of slow movements where the body weight is constantly shifting and the arms are describing circular arcs. Early development of T'ai chi ch'uan came from the Taoist religious tradition. The contemporary form was codified by Chang San-feng in the 12th century.

T'ai Chi master Da Liu showing the single whip and push forward T'ai Chi positions

T'ai chi ch'uan looks like dancing but it is not. This appearance comes from the flowing way in which the exercises are executed. There are 37 basic exercises and postures called forms which are learned at the beginning of training. Then these basics are repeated with variations, bringing the total number of exercises to between 65 and 108, depending on the T'ai chi ch'uan master supervising the instruction.

The flowing exercises can be speeded up into quick, sharply percussive movements. Springing from utter relaxation, these movements are particularly effective in combat because of the element of surprise.

Throughout T'ai chi ch'uan practice the emphasis is on centering the body, meditation and relaxation. Later, The study of the I Ching may be undertaken to give philosophic dimension to the T'ai chi ch'uan practice.

ACCESS

Two good books on Tai Chi Ch'uan are Cheng and Smith's *Tai Chi,* and DaLiu's *Tai Chi Ch'uan and I Ching;* both are illustrated. A film made in Taiwan of a master, is available for sale or rental from Tom Davenport, 235 2nd Avenue, New York, N.Y. 10003. Also available is a film by the T'ai Chi Society, 310 East 42nd Street, New York, N.Y. 10017.

A book to avoid on Tai Chi Ch'uan is Gia-Fu Feng's *Tai Chi— A Way of Centering & I Ching.* The Tai Chi section is uninformative and the translation of the *I Ching* is incomplete.

157   Martial arts

Zen Buddhism was at the core of the samurai way of life in medieval Japan. From the samurai conditioning come a number of martial arts. All of them attempt to instill the practitioner with a way in which to gain his own enlightenment and peace.

Some of the most popular martial arts include judo (the art of balance and leverage), karate (unarmed striking blows), aikido (self-defense through becoming your opponent—no fighting, or matches; only training), and iaido, stick and sword use.

ACCESS

Judo and Karate teachers abound. Watch your step. A good book on Aikido is called *Aikido and the Dynamic Sphere,* by Westbrook and Ratti. A list of Aikido Centers throughout the United States is printed in the January, 1971 Supplement to the *Whole Earth Catalog,* p. 34.

A judo championship competition

158   Calligraphy and Sumie

Black ink fresh ground in water from an ink stick on a stone block, a flexible pointed brush and a fresh piece of silk or rice paper are the only necessities. But these simple tools, in the hands of countless generations of artist-scholar-poet-philosophers in the East, have revealed the secrets of form and being.

Calligraphy by Shimzan Kamijo

Calligraphy as an art and a way of altering consciousness comes through aesthetic awareness, discipline and the control of the breath. Each configuration is executed in a long regulated exhalation of breath so that the flow is uninterrupted. Students are required to study and then copy the widely differing calligraphy masters. Once their talents are developed, they can begin to work on their own.

Each Chinese character, though a single unit, is made up of diverse parts in an asymmetrical arrangement. The way of seeing that calligraphy requires is a type of meditation, particularly when applied to painting. The subject is conveyed through its essentials, in a balance of shape and emptiness, with brush strokes of sufficient

power to reveal its basic nature, its breath—as well as its contours.

The expressiveness of *Sumie* (the Japanese name for brush painting) and calligraphy are unparalleled. A master can delineate any form, any gradation with a minimum of strokes, and, by only a slight change in pressure on the brush, completely alter the quality of a line or area of tone. Any subject may be treated, from the smallest sparrow to a range of mountains beneath the moon. Through the still, concentrated mind of the calligrapher great spontaneity is expressed with a few deceptively simple motions of the hand and arm. It flows on the paper almost without being noticed. Nothing has time to get in the way.

Caligraphy masters have spent years learning how "just" to write, "just" to paint.

ACCESS

Examples of sumie and calligraphy are on view in Awakawa's *Zen Painting* and Fontein and Hickman's *Zen Painting and Calligraphy*. An excellent introduction and manual is Yee's *Chinese Calligraphy*.

159 Flower arrangement

While Herrigel was studying the proper kyodo use of his bow and arrow, his wife was learning one of the ultimate Zen expressive forms: flower arrangement. Flower arrangement is much like the tea ceremony. There are many set ways and many prescriptions. The purpose is to let the "you" shine through the flowers, to let the you who arranges be the flowers which are arranged. No difference—you/flowers.

ACCESS

Herrigel's *Zen and the Art of Flower Arrangement* is the classic treatment in English. There is information on flower arrangement in both Sadler's *Cha-No-Yu* and in Okakura's *The Book of Tea*. The former deals with flowers only in relation to the performance of the tea ceremony, while the latter treats the subject more generally.

160 Sufism

Sufism is the mystic tradition of Islam. The basis of Islam is the absoluteness, the One-ness of God. Allah is the One Lord and every man is His servant and creature. The prophets, including Muhammad, were sent merely to call man to Him.

The Sufi is the one who does what others do—when it is necessary. He is also one who does what others cannot do—when it is indicated.

Nuri Mojundi

Like the Zen and Ch'an masters and the Hasidim (See No. 165), the Sufis, or Qadiris, maintain a lineage of knowledge through reports on the actions, behavior, and sayings of their masters. Below are some Sufi tales:

Bishr son of Harith was asked why he did not teach. "I have stopped teaching because I find that I have a desire to teach. If this compulsion passes, I shall teach of my own free will.

The candle is not there to illuminate itself.

Nawab Jan-Fishan Khan

A studious and dedicated seeker after truth arrived at the tekkia of Bahaudin Naqshband. In accordance with custom, he attended the lectures and asked no questions. When Bahaudin at last said to him: "Ask something of me," this man said: "Shah, before I came to you I studied such-and-such a philosophy under so-and-so. Attracted by your repute I journeyed to your tekkia. Hearing your address I have been impressed by what you are saying, and wish to continue my studies with you. But, since I have such gratitude and attachment to my former studies and teacher, I would like you either to explain their connection with your work, or else to make me forget them, so that I may continue without a divided mind."

Bahaudin said: "I can do neither of these things. What I can do, however, is to inform you that one of the surest signs of human vanity is to be attached to a person, and to a creed, and to imagine that such attachment comes from a higher source. If a man becomes obsessed by sweetmeats, he would call them divine, if anyone would allow it. With this information you can learn wisdom. Without it, you can learn only attachment and call it grace.

The man who needs information
Always supposes that he needs wisdom
If he is really even a man of information, he will see that he next needs wisdom.

If he is a man of wisdom, he only then is free from the need for information.

The Epitaph of Rumi:

When we are dead seek not our tomb in the earth, but find it in the hearts of men.

Translated by Idries Shah

In Islam there are 99 names of GOD:

1	ALLAH	47	Judge of Judges
2	The Compassionate	48	The Loving
3	The Merciful	49	The All-Glorious
4	The King of Kings	50	The Raiser from Death
5	The Holy One	51	The Witness
6	The Help in Peril	52	The Truth
7	The Peace	53	The Guardian
8	The Faithful	54	The Almighty
9	The Mighty	55	The Firm
10	The All-Compelling	56	The Nearest Friend
11	The Majestic	57	The All-Praiseworthy
12	The Creator	58	The Accountant
13	The Artificer	59	The Beginner
14	The Fashioner	60	The All-Powerful
15	The Forgiver	61	The Restorer
16	The Dominant	62	The Quickener
17	The Bestower	63	The Slayer
18	The Provider	64	The Ever-Living
19	The Opener	65	The Self-Subsisting
20	The All-Knower	66	The All-Perceiving
21	The Closer	67	The One Turned in upon Itself
22	The Uncloser	68	The Eternal
23	The Abaser	69	Providence
24	The Exalter	70	The Forewarner
25	The Honorer	71	The Fulfiller
26	The Leader Astray	72	The First
27	The All-Hearing	73	The Last
28	The All-Seeing	74	The Manifest
29	The Judge of All	75	The Hidden
30	The Equitable	76	The All-Governing
31	The Gracious One	77	The One Above Reproach
32	He Who Is Aware	78	The Good
33	The Clement	79	The Relenting
34	The Strong	80	The Forgiver
35	The Pardoner	81	The Avenger
36	The Thankful	82	The Ever-Indulgent
37	The Exalted	83	King of the Kingdom
38	The Very Great	84	Lord of Splendid Power
39	The Preserver	85	The Just
40	The Maintainer	86	The Gatherer
41	The Reckoner	87	The All-Sufficing
42	The Beneficent	88	The Sufficer
43	The Bountiful	89	The Provider
44	The Watchful	90	The Withholder
45	The Hearer of Prayer	91	The Propitious
46	The All-Comprehending	92	The Harmful
		93	The Light
		94	The Guide
		95	Eternal in the Past
		96	Eternal in the Future
		97	The Inheritor
		98	The Unerring
		99	The Patient

ACCESS

The primary interpreter of Sufism in English is Shah. Many of his works are already listed under Access for No. 18.

The Koran is the basic work of Islam, and Sufism is part of the Islamic tradition. A readable translation is by Pickthall, under the title *The Meaning of the Glorious Koran.* Other basic texts of Sufism include Al-Ghazali's *Niche for Lights;* and *The Enclosed Garden of Truth,* The Graves & Ali-Shah translation of *The Rubaiyyat of Omar Khayaam;* and Shabistari's *The Secret Garden* (Pasha translation). Poetry by Haifiz, Rumi, and Attar (especially his *Parliament of the Birds* allegory) is fundamental to Sufi study. Arasteh's study of Rumi has already been mentioned elsewhere (See No. 110). Corbin's massive *Creative Imagination in the Sufism of Ibn 'Arabi* is difficult but worth the effort. Matheson's *An Introduction to Sufi Doctrine,* Nicholson's *The Idea of Personality in Sufism,* and Burckhardt's translation of *Letters of a Sufi Master* are all good introductory texts. Arberry's account of this group, though scholarly, is informative.

Modern Sufi thought is represented by the twelve-volume *The Sufi Message of Hazrat Inayat Khan.* Especially noteworthy are Volumes 2, on sound and music, and 3, on education and human relationships. Samuel Lewis, who died in 1971, was an initiate of Khan's and also accepted by eight other Sufi orders. His *The Rejected Avatar* is a most unique tale.

A number of Sufi groups, organized around the teachings of Khan, meet regularly in major cities in the United States. The Islamic Foundation of New York is located at 1 Riverside Drive, New York, N.Y. 10023.

161 Gurdjieff

Georges Ivanovitch Gurdjieff was born in 1877(?) in Alexandropol near the Persian-Russian frontier. After training in the priesthood and medicine, Gurdjieff disappeared. Some say he went to Tibet to receive the high teaching from the masters that Madame Blavatsky (a nineteenth-century occultist) claims to have been in contact with; others report that he traveled among the Sufis and gathered his teaching through that association. In 1913, Gurdjieff showed up in Russia and taught groups in his own individual, enigmatic, unorthodox manner. One of his pupils was the writer, philosopher, and mathematician Ouspensky. Ouspensky recorded in his *In Search of the Miraculous* his encounter with Gurdjieff, their escape from revolutionary Russia with other members of the group engaged in "the work," and their settling in Paris in 1922. After 1924, Ouspensky taught separately in London.

Gurdjieff toured and lectured but always remained with his group in Paris. He considered himself a teacher of dance. He died in 1949.

The main tenet of Gurdjieff's thought is that of the four possible states of consciousness available to man, he (man) is capable of only two: sleeping and waking. The other two states, self-consciousness and objective consciousness, can only be reached through "the work." To reach these states man must awaken.

Blocking man's ability to awake is the fact that the individual is not one "I" but a multiplicity of I's. Individuals think that they do things, not realizing that they are machines. They have to "be" before they are able to "do."

Gurdjieff talked of the four ways: the way of the fakir,

Georges Gurdjieff

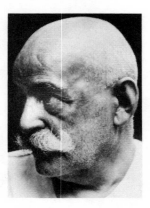

work on the physical body; the way of the monk, work on faith; the way of the Yogi, work on knowledge; and the fourth way, the way of the sly man, work on understanding.

Among the many exercises Gurdjieff taught his groups two of the most interesting were:

Self-observation: the ability to take mental photographs of oneself at various times. These are not just "photos" or images of details, but the whole picture of one's life at that moment. These pictures are to be studied so that the moods, postures, facial expressions, sensations, and so forth in every mental picture can be known.

Self-remembering: remembering who is performing the activity when the "I" is doing it. When Ouspensky tried self-remembering he found that it blocked his ability to think.

Gurdjieff aimed at creating a new man, an awake man. Others who studied with him, Ouspensky, Nicoll, Orage, also tried to continue this work in their different ways. Today, groups exist that carry on "the work." One of the advantages of the fourth way, according to Gurdjieff, was:

. . . *it is possible to work and to follow this way while remaining in the usual conditions of life, continuing to do the usual work, preserving former relationships with people, and without renouncing or giving up anything.*

One of the advantages of the Gurdjieff "work" is that it is not a matter of shifting between states of awareness and nonawareness. When done properly, "the work" continues at all times.

ACCESS

Gurdjieff himself wrote three books and a pamphlet. The pamphlet, *Herald of Coming Good* is short and not very exciting. The first book in his series, *All and Everything,* is all the title promises and more. It is a 1200-page recounting of life on earth as told by Beelzebub to his grandson as they speed by in a space ship—ingenious and difficult. *Meetings with Remarkable Men* is Gurdjieff's somewhat devious recounting of his early life and teachers. It somehow avoids convincing me that I've been given the real sources for all of his teachings. The third book, *Life is Real Only When I Am,* is a collection of his talks and lectures. It is yet to be formally published but is now being read aloud in many of the Gurdjieff groups. *The Teachers of Gurdjieff,* by Rafael Lefort, is Idries Shah writing under a pseudonym and attempting to lead us on an endless pilgrimage to nowhere. The point of the book is that Gurdjieff's teachings are not viable.

Gurdjieff's main pupil was Ouspensky. His *In Search of the Miraculous* is a record of his meeting and work with Gurdjieff. His own teaching is outlined in his *Psychology of Man's*

Possible Evolution (a series of talks) and *The Fourth Way,* a question-and-answer book. Maurice Nicoll's *Psychological Commentaries on the Teaching of Gurdjieff and Ouspensky* is in five volumes and is most complete. His own work, *Living Time,* is original and excellent. A modern account of teachings similar to Gurdjieff's is deRopp's *The Master Game;* deRopp is conducting a group in Santa Rosa, California. Ed van Tassel runs a similar group in San Francisco. Mr. Wolf runs a group in New York. Willem Nyland teaches groups in New York, Boston, Seattle, Santa Fe, and Sebastopol, California. His address is: Chardavogne Barn, Chardavogne Road, Warwick, N.Y. 10990.

162 Subud

Subud was founded by Mohammad Subuh. The center of Subud is a meeting, known as the latihan, which takes place twice a week and lasts for a half hour. People meet in sexually segregated rooms, and during the half hour no discussion or instruction takes place, no rules of conduct are enforced. The people at the latihan are free to do whatever they wish. They attend the latihan to submit to an acceptance of and receptivity to the power of God. Many who have attended latihans report remarkable experiences. Subud continues to grow as a group around the world.

ACCESS

A good account of Subud is given, with references for further reading, in Needleman's *The New Religions*. There are three major books on Subud. One is a collection of talks by the founder, called *Subud in the World.* Another is Edward Van Hein's *What is Subud?* The last is J. G. Bennett's *Concerning Subud.* Bennett was also part of the Gurdjieff–Ouspensky school and edited an interesting journal, *Systematics.* His two major works are *Energies* and *The Dramatic Universe* (4 vols.).

163   Krishnamurti

Krishnamurti was adopted at the age ot thirteen by founders of the Theosophical school. They proclaimed him the new avatar, the new World Teacher, and ordained the creation of the Order of the Star of the East.

Krishnamurti, 1928

Krishnamurti was Maitreya, the Buddha of the future. He was given such a fine education by this group of worshipers that several years after the proclamation Krishnamurti dissolved the Order of the Star and disclaimed having any knowledge, spiritual or otherwise.

He is now an accepted and sought-after Philosopher-Lecturer. His most profound insights include thoughts on death, desire, search, war, purpose, and the only meditation, the continuous meditation, being alive all the time.

Krishnamurti entertains questions at most of his appearances. Some sample dialogue follows (after a question on mental processes):

Krishnamurti: *I am speaking of something which you are refusing to face. It is very simple; the moment thought stops chewing its own tail, you're full of energy—aren't you? Because in that chasing, your energy has been dissipated. Right? Then you become very intense. No? What happens to a mind that is very intense, not under strain, but intense? What takes place? Have you ever been intense, about anything, have you? If you have what happens?*

Questioner: *Then you are not, as far as . . .*

Krishnamurti: *Wait. Wait. Sir, you say something and dissipate it. When you are intense, what takes place? There's no problem, and therefore you are not. You are only when there's conflict.*

ACCESS

Some of his books include: *Commentaries on Living* (3 vols.); *Education and the Significance of Life; The Only Revolution; Think on These Things.*

Needleman's *The New Religions* contains a chapter on Krishnamurti.

Krishnamurti speaks throughout the world. His schedule and other information is available from the Krishnamurti Foundation, 24 Southend Road, Beckenham, Kent, BR 3 ISD, England.

Meher Baba claimed to be the avatar, the Godhead in human form, come to earth for mankind. He claimed to be in the same line with Buddha, Jesus, and Muhammad. He did not speak for more than three decades. This was so because he felt that all the past masters and avatars had given the word and no one had listened. Meher Baba said that he would be the silent master. He did, however, communicate with his disciples, first through the use of an alphabet board and then through a system of hand gestures. His disciples spread the silent words of Meher Baba through books and pamphlets.

In the 1960s Meher Baba gained wide attention through his written pronouncements relating to psychedelic drugs. He said that though some drugs seemed to give religious or mystical experiences, this was just an illusion. The real spiritual way was to love God fully and completely, to give up one's entire self to God in love.

Meher Baba, 1932

A young man went to India and met with Meher Baba. He sought him out after several years of intense experimentation with psychedelics that had left him most anxious and distraught as to truth and real meaning in life. He reported, upon returning from India, that the meeting with Meher Baba produced two very profound experiences. One experience came when he entered the room where Meher Baba was sitting. He was totally overwhelmed by the perception of a very strong, unforgettable inner fragrance, unlike any odor he had ever smelled. He seemed to be smelling not with his nose but with his essence. The other experience was one of an outpouring of overpowering love throughout the room, love that seemed to come directly from the body of Meher Baba. He saw Meher Baba hold out his arms and

was immediately and mystically drawn into his embrace. He could never exactly describe the experience of holding and being helped by a man he felt was God. Meher Baba died, or "dropped his body," as Baba lovers say, in 1969.

ACCESS

Meher Baba set down his cosmology, cosmogony, and philosophy in *God Speaks*. Needleman's chapter on his movement, in *The New Religions*, tells most of the story.

165   Jewish mysticism

Jewish mysticism includes (especially) such groups as the Kabalists and the Hasidim. The Hasidim are relevant in many ways today and have an accessible literature. Much information is available on the *Bahir*, the first book of the Kabalists, assembled in the twelfth century. The development of this group ranged from ascetic, monklike study to messianic movements.

Hasidism became prevalent in Eastern Europe in the eighteenth century. Martin Buber has collected many of the outstanding tales of the early and later Hasidic masters. The Zaddikim, the rabbis and wise men who are the subject of these tales are identified by a variety of different names, which are standardized in the following quotes.

The Baal Shem said: "What does it mean when people say that Truth goes all over the world? It means that Truth is driven out of one place after another, and must wander on and on."

One sabbath, a learned man who was a guest at Rabbi Barukh's table, said to him: "Now let us hear the teachings from you, rabbi. You speak so well!" "Rather than speak so well," said the grandson of the Baal Shem, "I should be stricken dumb."

When the preacher Dov Baer realized that he had become known to the world, he begged God to tell him what sin of his had brought this guilt upon him.

Once when Rabbi Pinhas entered the House of Study, he saw that his disciples, who had been talking busily, stopped and started at his coming. He asked them: "What were you talking about?" "Rabbi," they said, "we were saying how afraid we are that the Evil Urge will pursue us." "Don't worry," he replied. "You have not gotten high enough for it to pursue you. For the time being, you are still pursuing it."

Before his death, Rabbi Zusya said: "In the coming world they will not ask me: 'Why were you not Moses?' They will ask me: 'Why were you not Zusya?'"

A community leader who was opposed to the rabbi of Kotzk sent him a message: "I am so great that I reach into the seventh firmament." The rabbi of Kotzk sent back his answer: "I am so small that all the seven firmaments rest upon me."

ACCESS

Buber's rendering of the Hasidic tales is referred to under access for No. 18. Scholem's *Major Trends in Jewish Mysticism* and Gewurz's *The Mysteries of the Kabalah* are good translations of Kabalistic thought. Elie Weisel retells many stories of the Hasidic masters in *Souls on Fire*.

The new Christianity, also known as the "Jesus freaks" and the "One-Way" movement, claims to be a return to the original spirit of Christianity. Its literature and public statements refer to the experience of Jesus Christ the man. Many of these groups live together in communal arrangements and often are socially structured along strong authoritarian patterns.

A prayer session of the Children of God, a new Christian group

One of the major tenets of the new Christian movement is its emphasis on drug-free life and drug rehabilitation. In this way it resembles Synanon, Phoenix House, Daytop and other "hard" narcotic-rehabilitation groups. Where the latter emphasize a neo-psychotherapeutic program, the new Christians substitute religious experience and Biblical dogma. Many of the groups have scripture and Bible study as their main activities. Other groups have ritual events like baptism at the core of their operations.

ACCESS

NBC's *First Tuesday* TV show did a highlight on groups in Texas, Cincinnati, and elsewhere. The California situation is described in Vachon's "The Jesus Movement Is Upon Us," in *Look,* February 9, 1971.

Astrology is one of the oldest of all sciences. It is concerned with systematizing the relationships between the movements of heavenly bodies and events on earth. Its results can be evaluated by experiment and mathematical or statistical modes of investigation.

There are seven different types of astrology:

Natal; involving character development and personality based on the configuration of the zodiac, sun, moon and planets at the moment of birth. These factors are also adjusted to the exact latitude and longitude at which birth took place.

National; concerning the developments of peoples, nations, and historical processes based on configurations similar to those used for individuals in natal astrology.

Horary; where questions are answered based on the time that the question was asked.

Astrometeorology; prediction of the effect of planetary influences on radio communication.

Medical; judging the nature and cause of illnesses and accidents, based on the relationship between the patient's birth configuration and the time of inception of illness or accident.

Election; choosing the best person at the best time and place for specific chores or duties. Especially for people who have to work together, as on jobs in industry or crews of airplanes.

Ontological; the use of all of the above to investigate philosophical and psychological relationships.

The astrologer begins by looking up in standardized reference books the positions of the planets, luminaries and constellations at a definite instant of time (as the moment of one's birth, in natal astrology). From this information he will then draw a map, known as a chart, which shows diagrammatically the positions of and relationships between the heavenly bodies.

In a natal chart, the map is divided into twelve sections, or houses. The time of birth determines what constellation or sign will be on the horizon, thus ruling the cusp or boundary of the first house. The other signs will fall accordingly over the other houses. The luminaries are then placed in their proper astronomical positions within the houses. Since each luminary of each house of the natal chart concerns different areas of human life, the interactions among luminaries (called aspects) and between luminaries, zodiacal signs and the houses, mirrors the development of the subject's personality and lifestyle.

The difficult task of drawing accurate conclusions from the chart's numerous positions and relationships is accomplished through the skill and sensitivity of the astrologer. He must combine his knowledge of the elements of the chart and their aspects with his insight into the person whose chart is at hand. The interpretation made by an accomplished astrologer delineates both important past events and future potentialities. The predictions are usually an indication of the positive and negative forces that will bear on the subject rather than forecasts of specific events.

The perspective astrology gives on the causes and nature of past, present and future events can distinctly alter our consciousness.

ACCESS

A good introduction to the subject is Louis MacNeice's *Astrology*. C. G. Jung's essay "Synchronicity" in Jung and Pauli's *The Interpretation of Nature and the Psyche* verifies the scientific basis of astrology. A good introductory text is the *A to Z Horoscope Maker and Delineator* by L. George. For more advanced work see the many volumes of Alan Leo. The finest contemporary astrologer/philosopher is Dane Rudhyar. See his *The Astrology of Personality,* and *The Planetarization of Consciousness*. A book for casting quick horoscopes with surprising accuracy is Grant Lewi's *Heaven Knows What.*

The astrological signs distributed throughout the body

168   Magick

Real magick is always secret.

ACCESS

To help you through the secrets read Colin Wilson's novel *The Sex Diary of Gerard Sorme.* His nonfiction book *The Occult* provides a look at contemporary magic and magicians. Also study the published work of the foremost magician of the twentieth century, Aleister Crowley. Budge's *Amulets and Talismans* and Christian's *The History and Practice of Magic* provide good background reading. Bardon's *Initiation Into Hermetics* and *The Use of Magickal Evocation* are for the more advanced student.

169   Alchemy

To the scientist the aim of alchemy seems only to be the transmutation of base metals into gold. Though some alchemists were concerned solely with this, many were serious and dedicated thinkers who used alchemical symbols and ideas to probe religious, philosophical and psychological problems. The "gold" of these men was wisdom and the creation of the whole, unmarred man. As Carl Jung has shown, the alchemists' symbols and methods were directly related to the workings of the collective unconscious and the individual psyche:

A 17th Century Dutch view of alchemy

Investigation of alchemical symbolism, like a preoccupation with mythology, does not lead one away from life any more than a study of comparative anatomy leads away from the anatomy of the living man. On the contrary, alchemy affords us a veritable treasure-house of symbols, knowledge of which is extremely helpful for an understanding of neurotic and psychotic processes. This, in turn, enables us to apply the psychology of the unconscious to those regions in the history of the human mind which are concerned with symbolism.

Carl Jung

It was through symbols that the alchemists expressed both their investigations of the elements making up human consciousness and the ways to integrate them effectively. The issues raised by alchemy are not dead. Some of our contemporaries consider psychedelic drugs to be this integrative principle, the philosopher's stone

of the new alchemy, and various masters have used alchemical methods in their own theoretical formulations—Gurdjieff's "Table of Hydrogens," for instance, posited a description of the elements of *matter* involved in man's consciousness.

ACCESS

Two introductory books are available, both called *The Alchemists*. One is by F. S. Taylor and the other by Caron and Hutin. *Mysterium Coniunctionis,* Jung's difficult treatment of the discipline, is found in Volume 14 of his collected works. Ralph Metzner's *Maps of Consciousness* contains a chapter on Alchemy.

170 Anthroposophy

Anthroposophy, literally, man's wisdom, was the name given to the work of the group that Rudolf Steiner formed in order to carry out scientific investigations of the spiritual realm. Steiner's was an incredibly able mind, producing singular works in many fields, including education, architecture, botany, and agriculture, and studies of such men as Goethe and Nietzsche.

Anthroposophy is Steiner's attempt to lay down a cosmic history and guide to the wisdom of the universe. It includes much of the knowledge that he gained through out-of-body experiences and astral projection.

Steiner developed a form of movement called eurhythmy, which means, literally, good rhythm. It was first used as an adjunct to the education of handicapped children. Steiner was interested in emphasizing the importance of rhythms, exercises, music and dance for developing what he called the "dulled sensual capacities." Eurhythmy is thought of by its practitioners as an art form and a therapeutic movement-exercise system, an organization of harmonious body movements to the rhythm of spoken words. The words, often in the context of highly emotional stories, are intended to provoke the inner forces to expression through movement.

ACCESS

Details on Steiner, his life and work, and anthroposophy are available from the Anthroposophical Society, 211 Madison Ave., New York, N.Y. 10016. Some recommended titles from the many volumes of Steiner's work: *Occult Science: An Outline; Theosophy: An Introduction;* and *Knowledge of the Higher Worlds and Its Attainment.*

171 Abilitism

Abilitism was developed quite recently by an ex-Scientologist, H. Charles Brener. It is a much looser, more well-rounded technique than Scientology. It aims to enlighten its practitioners through self-understanding.

Abilitism consists of two basic activities: "relating" and "enlightenment intensives." In the relating exercise two people sit facing each other, and while one talks about questions that relate to his existence, the other just listens. For 5 minutes this talking and listening go on, uninterrupted. Then the listener talks and the talker listens. This goes on with three or four talk/listen opportunities for each person in each session. Some of the sample questions include:

What is a problem you are now experiencing?
How do you stop yourself from relating to others?
What is something about yourself you hide?
How do others see you? How would you have others see you?

The enlightenment intensive usually runs for three days. The exercise is very similar to relating, but includes some new elements. You still sit opposite others, talking or listening attentively, but your talking is changed and so are the questions. The questions are:

Who are you?
What is life?

Rather than answer, you meditate and hold the question. As you hold it and attempt to maintain the question in your consciousness, various thoughts and images will come to mind. These spontaneous thoughts, which draw you away from the essential question, are what you tell the listener. Then you return your consciousness to the question. This goes on for 5 minutes. Then a bell rings and you listen to the other person relate to the same questions. This back-and-forth process goes on for 45 minutes, then there is a 5-minute break, a new partner is found, and the process is repeated. This process, with meals, exercises, and lectures goes on for 18 hours a day, from 6:00 A.M. to midnight.

There are also five-day intensives with the same scheduling. All conversation about anything but enlightenment is considered gossip, and is strictly forbidden during the intensives.

Abilitism represents an attempt to blend Eastern (non-talk) methods with Western (talk) methods. It now also uses some Yogic exercises and a health-food diet.

Brener has written a very poor, scientology-like booklet called *Abilitism: A New Religion* (co-authored with Richard Williams). Avoid this book if possible; it communicates very little of the discipline. The main headquarters is P.O. Box 798, Lucerene Valley, California 92356. There are also Institutes of Ability in Los Angeles, Oakland, San Francisco, Milwaukee, and New York.

172 Scientology

Scientology was devised by L. Ron Hubbard, a science-fiction author. It was originally called dianetics, and is a philosophical and psychological system. In America and Great Britain it is registered as a church for taxation purposes.

Scientology aims at moving people up through a complex and involuted hierarchal superstructure. The first objective is to be a *clear*. After that one can progress toward *thetan*. A clear can be an auditor and hear the problems of people who want to become clears. These aspirants are attached to what Hubbard calls an E-meter, which is a GSR indicator. (See No. 249.)

In addition to the fact that any operating GSR-measurement device will help a person know how his internal system is behaving (this is why auditing is successful), a number of other Scientology techniques *do* alter consciousness. Auditing is the best. In auditing the student tells the auditor everything that he can recall of what has happened to him. Whenever the auditor gets a response on the E-meter, he has the student tell that part again. Together, they work on the subject that elicited the response until there is no response for that subject. Then they move on. It's like vest-pocket psychoanalysis, and has a resemblance to certain procedures used in behavior therapy. The student is known as a *preclear* until he has successfully completed this auditing.

Two priests of the Scientology church with the E-meter

In some group processing, auditors use repetitious commands that are very effective in altering consciousness.

Often hypnotic in effect, these commands are frequently repeated for *hours* at a time. Some sample repetition phrases are:

EXAMINE YOUR CHAIR: SPOT SOME SPOTS: START LAUGHING, KEEP ON LAUGHING: LAUGH: COLOR TEMPERATURE WEIGHT: HOW CLOSE DOES YOUR BODY SEEM TO YOU NOW?

Scientology is very expensive.

ACCESS

Hubbard has written and/or published hundreds of works on Scientology. Introductions include *Scientology: A New Slant on Life* and *Dianetics: Evolution of a Science*. The instructions for auditors come from his *The Creation of Human Ability* which is not available to the general public.

An overview of scientology called *Scientology: The Now Religion* was published without Hubbard's blessings. A book tracing the negative aspects of this group is called *The Scandal of Scientology* by Paulette Cooper.

173 Arica

Arica is a training program developed by Oscar Ichazo. The name Arica is taken from the town in Chile where Ichazo trained his first group. The training consists of a variety of exercises that Ichazo integrated from many religious and mystical traditions, both Eastern and Western. Most of the exercises are experienced in the form of meditations. The focus of the meditations ranges over vibration, movement, sound, philosophical theories, planetary and galactic systems, music, kath (the center of the body, usually placed at or near the navel), tantra, kundalini and others.

The program is given over a variety of time periods. The 3-month intensive has classes 6 days a week, 10 hours a day. Other schedules last 6 and 9 months and weekend introductory workshops are offered. Those who complete the training often stay on to become part of the Arica staff of teachers. The basic course of the Arica training costs $3,000.

Ichazo says that the aim of the training is to produce a state of consciousness he refers to as the permanent 24. The number 24 refers to a state analogous to satori (in Zen Buddhism) or samadhi (in the yogic disciplines).

ACCESS

Ichazo has never published in English. John Lilly has described part of his experiences in Chile during the initial Arica training and some of the group exercises in his book *The Center of the Cyclone*. The main office of the Arica group is located at 24 West 57th Street, New York, N.Y. 10019.

A meditation session at the Arica Institute

Religious and miscellaneous

If you know of the existence of a religious or philosophical master or teacher that you feel will be just right for you, and you go to that master or find the source of that teaching, this journey is a form of religious pilgrimage. Another form is that practiced by the wanderer; he may make most of his life a search for the right teaching, the right teacher and the right time and place for learning.

The young man who went to see Meher Baba (see No. 164) went on a modern religious pilgrimage. He left Miami by plane, stopped first in Hawaii, and then went on to Formosa. From Formosa he begged, borrowed and connived his way overland across Asia, finally reaching India. This pilgrimage made his experience with Meher Baba, his master, all the more intense.

ACCESS

Baba Ram Dass's *Be Here Now* and his tapes, available through Noumedia (See No. 20), give his view of the religious pilgrimage. Other views include Hermann Hesse's *Journey to the East,* René Daumal's *Mount Analogue,* and the Sufi classic, *The Parliament of the Birds,* by Attar.

175 Faith healing

Physician, heal thyself! Patient, you may do the same. Though not all illness is caused by psychosomatic disorder, most are aggravated by a lack of understanding of the psychological conditions necessary for cure. The emotional environment developed by many faith healers is responsible for a great number of their successess. When the ill or lame patient knows that the healer he is to see has healed others, he feels it just might work for him too. If the healer possesses enough personal or charismatic power it often *will* work. This concept is similar to that which enables positive thinking methods to be so effective for so many people. It all has to do with the way we live: if we think something is so, we tend to help it become so, sometimes even in the face of extraordinary hardship.

ACCESS

LaBarre's *They Shall Take Up Serpents* deals with an unusual group in the Southern United States. Coe's *The Psychology of Religion,* Sargant's *Battle for the Mind,* and Kirkpatrick's *Religion in Human Affairs* also discuss the subject.

176 Seances

Seances are meetings of people who wish to receive spiritual messages. Generally an attempt is made to communicate with the spirit of a deceased family, friend, or acquaintance of someone present at the seance. At other times, a seance might try to contact a spirit having to do with the power of an event or structure, e.g., a house.

Though often pictured as a scene in which everybody sits at a round table holding hands, seances occur more often with the participants standing or sitting in a circle with nothing inside the circle, except perhaps some symbolically significant object, like a crystal ball. The group dynamics of the situation, plus the intensive energies being produced, often combine to bring about altered states of consciousness.

The medium is the person who directs the activities at a seance. Many are women. A medium claims to have the power to contact spirits; usually these spirits are supposed to be aspects of human beings who are now dead.

A medium will usually attempt to make contact with the spirit and to have the spirit indicate its presence to the others taking part in the seance. This demonstration is accomplished by some sort of unusual noise or movement in the seance room. Many seances have been broken up when the medium has been exposed as a charlatan who uses tricks to imitate a spirit presence. Many mediums in England have great followings because of their power.

177 Revival meetings

Revival meetings usually require a charismatic personality to bring them off. (See No. 175.) But most people
who attend them are already believers and trances are
usually the order of the day, or night. Faith healing,
ecstatic movement, snake handling, and holy rolling
are all instances of people experiencing extreme states
of consciousness change. If you become involved, it can
happen to you, too.

ACCESS

The Access material for No. 175 also applies here.

178 Charismatic speakers

[Greek *kharisma* = divine gift.]

Most of today's successful politicians are charismatic
speakers. When they address the public, their method of
delivery, their appearance, and their assumed social
position vis-à-vis the group to whom they are speaking
all combine to work a special kind of magic.

When you hear a speaker who can generate what seems
like electricity, when everyone listening to him is caught
up in the sound (not necessarily the content) of his
words, then you are in the presence of a charismatic
speaker. The next time you go to the political rally or a
religious mass meeeting (both George Wallace and Billy
Graham are good examples of charismatic speakers)
watch the crowd as you listen to the speaker. You'll see
them nonconsciously lean forward, nod, bob in their
seats, carry on subvocal dialogue, and grimace in reaction to things that aren't necessarily in the content of
the words being spoken. You will be observing the
special force of the charismatic speaker upon
his audience.

179   Crowds

On a city street some eight or nine people have gathered to investigate an unknown and otherwise unnoticed phenomenon. As other people walk by their eyes are drawn to the small group of people. Some walk over just to see what is going on. A crowd develops. The original group is standing crowded close together around a frantic man who is talking rapidly and breathing in gasps. More people are streaming toward the crowd. The attraction is magnetic. People who are part of the crowd are pressed tightly against one another, straining to hear what is being said at the center. All of the people in the crowd are focused on the same spot; their sensory attention is concentrated on the crowd, their crowd.

Suddenly, someone breaks from the crowd and runs down the street. Several people in the crowd give chase. Others stand and question each other in an attempt to orient themselves to the new events, to find out what's going on. People lose interest. They walk away. Others hang around, but there is no longer a center of activity; the focal point has disintegrated. The crowd breaks up.

In situations such as this, the consciousness involved is mass consciousness. Had the person who broke away from the crowd failed to escape, there might have been assualt, battery, perhaps even homicide. Crowds have the power to effect these sudden, often senseless acts.

ACCESS

Canetti's classic study, *Crowds and Power,* details all the altered states associated with groups. Also see LeBon's *The Crowd* for an earlier study of the same phenomenon.

An American crowd, 1939

180   Brainwashing

Contrary to popular opinion, the indoctrination technique called brainwashing, or thought control, does not work very well. It is applicable to short-term situations, but when belief systems are assaulted, temporary results fade away.

The temporary results are attained through the removal of familiar social and behavioral signals and through verbal assaults on the validity of personal reality-orienting systems. The methods used include repetition, contradiction, sleep deprivation, water deprivation and control of light and temperature.

When brainwashing is carried out over a long period of time, the intensity of the results obtained tends to lessen. But if exposure is for a week or so, it can result in extreme psychotic reactions, total disorientation, and in some cases, the onset of physical illness.

Technically, brainwashing can be called a form of intense hypnosis. The results usually produce a subject who is in a kind of trance. He seems confused, and his bewilderment colors all of his actions; his behavior is sluggish; he speaks only when spoken to, and his sentences are incomplete. All of this behavior is the result of the destruction of normal patterns of experience.

ACCESS

William Sargant's *Battle for the Mind* has most of the details, and presents them accurately and correctly. John Frankenheimer's highly entertaining film, *The Manchurian Candidate,* gives an exciting but somewhat exaggerated view of the results of brainwashing. See also the works of Robert Jay Lifton.

181   Flagellation

When the body is beaten the histamine content in the bloodstream skyrockets and one can get very high despite being hurt. Excessive beating is quite dangerous, of course.

Flagellation in a positive sense is used in steam baths, sweat lodges, and saunas to stimulate the circulation of the bather. After being in the steam bath or sweat lodge for some time the intense heat expands the skin and opens the pores. At this point it is best to flagellate the skin, usually with branches, in order to bring more blood toward the surface. This change in the circulation of blood helps the cleansing of the pores and brings about a tingling feeling in the skin. Some people have reported feelings of being high because of the change in blood flow brought on by a combination of heat and flagellation.

182   Body chanting

This technique is from Bernard Aaronson, who learned it from Shyam Bhatnagar, Pran Nath, and Harish Johari. The chant that was used on me was very similar to the *Live Very Richly You Happy One* chant described in No. 20.

For the spinal chant, the procedure is to lie down on a flat surface on your stomach. Your head rests on the ground, arms at your sides. The person who is going to chant places his or her lips approximately ½–1 inch over the base of your spine. There is a chant said for each chakra. (For details on the chakras and their locations see No. 148.) The chanter chants for at least 5 minutes over each spinal chakra. The teachers and therapists who are adept at this practice say that they experience the moment when a chakra opens and becomes activated. This is their signal to move on up the spine to the next chakra. No chanting is done for the seventh chakra, at the crown of the head. The person whose spine has been chanted over should be encouraged to lie still 5 or 10 minutes after the chanting has ended. The vibrational effect on the spine and the body as a whole can last as long as 3 hours.*

In addition to spinal chants there are frontal chants and full-body chants. When selecting places to chant over, remember that the vibrations will be releasing energy.

A most extraordinary method of body chanting is to have the one to be chanted on lie on either his back or stomach on top of some large speakers: the sounds that will come from the speakers will be chanting sounds that have passed through the body.

ACCESS

See Access for No. 20.

* The basic feeling of this vibrational effect is tingling and lightheadedness. The body seems much looser, colors are brighter, and most sounds seem clearer. It's a feeling of "loose clarity."

183 Happenings

Whether they are planned or totally spontaneous, happenings are events to experience. Mayhem, junk, a stage, crowds, paint, actors and actresses, the audience, sets, all out of the familiar, calm surroundings; all removed from the normal; all interweaving in sequences possible only through the employment of the imagination of many people simultaneously. Provocations. Accidents. Change.

Props to be used in a happening can include whatever *happens* to be on hand or they can be planned well in advance of the event. Alessandro Jodorowsky's event included such diverse elements as butcher blocks, animal carcasses, blood, hatchets, hot plates, men, women, incense, robes, scissors, plastic costumes, honey, rubber boots, goggles.

A sample of what went on during his happening, called "Sacramental Melodrama," follows:

I appear dressed in a shiny black plastic costume: pants and top like a sewer-cleaner's, rubber boots, leather gloves, plastic goggles. On my head a white motorcycle helmet like a great egg.

Two white geese. I cut their throats. The music breaks loose—a barrage of electric guitars.

Billy Kluver, president of Experiments in Art and Technology, preparing a happening exhibit by Andy Warhol

The birds thrash around in agony. Feathers fly. Blood spills on the two white women . . .

The pink woman, her feet still in the basin, sways her hips while the black one, like a slave, begins to cover her body with honey . . .

My body is then seen to be clothed in 20 pounds of beefsteak sewn together in a shirt.

ACCESS

A highly structured happening is described by Alessandro Jodorowsky in his "Sacramental Melodrama," which appeared in *City Lights Journal*, No. 3, 1966. A general work is Alan Kaprow's *Happenings*.

184 Future shock

Future shock, as defined for us by Alvin Toffler, is very much like the culture shock one encounters when traveling. Suddenly you're out of your familiar environment, out of your type of society. All the cues you once used to judge right from wrong, good from bad, no longer fit. In the new culture the old way of doing things won't do. The effects are dizzying, and often it's a relief to get home, to get back to the familiar, to know what works.

Future shock describes the effect of rapid change hurtling us faster and faster into a future world. Nothing lasts: rules, regulations, cultural cues, they're all falling by the wayside as we go, full speed, into our future. What worked yesterday can barely get us by today and will be totally inadequate tomorrow.

And there is no home to go back to; the retreat, through nostalgia, to a more familiar past, just makes life more difficult.

ACCESS

Alvin Toffler's *Future Shock* has many references to follow up for further investigation.

185 Short-lived phenomena

Global happenings, soil burns, mice plagues, lost tribes, black snow, bird irruptions, meteorite finds, volcanoes, tidal waves, earthquakes, tornadoes, beached whales, squirrel migrations, fireballs, butterfly invasions, star fish, and comets are all short-lived phenomena. The information on them will be reported to you as soon as it's known, if you so desire, by the Smithsonian Institution's Center for Short-Lived Phenomena.

ACCESS

The Center offers over 250 different reports every year on a daily, weekly, or monthly basis. To give an idea of price: daily notification in all areas (earth science, biological science, astrophysical science, and archaeological/anthropological science) costs $100. The prices go down from there to $5 for certain monthly notifications.

Smithsonian Institution, Center for Short-Lived Phenomena, 60 Garden Street, Cambridge, Mass. 02138, 617-864-7911, or Cable: SATELLITES NEW YORK

Also see the book: *The Pulse of the Planet* issued by the Center.

186 Sex with others

Some of the biggest difficulties in life are with sex. We have trouble making love to ourselves and we have trouble making love with others. This is all the more disconcerting when we know that sex can be a wonderful, delightful, exciting and pleasurable way to alter consciousness.

. . . to love a louse or the leg of a chair and to have sexual intercourse with it is all right with me. For goodness sake be fond of somebody or something!
R. H. Blyth

Sex with others begins with contact: touching. We treat our sexual relations as if they were entirely matters for our genitalia. Actually, our entire bodies are charged sexual outlets awaiting contact and stimulation. We need to touch more, to play more and to take our time. By slowing down we can savor our sensory and erotic experiences. With added time and care we can increase our awareness, our consciousness, our excitement and our fulfillment.

187 Prolonged sexual intercourse

The longer the better. After 10 or 15 minutes sexual intercourse becomes more interesting, as your movements become more subtle. After a half-hour or so, as with most other repetition phenomena, your consciousness will begin to change. Sensations begin to take on new ecstatic aspects as the one-hour mark is approached. Now only the sexual-body energy-environment exists. Now sensations blend and coalesce. Letting go to orgasmic climax is pyrotechnic, possibly divine, cosmically deep.

The man's problem with prolonged sexual intercourse is finding the technique that will help avoid a premature conclusion. Techniques include changing the speed of your movements, stopping movement short of orgasm, talking, changing your breathing, taking a series of shallow breaths, shouting or screaming, opening your eyes, thinking about non-sexual things until the crest of approaching orgasm passes, biting your lip, counting or holding your breath. The woman may choose to hold off her orgasm or she may go ahead and have any number.

After a certain time, which will vary from couple to couple, a threshold will be reached. At this point orgasm isn't just around the corner and the love making seems to take over body, mind and spirit. Then prolonged intercourse may proceed indefinitely.

Though it often seems that our skin envelopes shut us in, make us ultimately untouchable, we are not alone. Even on the most mundane level, this is obvious. When you take a trip you always come back. Perhaps not as happy as you would have liked, or as sane. But you come back, nonetheless. Back to other people. Sartre said, "Hell is other people." Heaven is other people, too. *We* are other people.

If the science-fiction fantasy became the science-fact reality and we were the subjects of a visitation by another species with whom we could establish communication, would we be ready? Would we know what to say or how to say it? Of course we would know how to ask *them* who they were, what their purpose was, and so on. But who are we? What is our purpose?

Information is a measure of one's freedom of choice when one selects a message.

Warren Weaver

John Lilly has done much in the field of extra-species communication. In his work with dolphins he may have opened the way for communication with a nonhuman, intelligent species right here on earth. Lilly has considered extra-species, extra-planetary communications and has concluded:

With the current picture as it is, I would advise any being greater or lesser than we are not to contact us. In our present state of development, we are still unsuitably organized and unsuitably educated to make contact.

ACCESS

See John Lilly's *Man and Dolphin* and *The Mind of the Dolphin*. And, of course, lots of science fiction. Arthur Clarke's *Childhood's End* comes immediately to mind.

John Lilly and a dolphin, during experiments in extra- species communication, 1961

PART THREE

DEVICES AND MACHINES

Nonelectric

The *I Ching* or *Book of Changes*, now the most important of the five classics of Confucianism, came to life as an oracular work more than 3,000 years ago. Its core is a series of sixty-four symbolic figures called hexagrams, each of which is one of the possible combinations of six broken and/or unbroken parallel lines. Broken lines stand for yin, the dark, feminine, receptive, negative principle, while unbroken lines stand for yang, the light, masculine, creative, positive principle. Each hexagram is an aspect of life or a life situation. Each line shows a different aspect of the situation pictured by the hexagram. Associated with each hexagram are commentaries which expound on its meaning. The most extensive of which was written by Confucious and his pupils.

As an oracle, the book may be consulted with either coins or stalks. Keeping the question constantly in mind, you cast the coins or stalks in a prescribed manner and, from the resulting configuration of unbroken and broken lines, find your hexagram. In most instances, some lines are changing lines leading to a second hexagram.

Consulting the "I Ching" with yarrow stalks

Jung considered the *I Ching* to be based on as valid an experimental method of investigation as Western science. He called the principle involved *synchronicity*, which means the occurrence at the same time of two events which, though unconnected by cause and effect, are nonetheless related.

Including information on government, numerology, astrology, cosmology, meditation, and military strategy, the *I Ching* transcends its divinatory function to become a philosophical guide to Chinese thought, both Confucian and Taoist.

When Jung consulted it regarding itself, it gave the hexagram *ting,* the cauldron, for which the judgment is "Supreme good fortune. Success."

This reflects the basic concept of the *I Ching*—that nothing in life remains static—all is impermanent—all is ever changing.

ACCESS

There are four worthy translations of the *I Ching*. The first was done by James Legge. It is now available in paperback and hard cover with a study guide by Chai. Legge thought that the Chinese were pagans, and his bias sometimes shows. However, his effort is somewhat closer to the original than any of the other English translations available. Z. D. Sung's *The Symbols of the Yi King* is somewhat outdated but makes points that none of the other translators quite capture. Blofeld's is good, in that it fulfills its stated purpose to serve for divination only. The most popular edition is the Baynes rendering of Richard Wilhelm's transliteration. This work is very usable but makes the *I Ching* seem more romantic, less gutsy than it really is. Pay attention to the boldface type: the image, the judgment, etc. Wilhelm's son, Hellmut, has provided the best introduction in his *Change: 8 Lectures on the I Ching.* This book should be read before consulting the real thing. Spend time also with Volume 2 of Joseph Needham's monumental *Science and Civilization in China: History of Scientific Thought.* Beginning on page 304 is a most astute analysis and consideration of the *I Ching:* one of the greatest books we have.

191   Tarot

The Tarot is another oracular device in the form of a deck of cards. Though its exact origin is not known, those who connect the Tarot with Hermetic philosophy and occultism trace the inception of its symbolism back to dynastic Egypt. Similar theories point to the fact that the cards were often used for gambling, which was the intention of the formulators of the Tarot system. Used in that way, even those unappreciative of occult significance would have use for the deck of metal or leather cards known as the Tarot.

The deck of cards now used for the Tarot are paper and are divided into two sections, known as the Major and the Minor Arcana. There are 22 cards in the Major Arcana and 56 (sometimes 52) in the Minor Arcana. The Minor Arcana is like the contemporary deck of cards. This means the Minor Arcana has four kings, queens, knights, and knaves (the knight does not appear in regular card decks—thus the fifty-six cards in the Minor Arcana), as well as aces, deuces, and so on up to ten. The four modern suits known as hearts, diamonds, spades, and clubs, are, in the Tarot, pentacles or money, cups, swords, and wands.

The 22 cards of the Major Arcana bear the following pictures and symbols:

1. Magician	13. Death
2. High Priestess	14. Temperance
3. Empress	15. Devil
4. Emperor	16. Tower Struck by Lightning
5. Pope	17. Star
6. Lovers	18. Moon
7. Chariot	19. Sun
8. Justice	20. Judgment
9. Hermit	21. Fool
10. Wheel of Fortune	22. World
11. Strength	
12. Hanged Man	

In some systems, 21 is the World and 22 the Fool, but when that is the case the Fool bears no number, or is known as the zero card.

The Tarot has been described as a philosophical machine, an instrument of cognition, and the algebra of occultism. It is all of these, to be certain, and more. Learning how to distribute the cards properly is a matter of the teaching consulted. Some use only the Major Arcana, some only the Minor Arcana, some both.

The various images of the Major Arcana are thought to be highly charged, archetypal symbols carrying a power that has been vested in them over centuries of use. By correctly reading the placement and appearance of the cards many claim to be able to describe events that have already transpired as well as gain impressions of events that will occur in the future. Ralph Metzner suggests using the images of the Tarot as a form of guided fantasy to see what kinds of associations come from the pictures on the cards. Pick out a card that has particularly positive associations for you and tack it to the wall. Live with the card and see what it guides you toward.

ACCESS

The most popular book on the Tarot is Waite's *The Pictorial Key to the Tarot.* Other useful works include Sadhu's *The Tarot;* Moakley's iconography and history, *The Tarot Cards;* and Gray's *A Complete Guide to the Tarot.* There are three interesting decks available. The standard is the deck designed by Waite and Colman. Two new decks include the Palladini deck from the East Coast, and the New Tarot for the Aquarian Age from California. *Maps of Consciousness* by Ralph Metzner has an explanatory chapter on the Tarot that is most informative.

192 Finnegans Wake

To many would-be readers, James Joyce's monumental opus is unreachable. For a select few who have discovered a simple method of entry, the book is a revelation of major cultural significance. The key is that the book is an oral record. It is meant not only to be read, but to be read out loud, to be shouted, to be sung, to be laughed; to be laughed at and to be laughed with and to be laughed through. In order to be known, *Finnegans Wake* must be heard. Speak the words out loud. The book will come to life.

Eric McLuhan has prepared one of a number of guides through this most fantastic work of words of the twentieth century. I hope that as you are reading this, final plans have been made to publish his *What the Thunder Said at Finnegans Wake: Joyce's Guide to the Media.* Many of the notes below are from this book.

Finnegans Wake is an account of the social dynamics and interplay of technology and culture in a variety of historical configurations. It is constructed as a total environment where the varieties of relationships described are expressed as resonance. A conscious awareness of the separate and interlocking sensory modalities is stressed. Joyce wanted the reader to approach the work with both visual and auditory perceptiveness, simultaneously. In addition, various evocations of space reach out for our tactile sense and consideration.

These are the words the reader will see, but not those he will hear.
> James Joyce, in a letter describing the Wake.

The metaphors and puns in the *Wake* attempt to liberate our linear modes of thought, re-enforced by years of visual, nontactile, nonauditory cultural indoctrination. Much of the characterization in the *Wake* describes the world changes and fluctuations between linear and nonlinear forms of information-processing brought about by media transformations.

Two parts of the *Wake's* construction make this clear: the five major characters: HCE, ALP, Shaun, Shem, and Izzy; and the ten thunderclaps, each of one hundred letters. These thunders are multilayered word compounds. They can be divided into three sections. The first section, the first three thunders, describes the detribalization of mankind through industrialization and the introduction of linear media. The second section, the fourth through sixth thunder, describe the totality of the civilizing processes that take place with industrialization. The last section, thunders seven through ten, describe what Joyce could see (the book was completed in 1939) of the coming eventual retribalization at the hands of the new world-surrounding electric technologies and media.

The characters play this history and future out in the following representations. HCE is everyman, detribalized, civilized, industrialized, our public, us. ALP is the woman behind the man (HCE) and the technological environment that helps to make the man what he is, often without his total awareness of the process. Izzy is her help, sometimes only by manifestation, who stands for the rising portions of environmental powers of transformation. The sons of HCE, Shaun and Shem, are the polarities of cultural transformation. Shaun, the bureaucrat, always needs the present/future orientation of Shem, the artist, to help move life out of the past's status quo.

As these characters play out our future destinies, the thunder intercedes at the moment of peak intensity, bringing at first fragmentation, as in environmental metamorphosis, and eventually, reunification of the human sensorium.

Joyce noted that he was writing the Wake *deliberately "after the style of" television—that is, his style is one that uses simultaneous and inclusive forms of awareness and extends to multiple-levelled pattern recognition.*

It has been noted that drug use is an attempt to mime, internally, the (to us external) structure, and effects, of our electronic environments—as it were, an attempt to play Perseus with the perceptions. Finnegans Wake *accomplishes this, not with chemicals or with pot, but with language: Joyce is as Perseus, the* Wake *his mirror (or "square wheel without spokes" which closes the time-gap of conscious-subconscious, of cognition and re-cognition) and ours for discerning, contending with and ultimately managing/controlling/programing our psychic as well as social environments and responses.*
Eric McLuhan

ACCESS

A section of Eric McLuhan's *What the Thunder Said at Finnegans Wake: Joyce's Guide to the Media* was published in Marshall McLuhan and Quentin Fiore's *War and Peace in the Global Village*. See also Burgess's abridged version of the *Wake*, his study of Joyce, *Rejoyce*, and, of course, the com-

plete *Finnegans Wake*. There is also a recording of Joyce reading from the *Wake* available through the James Joyce Society, c/o Gotham Book Mart, 41 W. 47th St., New York, N.Y. 10036. Other books that describe and analyze the happenings in the *Wake* include: *A Skeleton Key to Finnegans Wake* by Joseph Campbell and Henry Morton Robinson; *James Joyce: A Critical Introduction* by Harry Levin; and *A Reader's Guide to James Joyce* by William York Tindall.

**James Joyce,
author of "Finnegans Wake," 1928**

193 Incense

Incense can be any aromatic substance that is burned in order to produce an odor. Incense is one of the best devices ever made for "altering" the nose. Be sure to smell the incense before you light it. Many different kinds of incense are available and they all have a distinct odor both before and during consumption. Try many different kinds for different moods.

194 Sensory orgy

Take as many different things as you can think of and lay them out in an open space where everyone can freely get at them. Invite some friends to take part in a feast for the perceptions. A sense orgy can be anything that will help you revel in your own sensory apparatus.

Spices work very well, as do different kinds of fabrics, synthetics, stones, water, incense, oils, foods, sand, earth, skins and pelts, sticks, bells, and so forth. Wearing a blindfold often heightens the sensations.

ACCESS

A very complete list of spices and their properties appears in Shirley Roth's *Interior Ecology Cookbook*.

195   Intensive instrument playing

Music is a great consciousness alterer. If you can make music, do it all day and into the night. Drumming is especially useful in altering both breathing and blood circulation. Any wind instrument will definitely affect breathing in what can be a most extraordinary manner. String instruments, too, lend themselves well to changing consciousness, and cymbals are ideal. But nothing beats an organ.

196   Metronome watching

A metronome is a device that marks time with a steady beat. The frequency of the beat is adjustable. There is usually a hand that swings from side to side, marking the beat. The device is used in training for the playing of musical instruments; it is also a most effective hypnotic induction device.

To begin watching a metronome, don't set it too fast or too slow; too fast and you won't be able to stay with it; too slow and you'll lose interest. But in the middle you should find your own beat. Watch it sway and swing, left, right, back, forth. Deeper, longer, heavier and heavier. You're getting sleepy. Your eyelids are so heavy you can hardly keep them up. You feel like closing your eyes and drifting off, off, off . . .

ACCESS

Humanitas Systems, RD 2, Roscoe, New York 12776, offers a metronome, electric, light and sound variable for $28.43; and a Variable Pacer (metronome) ear bug for $14.95.

197   Stained glass

People go to church for a variety of reasons, many having to do with the alteration of consciousness. Yet our world has changed so much in the past century that it is difficult for churches to compete with all the other things in our environment: we just don't pay attention to church.

Stained glass, however, is a profound experience. It was the ultimate expression of light for an entire epoch of history. To sit in a church for a day, watching the multifarious changes in color, hue, intensity; the subtlety with which the light plays—that was divinity. There is a different light show everyday, and it runs on solar energy.

Design for stained glass

ACCESS

In Paris, go to Notre-Dame, and see especially the North Window. To sit in the cathedral at Chartres, France, reading Adams's *Mont-St.-Michel and Chartres* as the light changes the windows is a remarkable experience.

198   Hot and cold baths

Heat expands. Steam baths, sweat baths, saunas, they all open you up. As your pores open, whatever has been stopping them up flows out. This is cleansing, this is loosening. All heat allows you to move more.

Cold baths are deceptive. You probably think that the members of the local polar-bear club, the ones who get up at the crack of dawn in the winter to run and take a cold-water swim, are crazy. Could be; but they're also radically and swiftly changing their consciousness.

Cold baths are also great after a steam bath or a sauna. After you've finished sweating everything out, the cold water seals your skin tight. It feels great.

ACCESS

Sauna: The Finnish Bath tells you how to build it and use it properly. *Life in Harmony with Nature* by Adolf Hungry Wolf describes how to make an Indian sweat bath. An abbreviated version of the book is reproduced in the *Canadian Whole Earth Almanac*, Shelter Issue, Winter 1970, page 35.

199 Environmental control

Environmental control was pioneered by a group called USCO in the early 1960s. They recognized the fact that information is what shapes any environment. When you vary the information, say by adding more, creating an overload, then you change the environment. If you are aware of the changes they can be controlled.

Take a room and study the information that it dispenses. How does it feel? Sound? Smell? Taste? Look? If you change the covering on the floor you will change not just how the environment looks, but also how it sounds and how it feels. You will change the experience of the people who enter the new environment.

By changing images, lighting, and sound, and by keeping these changes in flow and flux, any environment may be controlled so that there occurs consciousness alteration. Exterior decoration leads to interior alteration.

For major environmental control, build a dome, zome, or bubble over your space. It will really change everything.

ACCESS

Contact your local light-show group. Or Gerd Stern (formerly of USCO) at Intermedia Systems, 711 Massachusetts Ave., Cambridge, Mass. 02139, for bigger jobs. For domes and the like check with Lloyd Kahn of Pacific Domes, Los Gatos, Calif. For Zomes and the like, Steve Baer, Lama, Box 442, Corrales, N.M. 87048. For bubbles, try Ant Farm, 247 Gate 5 Rd., Sausalito, Calif. 94965.

200 Sensory deprivation

Sensory deprivation is the removal of as many sensory inputs as possible. Usually this is accomplished by the use of complicated equipment that blocks all light sources, provides soundproof environments, creates restraints and temperature continua that limit tactile sensation, and deprives the perceptual processes of any odors or tastes.

A variety of different pieces of equipment have been designed, executed, and put to use to accomplish sensory deprivation. Usually they involve a soundproof, lightproof chamber. Within this chamber is a bathtub-like container large enough to hold a human. This tub is filled with water the temperature of which may be controlled. The subject of sensory "dep" is placed in the water and restrained in such a way that movement becomes nearly impossible, thus greatly reducing tactile input, one of our most constant sources of sensory data. (We are generally not aware of this, living, as we do, in a highly visual culture. But as you read this you are probably touching the book, your clothing, some furniture, the ground, etc. This perceptual information tends to become background in our sensorily overloaded environment.) This kind of sensory dep is thought of as quite severe and can be tolerated for only short periods of time.

You can accomplish a limited amount of sensory dep yourself by finding a darkened closet, filling it with pillows, making sure you will not be disturbed (unless you need help, which *must* always be present and available), making some ear baffles and a blindfold and whatever else you feel will limit your sensory input. Enter the closet and do your best to limit all movements, even twitching and scratching. Don't stay in for too long! Usually a couple of hours will produce effects that are both inescapable and dominant.

When sensory data from the environment is cut out, inner sensory data become available, and can often be frightening. Most people who have taken part in sensory dep experiments have had unpleasant experiences. There is evidence, however, that the set of the subject as well as the manner in which the experimenter presents and administrates the experiment greatly shape and determine the subject's experience.

When you remove visual input you can expect, after a while, to experience new visual sensations, either hallucinations or, possibly, the appearance of phosphene patterns. When you limit auditory input you can expect to hear sounds that are always there, but are overwhelmed by the sounds of the environment. You will hear your breathing, your heart, the circulation of blood in and around the ears, and a variety of other sounds. This seems quite simple, but never having really listened to these sounds before, you can experience them as deafening and overpowering. They never stop.

Many people who participated in long-term (more than 24-hour duration) experiments found relief from the negative effects of SD by sleeping and playing games and engaging in mental exercises (learning the alphabet backward, mathematical problems, etc.). Once sleep time was exhausted and the exercises could no longer be maintained, the subjects would demand to be released. Most people find SD intolerable. Without proper controls it can be dangerous.

ACCESS

The original standard text is *Sensory Deprivation* by Solomon, Kubzansky, Leiderman, Mendelson and Wexler. A less formal account is Jack Vernon's *Inside the Black Room.* The most up-to-date review of what's been going on in formal research is Zubek's *Sensory Deprivation: Fifteen Years of Research.* The latter has a complete bibliography.

201   ASCID

ASCID stands for Altered States of Consciousness Induction Device. It is also known as the Witches' Cradle. The ASCID was developed by Robert Masters and Jean Houston of the Foundation for Mind Research. The device was suggested in historical accounts of witches. Evidently the witches learned about it by the Inquisitors' practice of putting an accused witch in a bag and stringing the bag up over the limb of a tree. This made the bag swing in a pendulum-like motion while the witch inside the bag was confined and in a sensory-deprivation-like position. The witches then adapted this procedure for their "transportation" to the "Witches' Sabbat."

Masters and Houston developed a metal swing in which the subject stands upright. This swinglike container tends to swing to and fro, and left and right, greatly exaggerating the movement of the occupant. The occupant is strapped into the ASCID and is blindfolded. Some experimenters also use ear baffles. Most people who try an ASCID experience an altered state of consciousness, characterized by increased visual imagery and by highly realistic fantasy trips to other places, other lands, and other worlds. The altered state usually begins within 20 minutes.

Jean Houston with a subject in the ASCID, or witches cradle

A variation of the vertical ASCID is the horizontal model. In this device the occupant lies down and a swinging motion begins. It is very much like the experience of being rocked as a child, and many report regressive experiences. It helps to induce visual imagery, though usually of a much less dramatic nature than does the vertical model. It is also noted as an aid for inducing sleep.

ACCESS

The work of Masters and Houston with the Witches' Cradle will be written up in their *New Ways of Being*. Some mention of the experiments is in their paper mentioned in Access for No. 143. Aaronson and others at the New Jersey Neuropsychiatric Institute are also conducting a study, which will eventually be published, with their horizontal ASCID. The Erickson Educational Foundation, 4047 Hundred Oaks Avenue, Baton Rouge, La. 70808, has the construction plans for the ASCID and makes them to order for $300.

202 Body confinement

Most body confinement takes place as a result of medical procedures. It may be confinement in a respirator due to polio or respiratory ailments, confinement in traction, or confinement in body casts. All of these devices, like sensory-deprivation equipment, create an SD experience, because of the reduction of sensory input. Auditory and visual hallucinations are often reported.

Other kinds of body confinement are described in what is known as the bondage branch of sexual literature. Many people derive sexual pleasure from being tied and bound so that they are totally confined and unable to move. Havelock Ellis has written that the restraint of emotional and physical activity tends to heighten sexual excitement.

ACCESS

Further data can be found in two articles: Leiderman's "Sensory Deprivation: Clinical Aspects," in *Archives of Internal Medicine, 101,* 1958, pp. 389–96; and Mendelson's (et al.) "Hallucinations of Poliomyelitis Patients During Treatment in a Respirator," *Journal of Nervous and Mental Diseases, 126,* 1958, pp. 421–28.

Sexual bondage is treated most completely in *The Joy of Sex* by Alex Comfort.

203 Visual illusions

In No. 25 the nature of visual illusions is discussed. Here I will describe some devices that generate them.

One device is an ordinary desk lamp fitted with an opaque shade and an on–off switch that can be operated every second. Seat yourself so that you are about 18 inches away from the lamp and gaze at the area on the surface of the desk under the lamp. Begin to switch the lamp on and off about once every second. After a dozen on–offs a small disk of light will appear, just below the bulb, whenever the lamp is turned on. When turned off, a shadow, circular in form, will sweep across the field of vision, and the light will contract into a disk and fade away.

By placing a pattern similar to the one below on a phonograph turntable and operating the turntable, under bright illumination, at 78 rpm, the black sections of the drawing will become slightly purple. Reduce the speed to 45 rpm and a yellow haze will appear. At 33 rpm most color perception will recede.

The combination of a variety of op art patterns and a phonograph turntable or other spinning device can produce very powerful and effective visual illusions.

ACCESS

Edmund Scientific of Barrington, New Jersey, sells visual illusions mounted on cards among other things. Send for a free catalogue. Both of Gregory's books, *Eye and Brain* and *The Intelligent Eye,* as well as the book *Visual Illusions,* will give you a lot of ideas. For $75, Psychophysics Labs, of 31 Townsend Terrace, Framingham, Mass. 01701, will sell you an Illusionator kit which provides eight or more separate illusions. Also included are some op art patterns which help to stimulate mild hallucinatory effects. See also No. 25 and C. L. Strong's article, "Generating Visual Illusions with Two Kinds of Apparatus," in the March 1971 *Scientific American.*

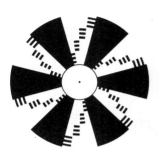

A device for generating visual illusions

204 Ames perceptual demonstrations

Even when we know that what we are perceiving is not true, we still perceive it. This sounds like a riddle, but actually it was what led Adelbert Ames, Jr. to construct a number of perceptual-demonstration devices so that we could see just how our senses often perceive what is not actually present in the environment. Even when we know the truth about what the demonstration shows, it is impossible to inhibit the experience of the illusory or distorted image.

ACCESS

The Ames Demonstrations in Perception, by William Ittleson, tells you what these devices will do to your perception and exactly how to build each one.

The Ames Perceptual Demonstration room showing monocular distortion

205 Mandalas

Mandalas are circular images often used as devices to alter consciousness and to increase awareness, especially during meditation. The Tibetan Buddhists used their religious paintings of mandalas, known as tankas, as models for the universe in miniature. Other cultures have used the mandala form in art, architecture and dance as means of expressing wholeness. The earth and the moon and the sun are mandalas. The clearest images that we have of atoms and their constituent entities are in the mandala form, as are galaxies and galactic systems like the Milky Way.

Most mandalas used for meditation have centers so that the meditator has a point on which to focus, to concentrate his efforts and energies. Then by letting his own energy move out from the center of the mandala he can experience the movement of energy, through form-taking, throughout the cosmos.

ACCESS

Masters and Houston's *Psychedelic Art* contains some interesting mandalas and some examples of the works of artists of the "fantastic realism" school whose paintings may assist in changing consciousness. Giuseppe Tucci's *The Theory and Practice of the Mandala* is most complete. C. G. Jung's *The Archetypes and the Collective Unconscious* contains mandalas drawn by patients who were using the form as a means of self-expression and self-discovery. Some of the painting were done by Jung himself. Jose and Mirium Arguilles have produced a beautiful book devoted to the subject of circular paintings and images called *Mandala*.

The central mandala of the Tibetan Wheel of Life

206 Communes

Concomitant with mass alterations of middle-class consciousness in the last decade by way of drug usage, new sexual expression and future shock, came the first beginnings of an attempt to retribalize society by communes. Communes afforded an opportunity for those who wanted to experiment with different life-styles to gather together and put their theories into practice. Some have tried not having any theories at all and have been founded on the rule of no rules.

This came about, in part, when certain groups found that altering consciousness by way of drugs and other methods, required new ways of living together. Some felt that the old structures, like stable homes and family situations, no longer fit their experiences of reality. They needed to retreat from society in order to test the social implications of their experiences and new modes of consciousness and awareness. Communal living seemed to provide a safe way to try out new ways of being and at the same time served as a statement against social forms that many communards felt were the manifestations of a highly structured, linear, bureaucratic culture. They felt that their communes were a sign of life in a dying society.

By being forced to live closely on a day-to-day basis with people outside their immediate families, members had the opportunity to experiment with different ways of experiencing reality. Many communes have failed, some due to idealism, others due to economics or poor organization; but some continue.

ACCESS

Alternatives Foundation publishes a number of periodicals keeping up with what's happening in the commune community, but not necessarily in the community community. Their address: 2441 Le Conte Avenue, Berkeley, Calif. 94709. A fine Canadian periodical in this field is *Alternate Society*, available from 10 Thomas Street, St. Catherine, Ontario, Canada.

207 Gymnastic equipment

It's hard to get higher than you get on a trampoline.
Bouncing around in the sky.
Jumping and floating and almost flying.
Rings. Swings.
See-saws and trapezes.
They're all great.
Ask any kid.

208 Scuba and skin diving

Skin diving takes you down into another world, right here on earth. Men who go to the moon are called astronauts of outer space; many who delve into their own minds are called astronauts of inner space. Perhaps skin divers and others who go deep into the sea should be called astronauts of under space.

The planet earth is 80 percent water. Species unfamiliar to your eye exist by the thousands in the oceans and seas of the world. Using the proper gear and technique, a technique that can be learned in schools throughout the United States, you can explore this world with all of its sensory delights and mind-boggling sights and experiences.

Technically, skin diving is underwater swimming with a snorkel breathing device. SCUBA stands for Self-Contained Underwater Breathing Apparatus.

209 Boffing

Only in the case of boffing, to quote its inventor, Jack Nottingham, is "the sword mightier than the pen." Boffers are styrofoam swords that allow for lots of nondamaging, nonhurting, yet real physical contact. Use them with love. They not only allow one to release anger and find energy, they also teach coordination, style and skill.

Boffers are especially useful for couples or friends who need opportunities to express real aggression toward each other without endangering the relationship. By fencing with boffers the aggressive feelings are truly expressed in an atmosphere of real "fun and games." It is difficult to really hurt someone with a boffer, yet if you get hit with one you know you've been hit, even though there is no pain. The very act of hitting and being hit with something that doesn't hurt is magnificent. One of the great inventions of the twentieth century.

ACCESS

Boffers are available from their inventor, Jack Nottingham, at 190 Emmet Court, San Francisco, Calif. 94110. Two swords, two hand protectors, two goggles, and instructions cost $11.

210 Bells

Ringing bells can get you high. The bigger the bell the better. In the old world the ringing of bells was the focal point and ordering process of town life. But those were real bells, with tone and intensity, not like our school bells and alarm clocks, which sound dull, thudding and mechanical.

Get yourself some bells. Large ones are best, but small ones are good too. Ring them and listen for the special sound that will make you feel the bell's vibrations and your own.

Gongs are also great. James Coburn, the movie actor, has appeared on a number of television shows demonstrating his ability to induce altered states of awareness, in himself and others, by playing gongs.

A large church bell

211 Masks

The wearing of masks is a definite device for the alteration of consciousness. This is true both for the wearer of the mask and for the one who perceives the masked figure. Think of the Lone Ranger, of the Noh theatre of Japan, of Halloween, and you may gather the strength of mask wearing. The mask is often symbolic of desired powers or attributes. Masks are often worn in tribes to show tribe members the powers the wearer has gained by donning the mask of an animal or spirit.

A 19th Century Austrian mask, used in the "Chasing of Winter" festival

Pick a spirit, mythological character, animal, or creature with whom you identify; or ask your friends to pick one that they think fits you. Then go and make up a mask that you feel conveys the feelings of that character. Make it out of paper, clay, or tinfoil, papier-mâché, or simply paint your face with water-base paints.

When you can be alone, wear the mask. See the power that it gives you. Feel the energy of the creature portrayed by its image enter you.

ACCESS

See Jung's *Man and His Symbols* for an interesting discussion of the use of masks and the mask as *persona*.

212 Rock throwing

Rock throwing can be one of the most fulfilling ways to express your anger. You can throw rocks against other rocks (watch out for the flying particles). You can throw rocks against the ground. You can throw rocks into the water, much like the shot put or weight throw in athletic competition. You can rip weeds out of the ground or express your fury by shredding up dead leaves.

In tribal Malaya people express their anger in a most ecologically unsound manner: they hack at trees. When a tribesman becomes angry he goes out into the jungle and hacks at the trees until a trance-frenzy develops, allowing for complete catharsis. Then he can return to the tribe with a more balanced life attitude.

213 Automobile destruction

Ecologically sound, and even beneficial until auto
and gas companies improve their products. Required:
open space, an automobile, implements of destruction
(e.g., sledge hammer, ax, club, crowbar, acetylene torch,
etc.). Be careful: automobiles may be dangerous to your
health: this is true for their destruction also. (There is
danger of being injured by flying pieces of broken
glass or being cut by shredded metal.) This may be
the Western answer to hacking at trees. Destroy a car.
Make sure that you recycle all the junk.

214 Kayak disease

Next time you're in Greenland, if you go out hunting
in a kayak and you stay out for more than three days,
well, that's usually when kayak disease sets in. Terrible
hallucinations, both auditory and visual, may affect
you; extreme disorientation may also ensue. Be careful.

ACCESS

Kayak disease is described in G. W. Williams's "Hypnosis in Perspective," which appeared in LeCron's *Experimental Hypnosis*.

215 Engine rough

Engine rough is part of the highway- or road-hypnosis experience. It is usually encountered by truck drivers or others who must spend long hours on the road. Engine rough is the auditory sensation that occurs from over-exposure to a repetitious engine sound. Its effects are very similar to those of other auditory hallucinations. Highway hypnosis is worse than falling asleep at the wheel. The trance produced is usually not corrected merely by awakening. It is especially prevalent and dangerous during driving rain, hail, sleet, or snow.

What happens is that the constant, repetitious sound of the engine forms a background, much like music. Out of this background come other sounds, all of which are illusions. These sounds range from human voices to automobile-horn blowing. The effects can be very dangerous. Similar sensations occur to the fatigued driver, though he might just fall asleep. Engine rough can cause a driver to react to the illusory sensations, often provoking accidents and shock reaction. It is not recommended to pursue this altered state of consciousness.

ACCESS

Engine rough and other forms of "highway hypnosis" are dealt with in A. L. Moseley's article abstract "Hypnogogic [sic] Hallucinations in Relation to Accidents," which appeared in the *American Psychologist*, No. 8.

216 Breakoff

A breakoff phenomenon is peculiar to high-altitude jet pilots. It is a form of sensory deprivation, with the usual accompanying hallucinatory experiences, and is a result of lack of orientation points and stimuli at high altitudes.

When flying through weather of high barometric pressure, i.e., empty, cloudless skies, or when flying for extended periods on instruments through intense cloud cover, the pilot has, literally, nothing to look at except the inside of the cockpit. Often the hallucinations involve movement illusions, since breakoff takes place when the pilot cannot tell whether or not he is moving.

ACCESS

A. M. H. Bennett has written the authoritative article "Sensory Deprivation in Aviation," which appeared in Solomon's (et al.) *Sensory Deprivation*.

217 Gliding

Gliding is different from flying because of the almost total silence it involves. The only sound heard, as you soar on the wind currents and air pockets, is the air itself, as it whooshes over the wings and past the cabin. Also known as sailplaning and soaring, gliding allows for incredible experiences: altitudes of over 45,000 feet, speeds of over 160 miles per hour, and some of the most fantastic dives in all aviation. You can glide for over 600 miles without landing.

The way to soar is to locate a soaring club and learn how; buy, rent, or borrow a glider; get hitched up to a small engine-powered plane that will tow you up to at least 3,000 feet and then let you go; and then steer your way toward a thermal current so that you can join the birds.

ACCESS

Peter Dixon's *Soaring* gives full details, a list of schools that teach gliding, and one of gliding clubs throughout the United States.

218 Sky diving

What could be more consciousness altering than jumping out of a moving airplane, "flying" down to the ground, landing, and then being alive to do it all over again?

A married couple exchange a kiss during a wedding anniversary sky dive

219   Land diving

On Pentecost Island in the South Pacific, when a man has something he wants to get off his chest, when he has something that he wants to tell all of his fellow tribesmen, he climbs to the top of an 83-foot tower, affixes spring vines around his ankles and holds one hand above his head. This is the signal that he wishes to speak and the dancing and singing some eight stories below him come to a halt. All are attentive to the complaint or cry or story. It might be that he has paid too high a price for a pig or is very proud to be a member of the tribe.

After finishing his speech, he raises both hands above his head, claps them three times, and dives head first toward the softened earth some 80 feet below him. As his head reaches the soft earth, specially prepared for his landing place, the vines (called lianas) attached to his ankles snap tight, and the platform above collapses from the strain to absorb the shock of the fall. His head barely touches the earth as he rebounds and is held tight by the vines, swinging in an arc.

This surely must be one of the most extraordinary ways of altering consciousness.

ACCESS

Kal Muller tried land diving in the New Hebrides, on Pentecost Island, and told about it in the December 1970 *National Geographic*. *National Geographic* also made a television special on these islands that included a sequence on land diving.

220   Skiing

Skiing, with its speed and grace, is a fine way to alter consciousness and sharpen perceptual awareness. What contributes to all of this is the heightened experience brought on by the extreme cold, the dazzling brightness of the sun, and the sensorily deprived experience one has in being in such a pure white environment.

As you whoosh through the snow your skis will make a smooth churning sound as they carry you speedily on your way; you feel your body smoothly steering you and your skis as it twists, turns, bends, and stretches. You become your skis and the snow.

221　Space travel

Perhaps in years to come one might be required to explain why space travel is such a remarkable experience. I don't think any explanation is required at the present time. It seems quite obvious that in its newness it must be unbelievably exhilarating and mind altering.

Much research in sensory deprivation has been done in connection with preparing for and carrying out manned space flight.

In space, apparently, the human eye can detect the more energetic primary cosmic rays. With the space craft dark and his eyes closed, Neil Armstrong reported seeing flashes at the rate of about one a minute. Buzz Aldrin reported pointlike flashes and occasional streaks. . . . The Apollo 13 astronauts reported in their debriefing that they all saw the flashes, but only when they were relaxed.

John P. Wiley, Jr. in "Sky Reporter"; Natural History,
January, 1971

222　Biorhythm

Biorhythm, or bio-chem phasing, operates on the fact that man undergoes three very distinct and measurable biological cycles. Biorhythm records and charts the 23-day cycle of physical strength, endurance, energy resistance, and confidence; the 28-day cycle of feelings, intuitions, nerves, sensibility, cheerfulness, moodiness, and creative ability; and the 33-day cycle of mental alertness, intelligence, memory, logic, reasoning power, reaction, and ambition.

By charting these different cycles, lines of stress appear on days when a critical position (the intersection of two, possible three of the cycles in one period) is achieved. In this way, a person can be made aware of his good and bad periods, for initiating new plans, projects, and so forth. In Europe, some doctors use biorhythm as part of diagnostic procedure and in preplanning for surgery. Biorhythm, employed in this way, is similar to medical astrology, since the charts are drawn according to date and time of birth.

ACCESS

The best book on the subject is *Is This Your Day?* by George Thommen, who tells you all you need to know. Charts are available from Bio-Chem-Phase-Charts, P.O. Box 4171, Grand Central Station, New York, N.Y. 10017. A one-year chart costs $9.50; a six-month chart, $6.50. However, it's much cheaper to make you own chart, based on the models and data in Thommen's book, which costs 75¢.

223 Trepan

Trepanation is an ancient process, an operation whereby a hole is drilled in the head and part of the skull removed. This is done in order to increase the volume of blood that reaches the brain. Bart Hughes of Amsterdam claims that the operation will not only make anyone undergoing it "high" for life, but will also cure all mental illness. However, most doctors will not perform this operation.

ACCESS

T. Lobsong Rampa describes his pre- and post-trepanation experiences in *The Third Eye*. The data on Bart Hughes is in an article by Joe Mellen (who claims to have been trepanned), "Hole in the Head," which appeared in *Other Scenes*, November 1970.

Electric

224 Sensory overload

Just as our sensory equipment reacts when we deny it data from the environment, it will create an entirely different reaction when overloaded with environmental data. In speaking of sensory deprivation in No. 200, I mentioned that the senses cue in on internal information when cut off from the usual flow of sensation produced by the environment. Internal sensations are usually distinguished and experienced as hallucination, illusion, distortion of "normal" perception, and disorientation. With sensory overload, some of these same sensations appear, only in different forms and configurations.

Our cognitive apparatus is constantly selecting and screening the stimuli that bombard us from the environment. We focus our attention on one figure, image, or event and the other perceptions fall into a background configuration. Sensory overload is the state that occurs when so many images are competing to become the center of our attention that we are unable, consciously or unconsciously, to make a choice. We are overwhelmed, carried off by the stream and flow of bombarding imagery and sensation. We literally don't know where to turn.

This state can lead to visual and auditory hallucinations (seeing and hearing things that do not originate from given stimuli), illusion (taking given stimuli from the environment and perceptually misapprehending them so as to change their nature), and extreme disorientation. Occasionally, sensory overload leads to creative breakthroughs, increased mental imagery, problem solving, synesthesias (perceiving an image with a sensory receptor not designed to receive that image: seeing sound, feeling color, etc.), and even to psychotic experiences.

The major social examples of sensory overload are the light shows that accompany concerts of rock music and happenings. Some theater and cinema presentations have recently been incorporating concepts of sensory overload into their productions. (TV as a sensory overload is discussed separately in No. 246.) Many people consider some aspects of contemporary global urban life—increased activity, lights from advertising displays, and overwhelming noise pollution—to create a permanent state of temporary overload, even for those who do not desire to exist under such conditions.

A good example of the deliberately constructed sensory overload environment can be found at the Foundation for Mind Research in New York City. Robert Masters and Jean Houston, with the help of lumia artist Don Snyder, have created a total audiovisual environment, as well as a portable audiovisual-olfactory-tactile device.

The environment is composed of an 8 x 8 foot semicircular rear-projection screen. The subject sits behind this screen, very close to the center of its curve. In this way the visual images occupy his total field of vision and the sensation of being "in" the images is accomplished. The visual images are from 2 x 2 inch or 35 mm slides. The slide-projecting equipment is computer controlled and linked to the sound track being played. The subject hears the sound track either through a set of individual headphones or through speakers situated on either side of him. The rate of speed of the dissolve, that is, the intervals at which the slides change and new images are shown on the screen, varies from 1 to 20 seconds. The slide changes are geared to the sound track.

For software in the visual area, the Foundation uses slides hand painted in transparent colors, so that many slides are original works of art. Images from such painters as Bosch, Breughel, Fuchs, Klarwein, and Tchelichew are also shown. The sound track is usually electronic music augmented by Zen and Sufi chanting.

The Foundation has also developed an environmental overload device which makes it possible to control and overload visual, auditory, olfactory, and tactile stimulation. This device is like a small version of the curved rear screen, except that it is shaped like an elongated bubble which fits over the head. When images are projected on the head covering, the subject is, literally, inside of the pictures being presented: the images form a total surround. There are earphones inside of the device as well as a series of air hoses. These hoses not only bring fresh air to the subject but can also be used both to introduce odors and to change the flow of air speed, thereby altering the tactile experience.

This device is still in the experimental stage. When completed, all of the different sensations will be computer controlled so that when the Tibetan tanka mandala image fills the visual field, the chanting will get louder over the sound track, the odor of temple incense will fill the device, and the air will come rushing at the subject's face timed to the beats of the chant.

ACCESS

Sargant's *Battle for the Mind* and London's *Behavior Control* discuss the more formal aspects of sensory overload and bombardment. The Masters and Houston references may be found in Nos. 143 and 201.

225 Natural sounds amplification

You are constantly making noise. Your heart beats and pumps as your lungs fill and collapse. The blood rushes through your veins and arteries. You breathe. If you've ever had your head in anyone's lap for a sufficient amount of time you know that the stomach and intestines do not go about their procedures in total silence. Your bones screech and creak, and occasionally crack. When you scratch your skin your nails make cacophonic symphonies.

Stethoscopes are the best instruments available for listening to sounds within the body. All of the noises noted above can be made clearly audible with a stethoscope. But what is really an extraordinary experience is to connect a stethoscope to a sensitive microphone and amplification equipment and "broadcast" your own internal music.

John Cage describes entering an echoic chamber, a totally sound-proofed room. He heard two sounds, one high, the other low. When he discussed these sounds with the engineer in charge, Cage was told that the high sound was that of his nervous system and the low one that of his blood circulating.

ACCESS

Stethoscopes may be purchased at any medical supply center.

In 1944, Margolin and Kubie published the study "An Apparatus for the Use of Breath Sounds as a Hypnogogic [sic] Stimulus." The article describes their construction of complicated laboratory equipment to amplify the sound of a subject's breathing and the use of that sound for the purpose of hypnotic trance induction. (*American Journal of Psychiatry, No. 100*, p. 610ff.)

As suggested in No. 182, sounds coming through a speaker may be used as a massage. Amplification of natural body sounds will serve this purpose as well as chanting.

The Piper Brace Co., 811 Wyandotte, Kansas City, Mo. 64105, offers a blood-pressure cuff (velcro hold sleeve) and stethoscope. The price for the cuff is $20.70. The stethoscope (only available when ordered with the cuff) brings the total to $23.60, a good buy for anyone who is interested in experimenting.

John Cage's story comes from his lecture "Experimental Music," in his book *Silence.*

226 Prolonged radar screen observation

Prolonged observation of radar screens, plus the threat of advanced Chinese brainwashing techniques used during the Korean War, were the impetus for the first experiments into sensory deprivation. Watching a radar screen is a form of sensory deprivation. What is most alarming about radar-screen watching is that after several hours even the most competent operators see blips that aren't there.

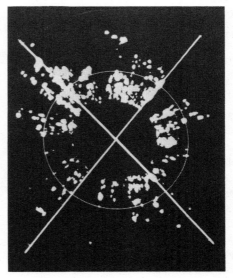

The radar scope used by all-weather airline controllers

ACCESS

See Heron's article on "The Pathology of Boredom," in *Scientific American, No. 195*, 1957, pp. 52–56.

Motion pictures are more and more actively designed to turn you on. For a while, they just attempted to re-create psychedelic drug trips on screen. Now the total design and execution of entire films attempt consciousness-altering.

Flicker Film by Tony Conrad is a good example. This is a short subject that uses frames of pure white and black, alternating on the screen, to produce a stroboscopic flicker effect. Most people watching the first few minutes of the film are bored and start to complain. But after about 5 minutes the white and black images flickering on the screen make the viewer begin to see colors where there are none. What Conrad has done is to create a film that stimulates the eye, the optic nerve, and the brain to produce its own color.

Other interesting films include those made by the Whitney brothers, who produce short subjects of computer-generated mandala patterns that change and transform with great intricate motions. Jodorowsky's *El Topo* portrays a man's search for a master within himself by his meetings with masters of the Yogic, Gurdjieffian, Sufistic, and Taoistic persuasions. Peter Brooke's screen version of *Marat/Sade* brings madness to life on the screen. Chris Munger's short *X-Ray* takes you on a journey inside your own body. Charles Eames's *Power of Ten* takes you from a picnic table in Florida out to the furthest reaches of the cosmos in the space of less than 10 minutes.

And motion picture theaters are great places in themselves. There you are, sitting in near-total darkness, surrounded by hundreds of other who have gathered together to participate in a highly ritualized social event. The main content of this event is to watch larger-than-life images as they are projected on a screen and reflected back to your eyes. All of this is done in relative silence.

ACCESS

Gene Youngblood's *Expanded Cinema* gives further details on the link between cinema and consciousness.

Some films that will change almost everyone's consciousness: *The Powers of Ten* (Charles Eames's adaptation of Boeke's book, *Cosmic View*. Eight minutes that transport you visually to the outer ranges of the universe.) Purchase: $125, from Eames, 901 W. Washington Blvd., Venice, Calif. 90291. Rental information from the University of Southern California, Film Distribution Section. *Flicker Film* and *Straight and Narrow* (Tony and Beverly Conrad's films, both shot entirely in black and white, make most viewers see colors. Much like stroboscopic phenomena.) From Film-Makers' Co-operative, 175 Lexington Avenue, New York, N.Y. 10016. *Binary Bit Patterns* (Michael Whitney, whose films and those of his relatives are described by Youngblood. This is one of the new computer language films.) Creative Film Society. *Lapis* (James Whitney). New American Filmmakers Series, Whitney Museum of American Art, Madison Avenue, New York, N.Y. 10021. *Crystals* (Herbert Loebel's film of microphotography.) Pyramid Films, Santa Monica, Calif. *X-Ray* (Chris Munger's view of how man functions, from inside). Whitney Museum, New York.

228 Stroboscopes

Stroboscopes are devices that create pulsations of light at regular and fixed intervals varying from one flash for every several seconds to several flashes per second. In order to experience hallucinations, one sits in front of a stroboscope with the eyes closed. When the machine is turned on the flashes of light should be aimed at the closed eyes. The stroboscope's varying speed mechanism should be set between 8 and 25 flashes per second. It is in this area that most people experience visual images. The speed where most imagery is reported is 10 flashes per second. The varying of speed will vary the images produced.

The above instructions apply only to the modern type of stroboscope, the xenon strobe. This strobe produces a type of "artificial lightning"; a very bright flash of white-to-violet light.

Another, older type of strobe produces a different form of sensation. This is the neon strobe which produces a reddish light which is not as bright as the light flashes of the xenon strobe. With the red-lighted neon strobes, hallucinatory effects are possible with the eyes *open*.

When the strobe is flashing at the speeds indicated above, the observer will notice an image that seems to float just above the strobe. This image will vary in color through the entire red-to-green section of the spectrum as the speed of stroboscopic flash is varied.

Stroboscopes are used in the laboratory to divide motion activity into discrete elements, making the object illuminated appear to be not in motion. The same effect will be gained if you or anyone you please is placed under strobe illumination. You will appear to be not moving when you are. All of your motions will be broken down and frozen in time. Dance halls use strobes to illuminate the dance floor for just this purpose.

ACCESS

Strobes are sold wherever equipment for light shows is sold, at theatrical equipment houses, and through scientific-instrument supply centers. Finding an old neon strobe just takes hunting around. Or you can put a red shield over the face of a xenon strobe, which will make it approximate the effects of a neon model.

A strobe which synchronizes its flashing with your brain waves is called the Brain Wave Synchronizer and is marketed by Schneider Instrument Co., Skokie, Illinois.

229 Dream machine

In the early 1960s, when W. Gray Walter had recently published his book *The Living Brain,* which detailed the effects of stroboscopic flicker phenomena in producing hallucinations, Ian Sommerville and Brion Gysin devised the Dream Machine.

The Dream Machine is a homemade flicker-producing instrument. All that is necessary to make it is some cardboard or poster paper, a light bulb, and a phonograph that will revolve at 78 rpm.

Make a cylinder 10 inches high from the cardboard. Make sure that the cylinder will fit on the phonograph turntable. Then cut ten horizontal slots, five on each side of the cylinder. The slots should be each 1½ inches apart and measure about 4 inches long and ⅜ of an inch wide.

Suspend an electric light bulb (100 watts) inside the cylinder on the turntable. Be sure the light bulb is level with the slots in the cylinder. Start the turntable at 78 rpm so that the cylinder revolves at this speed. The bulb is stationary. Bring your *closed* eyes as close to the slots as possible. You will see images similar to those produced by a xenon strobe.

ACCESS

Articles by Ian Sommerville on "Flicker" and by Brion Gysin on the "Dream Machine" are included in *Olympia* magazine, No. 2, January 1962. The magazine is now defunct. A sample Dream Machine to be cut out was included. It is possible that the Gotham Book Mart, 41 West 47th Street, New York, N.Y., may have copies for sale. The original price of the issue was $1.

230   Continuous light and sound

Continuous light and sound environments are the work
of La Monte Young and Marian Zazeela. They maintain,
at their studio in New York City, an environment of
constant-periodic sound-wave forms generated by an
electronic synthesizer. Young has analyzed a series of
rational-frequency ratios and will adjust his synthesizer
so that a number of frequencies are sounded constantly.
These frequencies, somewhat like electronic chords to
the ear, have been played at the Young–Zazeela studio-
home 24 hours a day, 7 days a week, since September
1966. They work, play, eat, talk, socialize, sleep, dream,
and make love while these frequencies fill the air.
Young and Zazeela call this kind of sound environment
"House Hums."

**A continuous light and sound environment designed by
Robert Masters, Jean Houston and Don Snyder**

In addition to these constant, everpresent frequencies,
the studio is always in a state of flux with a variety of
moving and alternating lighting effects. Some lights go
on and off, others change color, tone, intensity, and hue
(as do the sounds, when Young adjusts the synthesizer).
It takes about 20 minutes to get "high" in the studio,
just from the flux of light-and-sound frequencies. When
desired, alteration of consciousness can be achieved in
seconds, by specific changes in frequency.

Other continuous light and sound environments have
been designed and executed by Robert Masters, Jean
Houston and Don Snyder.

ACCESS

La Monte Young and Marian Zazeela have produced a record
of their sound ($8.50) and a book of their *Selected Writings*

($3.50). Both are available from P.O. Box 190, Canal Street
Station, New York, N.Y. 10013. Their environmental installa-
tions for continuous light and sound cost between $7,000 and
$10,000, or higher, depending on your needs. Contact them
at the address above or through their gallery: Galerie Heiner
Friedrich, 20 Lindenstrasse, 5 Cologne 1, West Germany.

Masters & Houston maintain their environment at their Institute for Mind Research in New York.

231 Riley room

Terry Riley, a musician and environmental artist who has worked with La Monte Young, has constructed a most ingenious room of images and repetition. Within the walls of the room are about nine different outer chambers and one central chamber. All of the chambers are connected by doors which lead to the other chambers, to the outside of the entire room, and to the chamber in the center. The walls and doors are made of a polymylar that can be called both reflective and transparent. That is, when looking at a door one can see through the door to the other side and at the same time see one's own reflection in the door.

In each chamber are a number of microphones connected to a delayed recording and playback device and a number of speakers. When I say something in, for example, Chamber One, 5 seconds later my words are played back over a speaker in Chamber Three. When only one person is in the Riley room this is a most delightful effect. When a series of the chambers are occupied and the occupants are constantly talking, and opening and closing doors as they go from chamber to chamber, the effect is devastating to normal consciousness and rational functioning. It becomes impossible to tell who said what, where, and when; meanwhile the interplay between real image and reflection adds to the general quandary.

Riley called the room "The Time-Lag Accumulator," a sonic gallery module.

ACCESS

Terry Riley installed this particular room for an exhibit at Automation House, 49 East 68th Street, New York, N.Y. 10021. The original was executed for the Magic Theatre Exhibit in Kansas City. A book describing this exhibit, also called *The Magic Theatre*, written by Ralph Coe, was published in 1970.

232 Infinity room

Stanley Landesman is an artist who has constructed a room that gives the feeling of being in infinite space. Through an arrangement of glass, thousands of amber light bulbs, and mirrors, Landesman has created an effect of endlessness. When one steps into his Infinity Room one immediately notices that all the walls, the entire ceiling, and the very floor one is standing on are covered with row after row of amber bulbs. These rows of bulbs, thanks to the invisible arrangement of the mirrors, give the depth impression of continuous backward recession from the wall. That recession never ends. Being in the room gives a feeling of total suspension, total stoppage. The effect is instantaneous. All one's preconceived notions about *real* space are left behind, outside the room. This warping of the space sense also affects one's experience of time. With no spatial landmarks and no boundaries, time, too, goes on toward infinity.

ACCESS

Stanley Landesman may be contacted through his gallery: Leo Castelli, 4 East 77th Street, New York, N.Y. 10021. The Infinity Room is also described in Ralph Coe's *The Magic Theatre*.

233 Psychedelic bathtub

Harry Hermon, a researcher into psychedelics and altered states of consciousness, has developed a psychedelic bathtub that might more properly be called a psychedelic bathroom. The room where the bathtub is located is fitted with a variety of light-and-sound fixtures, including a revolving mirrored ball with spot, color wheels, and strobes. On the walls are a number of mounted moving *moiré* patterns (See No. 237), and other colored lights that may be varied as to intensity and operation.

The subject is told to undress and run his bath. While the bath is running, an especially luminescent bubble bath preparation is added to the water.

When the bath is drawn, the subject gets in and relaxes. Then the lights start to move, the *moiré* patterns begin shimmering and revolving, the strobes flicker at a variety of different speeds, the mirrored ball sends beams of rainbow light shooting across the room, and all of the above reflect and shine onto and through the multicolored soap bubbles. When sounds—chants, electronic music, or random noise patterns—are added, the bathroom becomes a fantastic room, and the subject becomes high.

With a little effort, the purchase of the correct equipment, and the proper design implementations, the psychedelic bathtub can be assembled almost anywhere.

ACCESS

Harry Hermon is the Director of the Institute for Psychedelic Research. He lives and maintains a private practice in Brooklyn, N.Y.

234 Magnets

Large industrial magnets have tremendously powerful force fields surrounding them. When entering these force fields one's own fields become greatly affected and the pulls and tugs, seeming to come from out of thin air, are unique and interesting. Be careful not to be wearing or carrying anything that will be torn from you by the magnet's force.

235   Negative ionization

Our atmosphere is constantly being ionized. Cosmic rays, radioactive soil elements, ultraviolet radiation, thunderstorms, winds, and the friction of blowing dust and particulate matter cause ions in the atmosphere to be positively or negatively charged.

Positive ionization is heaviest in urban areas. Negative ionization is most prevalent in the desert, on the open seas, at the tops of mountains, and in any spot where a thunderstorm has just occurred. Positive ions make the air feel stale, and cause fatigue and depression. Negative ions give feelings of alertness and mild excitation.

A machine that produces negative ionization periodically is often attached to industrial-sized air-conditioning units. Some of the literature on these units claims that astronauts are trained in negatively ionized environments, and that the main caucus rooms of the Democratic and Republican Presidential nominating conventions are also negatively ionized.

It is surmised by researchers on negative ionization that their presence in the bloodstream enables more oxygen to reach our cells and tissues and allows it to get there quicker. Positive ionization has the opposite effect.

ACCESS

Idries Shah (See Nos. 160 and 161) is a director of Medion Ltd., Box 1, Oxted, Surrey; Oxted 3127, England. Medion markets negative-ionization machines. The small portable model that operates on wall current is a little more than $60. A similar model that runs on batteries is $72. A larger model that will negatively ionize a large room costs a little less than $130. I have personally used the small model; it works. Philip K. Dick has written a novel, *Ubik,* that has part of its plot centered around the effects of negative ionization.

236   Prosthetic devices for the blind

Machines are now being made to give the blind the equivalent of sight. These prosthetic devices work on the transfer of sensory images and on the stimulation of phosphenes.

The main devices now under development are those that attempt to create tactile images of the visual field, so that the blind person can learn to translate the tactile impression into a visual cognition. Two types of devices have been shown. Both operate on the same principle, but one transfers the image to the back and the other to the forehead. It works this way: a photoelectric camera on the blind person's head or shoulder scans the visual field. What it "sees" is translated into a number of tactile impressions that literally draw a picture, in "touch," on the blind person's back or forehead. The blind person then attempts to translate this tactile imagery into an impression of how the environment looks to the camera. At this time, results are rudimentary.

The other group of devices now being researched has to do with the evaluation of phosphenes (See No. 34), their size, shape, color, and how these elements can be manipulated to give a "visual" image that will correspond to the blind person's environment.

ACCESS

A brief description of some of the machines in operation is to be found in a *Popular Electronics* (January 1971) article, "Electricity and Physiology," by Webb Garrison.

237 Moiré patterns

Moiré patterns are everywhere in our environment. The easiest way to see one is to take two identical black pocket combs, align them, and then move one back and forth. The patterns made by each comb's teeth will combine to give an impression of a third and moving pattern.

We also see *moiré* patterns on the highway as we drive. Two different types of fencing or two different sets of posts will create the same effect as the pocket combs do, with the automobile supplying the movement.

Moiré or watered silk was invented by the Chinese. The *moiré* pattern sensation can be stimulated by many other patterns, such as those presented by op art.

One of the more ingenious uses for these patterns is to mount them on a wall attached to a vibrating and/or rotating device. Though *moiré* patterns do not always have to move to produce their hallucinatory effects, when they do move these effects are greatly heightened.

A Moiré pattern

ACCESS

Gerald Oster's (with Nishijima) article on *moiré* patterns appeared in the May 1963, issue of *Scientific American, No. 208*, pp. 54–63. Oster's book on the subject, *The Science of Moiré Patterns*, as well as a number of *moiré* pattern kits and reproductions, are sold through Edmund Scientific Co., 101 E. Gloucester Pike, Barrington, N.J. 08007.

238 Electrical phosphene stimulation

Gerald Oster has discovered that phosphenes, which can be stimulated manually with the hands or in a shower (See No. 34), can also be elicited through electronic stimulation. Don't do this unless you are aware of what you are doing, and have a good knowledge of the anatomy and physiology involved. Electrodes connected to an audio generator or oscillator are also connected to the side of the eye, at the temple bone. Electrode paste is necessary. The generator is applied at a subaudio level, down to about a cycle per second in frequency.

A potential of 2–3 volts gets a very good response in terms of phosphene production and is not tactilely experienced by the subject. DO NOT EXCEED 10 VOLTS! This will lead to irritation. Make sure that you can contact an expert at any time that help might be needed. This is an experimental procedure; the manual stimulation of phosphenes is very effective and much easier.

Flashes similar to phosphene stimulation have been elicited when a subject was exposed to neutrons of energy in the 25-million-volt category, generated by a cyclotron.

And if a plate of zinc be placed between the gums and the upper lip, and a plate of gold be placed in the upper part of the tongue, when the gold is brought into contact with the zinc, the person sees immediately a flash of lightning.

Dr. R. J. Thornton, 1813

ACCESS

See Access material for No. 34. The data on the cyclotron-generated flashes appear in *Science*, May 21, 1971, pp. 868–70. Dr. Thornton's quote is from "Animal Electricity," in his *The Philosophy of Medicine*.

239 Seeing your eye

Oster also shows how to see the internal structure of the eye and the eye lid. Take a length of fiber optics light pipe and place one end on the lens of a very powerful source of light (e.g., a high-intensity reading light). Put the other end of the light pipe on the lid of your closed eye. You will have to move the end that is on your eye lid around, since the eye never focuses on any one place for very long. What you will see as you move it around is a show of internal cinema that rivals the best hallucinations: the structure of the circulatory system of the eye lid and part of the system of nerves, veins, and arteries of the eye itself.

ACCESS

Fiber optics light cable is available from Edmund Scientific, Barrington, N.J. 08007.

240 Electrical stimulation of the mastoid

When NASA was trying to determine what to do to ease the feelings of nausea that astronauts who are in a spinning, tumbling capsule experience, they considered the production of countersensations to mask the effect. One of the experiments was the generation of an electrical charge to the astronauts' mastoids which, controlled properly, would give them the sensation of spinning in the opposite direction. This would have neutralized any spinning or tumbling effects.

This idea was abandoned and retro-rockets were finally adopted to deal with the problem. Oster picked up his idea from NASA's research. In his lab, he can hook people up to an audio generator and produce low-voltage, low-frequency stimulation to the mastoid. This stimulation must be phased to create a beat, generating a third sensation made by the proper phasing of two different frequencies. (Beat is also the basis of *moiré* sensations.) At 8,000 cycles or more the subject feels the room beginning to spin in one direction. When the phasing is reversed and the tuning slowed, the subject experiences the room spinning in the opposite direction.

ACCESS

The audio generator used in the experiments described was a Heathkit Audio Oscillator.

241 Beat head hole

We can make the brain hear a new third pattern when only two frequency patterns are reaching it as input by the creation of a beat and the use of phasing. If we hook up tone-producing equipment to a stereo amplifier, one frequency is sent on one channel to one ear, and another frequency on another channel to the other ear. The frequencies are adjusted until the subject has the feeling that there is a large empty space in the center of his head. This initial perception is frequently of an elliptical space. Adjustment and tuning of the frequencies can change the perceived shape from an ellipse to a circle to something that feels very much like a rectangle.

242 Russian sleep

Russian sleep, or electrosleep as it is often called, refers to the use of electrical machines that enable people to live with less sleep than they would normally require. Russian sleep involves the direct manipulation of the electrical charge and power of human brain waves. This manipulation is accomplished by machines that are available in the United States only to those who meet government research qualifications.

The sleep machine is very similar to an audio generator. It sends out an electrical current through electrodes that are attached to the subject's temple and forehead. Usually, a square-wave of one millisecond duration, at a rate of 100 hz, is produced. Treatment usually lasts for a half hour.

The Russians use this equipment to replace sleep. The American research has so far been applied to people suffering from insomnia, anxiety, depression or drug addiction. The machine is used to help them relax so that they can get to sleep without the aid of barbiturates.

New research indicates that the sleep experienced during electrosleep is all delta brainwave non-dreaming sleep. Many of the Russian subjects, after using a sleep machine to replace nightly sleep, began to spontaneously dream in their waking hours, creating potentially dangerous situations. The bodies of these subjects were demanding a certain amount of dreams each day, dreams denied them by the use of the machines.

ACCESS

Garrison discusses the apparent lack of American interest in electrosleep equipment in "Electricity & Physiology," *Popular Electronics*, January 1971.

I personally wrote Lafayette Electronics asking about the purchase of their Model 7200 Somniatron. They replied that the electrosleep machine is classified by the Food and Drug Administration as experimental apparatus and available only to qualified and approved researchers.

243   Electric clothing

Electric clothing was introduced by Diana Dew in the late 1960s. Wearing a dress of her own design and making, she appeared as a walking, bleeping, flashing body. Her dress was wired to a battery worn around her waist. The eye delighted as different parts of her dress lit up, flashed, changed color. Although miniaturization now makes less cumbersome batteries available, further development has been slow in this area.

ACCESS

A selection from Tom Hyman's profile of Diana Dew and her electric clothing appears in M. McLuhan and Q. Fiore's *War and Peace in the Global Village.*

244   Motion and sound sensors

Motion sensors may be attached to you (or to anything else you'd like) and will report, by way of an auditory feedback signal, whenever motion occurs. This helps you to keep still, and also increases your awareness of how often you move without knowing it.

Sound sensors work on the same principle. Connect them to whatever you would like to monitor; any time a sound is created, you will be informed by a beep, or a buzz, or a light. They can be used to increase your awareness of what true silence is.

ACCESS

Humanitas Systems, RD 2, Roscoe, New York 12776, sells a Series 300 Motion Sensor with audible feedback for $59.95. They will also design and build sound sensors to your specifications. Prices vary according to the system desired.

245 OKPLD

OKPLD stands for the Optokinetic Perceptual Learning Device for Sensory Stimulation and Learning. The device, now patented (No. 3,496,649), was developed by Eleanor Criswell while she was working toward her doctorate at the University of Florida.

The OKPLD is a paper drum 6 inches high and 8 inches in diameter which is affixed to a three-speed phonograph turntable. Attached to the drum's vertical sides are paper bands with a high-impact, highly detailed design (newsprint will do, and black and white is preferred). A high-intensity light should be available for the operation of the OKPLD.

You sit facing the OKPLD so that your gaze falls on one side of the drum, watching with an intent but relaxed gaze. The drum is revolved at 33⅓ rpm. for 3–5 minutes. During this time, you watch the design; it is best to count while watching. Criswell suggests that you say: 1—I am, 2—I am, 3—I am, etc., through 10 and back to 1 again.

While you are watching the revolving drum the light is illuminating the area, and you are enhancing your perceptions for the rest of the day. You should have a timer nearby to make sure you keep viewing for about 5 minutes. At the completion of a viewing, when the turntable and the drum stop, a motion after-effect will be manifest for a brief period of time.

This effect and the enhancement of sensory awareness are the most frequently reported alterations of consciousness achieved by the OKPLD.

ACCESS

Eleanor Criswell was granted Patent No. 3,496,649 in February, 1970, for her OptoKinetic Perceptual Learning Device. To get a copy of the patent send 50¢ to the Commissioner of Patents, Washington, D.C. 20231. Additional information on the OKPLD is available in *Dissertation Abstracts, 30, No. 5,* 1969, 1862-A.

It may be possible to construct your own OKPLD, using black poster paper for the drum and newsprint for the bands or strips.

246 TV

Television is already a consciousness expander, especially in color. We are yet to discover exactly how television effects us neurally:

Television, as direct experience, can be considered in this instance on two levels. First, it is a potent source of light. The cathode-ray experience is the only instance where man looks directly into a light source for any sustained period, possibly averaging four hours a day. Light is actually projected onto the retina by the cathode-ray tube. Second, man responds not only to light perceived by the sense but also to invisible factors of biological rhythms such as the phylogenetic flicker. Television alters this rhythm violently.

John Brockman

When we go to the movies we see light reflected from its source to the screen, and then into our eyes. When we watch TV we look directly *into* the light source.

The TV repairman uses an electromagnetic "magic" wand to stabilize color-TV operation. You can ask your repairman how to get one. When the wand is passed in front of the screen all of the color images produced by the tube follow the wand. You can program your own free-form color abstract-pattern art. (Art of this sort has been exhibited by Nam June Paik, and others.)

TV used as a feedback device is a magnificent consciousness-alteration technique. Many forms of therapy have recently been combined with TV videotape. A recording is made of the therapy sessions. In addition to patient/therapist/group interface, all of those present are able to observe their behavior and interactions when the video tape is replayed. When you are able to see how you act you start to act differently. A rather startling, imaginative, and fun way to use videotape feedback is through a delay system. A TV camera is mounted directly over a monitor. But the image is taped and appears on the monitor after a delay of about 5 seconds. The subject standing in front of the camera and monitor sees his image as it was 5 seconds before, and differently than he's accustomed to seeing himself.

When we look at ourselves in a mirror we see a reversed image, a reflection. We see not what is going on, but the opposite of what is going on. When I stand in front of a mirror and raise my right arm into the air over my head, the image in the mirror raises his left arm over his head. Since we see ourselves in mirrors all the time we unconsciously adjust for this reversal.

With a TV image this doesn't happen. When a TV camera records the raising of my right arm the image on the TV screen raises his right arm, too. When this re-reversal, as it were, from mirror images is coupled with delay there often occurs a wonderful experience.

Cable TV (community antenna television) will probably be the next video development. CATV will let you talk back; it is TV with the ability for dialectic. You can use it to get information and then to ask for more information; or to give the system behind the TV your own information, as in polling or voting.

ACCESS

TV as a vehicle for the change of consciousness, both individual and global, is covered in Gene Youngblood's *The Videosphere*. Current and future events in TV are reported and commented on in *Radical Software*, a quarterly periodical available from 24 East 22nd Street, New York, N.Y. 10010. John Brockman's remarks on TV and other topics in *By the Late John Brockman* are useful and interesting. Portable TV equipment is available from a variety of sources. Some of the best comes from Sony.

247 Repetition tapes

Repetition tapes were discovered by R. L. Gregory of England and Richard Warren of the United States. A repetition tape is a loop tape that repeats, exactly, the same sound, word, or phrase over and over again, indefinitely.

My first exposure to them was through John Lilly. Lilly played a tape with the word "COGITATE" repeating over and over to a roomful of more than 100 people. Everyone heard the tape change into another word. My own experience was of being able to let the word change into other words, but of always being able to return to the initial perception: that of hearing "COGITATE." After about 8 minutes of listening I became tense and nervous; I was tired of listening to the same word repeated over and over. Suddenly, the tape changed. It said "MELT INTO IT." I did some mental double-checking and discovered that this change had occurred on the tape, not in my brain. I could not return to "COGITATE" totally for another minute. Then I heard nothing but "COGITATE" until Lilly turned the tape machine off, after some 10 minutes. I turned to a friend to compare notes.

"Tape changed, didn't it?" I said.

"It sure did," said my friend. "Count to ten."

"What?" I said in disbelief.

"The tape changed from saying 'COGITATE' to saying 'COUNT TO TEN.' I heard it change. It wasn't me."

Everyone in the room heard it change to a different word or phrase. However, the tape *never* changed. It always said "COGITATE."

Lilly reports that almost all people's brains will function this way in order to cope with a boring, unchanging, repetitious image. The only people who have never heard such tapes change are the congenitally blind. It is thought that this is because of their need to correctly perceive auditory cues in their environment. The sighted can afford auditory hallucinations.

ACCESS

The origin of repetition tapes is discussed in Nigel Calder's *The Mind of Man*. Lilly's loop and repetition tapes, and others prepared by Stanley Keleman, are available through Big Sur Recordings.

248   Computer/human interface

Computers and computer applications have been used for almost a decade in educational services, including teaching machines. The new developments in computer education will depend on the development of the educational console, which will be able to construct a personal response for the user.

Computers have also been used in diagnostic and therapeutic procedures. There is a report of a computer which is fed data on the activities of mentally retarded children by teachers who observe the children's behavior. The computer, after absorbing the data and comparing it to past information on behavior, makes recommendations on aspects of behavior that should be reinforced.

Many types of therapy are built upon language manipulation by the therapist and his ability to point out ideas (in language) to the patient. It is reasonable to assume that the next step will be to replace the therapist with a computer. The computer would be programed to mimic the behavior of the therapist or counselor. Experiments in this field are now under way.

An IBM 360-40 computer used in banking

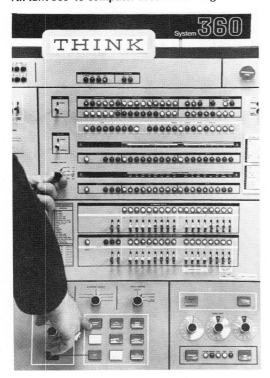

249   Bio-feedback

Feedback is information. When a process is being performed and the resulting knowledge of the process is made accessible to the performer, then feedback takes place. Feedback involves a knowledge of certain results being reintegrated back into a system.

Bio-feedback is a new frontier in research and creativity, combining the activities of consciousness, psychology, philosophy, electronics, and physiology. What bio-feedback does is apply feedback technology to internal, visceral systems. These systems are usually out of our conscious, voluntary control. Bio-feedback brings our internal functions into the area of consciousness, and thereby allows learning and control to take place.

Applications of this method hold great promise for the treatment of illness and for use in rehabilitation. Great excitement has also been generated because of the possibility of its use in altering states of consciousness.

For centuries, select groups of men have known that it is possible to become aware of, and control, internal states. Yogis in India, Tibet and elsewhere can speed up and slow down breathing, heart beat and pulse, and blood circulation, as well as control other functions. The Yogi Swami Rama recently came to the United States to demonstrate some of his awesome abilities of psycho-physiological control. One astounding demonstration was that of his ability to control the temperature of his hands; he could, within 2 minutes, raise the temperature on one part of his hand 10 degrees higher than the temperature on another part of the same hand, some 2 inches away! This Yogi has been tested by the Greens of the Menninger Foundation in Kansas, people currently pioneering in the study of voluntary control of internal states.

In many ways, bio-feedback mimics the Yogis' experiences in training. A Yogi spends years learning how to zero in his consciousness on a physiological indicator, say the heart beat. After learning to become aware of his heart beat he can then learn to use this awareness to control the *way* in which his heart beats. Bio-feedback works much the same way, in that the subject can be connected to a feedback device, an EKG (electrocardiograph), for information about his heart. When he can measure and compare, internally, the states that are being reported by the feedback device, the next step will be to use that feedback information to control the state being reported. If his heart beats too slowly, he can speed it up; if it beats too fast, he can slow it down. Yogis take years to learn this kind of awareness and control. Technological instrumentation now allows this kind of learning to be acquired in a matter of months, even days.

Feedback learning and control work is now being conducted in a variety of research areas. These include:

BRAIN WAVE Using electroencephalographic devices, subjects are taught to control and manipulate their own brain waves. This research was initiated in the United States by Joe Kamiya. Most of the work in brain-wave feedback has centered on one particular brain wave, alpha. (There are four main varieties of brain waves: *Beta,* with a frequency ranging from 14 to 50 cycles per second; *Alpha,* with a frequency ranging from 8 to 13 cycles per second; *Theta,* with a frequency ranging from 4 to 7 cycles per second; and *Delta,* with a frequency ranging from 0.5 to 3.5 cycles per second. Beta indicates mental and visual activity. Alpha is present during relaxation and some dream states. Theta is sometimes present in dream and other sleep states as well as in some relaxed waking states. Delta is indicative of deep sleep.)

Subjects were trained with EEGs (electroencephalographs) or the like by being given a feedback indication of when they were producing alpha. Subjects learned quickly and most could generate alpha at will after several hours of intensive training. Studies of the EEG states present in meditating Zen masters and monks, and in Yogis, indicated that alpha, and some related theta states, were the results of the years spent in meditative practice.

As research has continued, experimenters have become interested in a borderline area between alpha and theta, an area identified by brain waves ranging from 6 to 9 cycles per second, with amplitudes of more than 50 microvolts. (Most brain waves produce power in the range below 25 microvolts.) Several experiments are now being conducted to establish a link between creativity, ESP, and other factors and this borderline brain-wave area.

What must be stressed with reference to the future of brain-wave feedback is that all studies, formal or informal, professional or nonprofessional, are being pursued in an area of relative ignorance. Though subjects can now learn to generate alpha and other brain-wave patterns at will, in short periods of time, and though the resultant states of consciousness are described with adjectives ranging from relaxing to psychedelic, most researchers indicate that the field is currently in its infancy. No one is yet sure what the difference is between alpha generated from the left cerebral hemisphere and that emanating from the right cerebral hemisphere.

Recent studies in brain implantation and ESB (electrical stimulation of the brain) indicate that alpha itself is generated from within the septum, deep inside the brain. All EEG measurements, by both professional and amateur equipment, are taken from outside the skull. The ability to place electrodes intracerabrally will probably usher in the second, third, or fourth generation of brain-wave feedback research.

A number of centers have appeared throughout the country, usually supported by the pseudo-scientific research of self-professed psychologists (with and without degrees), which claim to train individuals in controlling brain-wave states without the use of feedback instruments. Usually they quote Kamiya and other authorities out of context and without permission to support their claims. They all have thousands of successful graduates. Their courses cost hundreds and sometimes thousands of dollars. The basis of these courses almost always centers around a mild form of hypnotic induction. Be wary of the smooth-talking salesmen who are now "brain-wave teachers."

EMG EMG (electromyographic) feedback is used here to describe work being done using muscle feedback to control tension states. The subject is connected to an EMG and hears a tone that varies according to the electrical activity present in the muscle or muscles wired for feedback. When we are aroused in exercise, fright, flight, or anxiety we take on a high degree of muscle tension. Even when not in these states, during waking hours most people have a high degree of muscle tension. If that tension can be drastically reduced, as it can by EMG feedback, then a relaxed and sometimes altered state of consciousness ensues. This work has been pioneered by Thomas Budzynski and Johann Stoyva.

GSR GSR is an abbreviation for galvanic skin response. A GSR machine measures the electrical resistance of the skin. It is also called a galvanometer. It is not certain what areas of tension GSR reports. What is probably measured is electrical activity associated with certain vascular changes in the circulatory system. One subject had a GSR attached to his finger. The feedback mechanism was producing a loud but low whine. Another person said: "What if I were to hit you [the subject] in the stomach right now?" He made no motion. As the subject considered these words the whine increased in intensity and pitch until it was a piercing howl. As they talked and the subject discovered that the other man had no intention of hitting him, the feedback sounds returned to their original whine.

HEART BEAT, BLOOD PRESSURE, AND RESPIRATION Through the use of feedback coupled with an EKG, people have been learning to control their hearts, to make them go faster and slower, to make them beat more evenly and regularly, and to detect any changes in operation. Blood-pressure feedback, through the use of a blood-pressure cuff, has enabled people with high and low blood pressure not only to change their blood pressures, but at the same time to become aware of the states that raise or lower these pressures to begin with. Breath bags, mirrors, and other devices have been used to show a subject the workings of his breathing mechanisms.

Some researchers have been working in areas which include voluntary control learned through feedback of temperature, both for the entire body and for separate parts of the body; sweat-gland activity; eye movements, etc. The Greens train their subjects to control three major neuroanatomical regions, craniospinal, autonomic, and central.

Certainly, the future of bio-feedback lies in this area of feedback training and control in combination. To isolate just EEG, EMG, or blood pressure will not bring anywhere near as dramatic results as learned voluntary control in all three areas.

Looking into the future a bit I can envision a living room "altered-state console" that looks much like the present hi-fi cabinetry. There will be easily applied electrode configurations and a variety of altered states that can be programmed simply by pushing buttons on the console. A combination of auditory and visual feedback will be available. An example might be a low EMG, high alpha EEG trip or perhaps a low EMG, low alpha combination (this tends to produce bright, extremely vivid visual phenomena if the alpha is obtained from the occipital region exclusively [generated from a point near the center of the back of the skull]).

Thomas Budzynski, 1971

That man really lives who brings the greatest fraction of his daily experience into the realm of the conscious.
Martin H. Fischer in an article entitled "Spinal Chord Education" in the Illinois Medical Journal, December, 1928

ACCESS

The first article by Joe Kamiya was his "Conscious Control of Brain Waves" which appeared in *Psychology Today* (April 1968, Vol. 1, No. 11). Another of his papers appears in Tart's book, along with the supporting evidence in the form of the papers which evaluate the EEG readings of meditating Yogis and Zen Masters. "The Psychology and Physiology of Meditation and Related Phenomena: A Bibliography," by Beverly Timmons and Joe Kamiya, was published in *The Journal of Transpersonal Psychology*, No. 1, 1970. It is most complete in its listing of references to bio-feedback.
That same issue of the *Journal* also has the report on the work of the Greens with conscious control of internal states.

Many significant feedback equipment systems are now on the market. New machines are being invented and marketed every day. Make sure of the product you are trying or buying. If the machine is safe but doesn't work, at least it will get you to sit still, do nothing, and try to relax. This is helpful and can lead to meditation; it explains why many people have purchased malfunctioning brain-wave feedback devices and been perfectly happy with them. The best machine available for brain-wave feedback is the EEG Bio-Feedback Research Apparatus from Intelex, 2277 Canyon Drive, Hollywood, Calif. 90028. It is the closest thing to laboratory EEG equipment that can be purchased for under $10,000. It also incorporates many feedback-oriented design features not found on lab EEGs. The price is $4,980.00. The equipment was developed

by Edward Wortz and David Nowlis. Wortz works for Garrett, an aerospace research and manufacturing concern.

Another EEG-type machine is the SA4 EEG Amplifier, available from Mousseau Scientific Instruments Ltd., 30 Capital Drive, Ottawa 12, Canada. The price is $995.00

The equipment listed above is of professional quality and is now being used in ongoing experimental work in brain-wave feedback.

The devices listed below have more of an appeal to the general market. They are less expensive and less sensitive to subtleties of EEG transmission. However, where indicated, they work—that is, they report a fairly accurate EEG reading from places on the outside of the skull.

Psychophysics Labs at 41 West 71st Street, New York, N.Y. 10023, sells brain-wave feedback machines. They carry the Toomim Alpha Pacer, one of the smallest of the brain-wave feedback devices. It works well, but has a rather annoying feedback tone; it has potential for light feedback. $195.00.

Psychophysics Labs also markets the Aquarian Alphaphone. The model of this machine featured in *Life* magazine suffered from a tendency to report artifact. A consultation with the engineer from Bio-Feedback Technology has produced a second-stage model of the Alphaphone, with good EEG response and an interesting tone. No light feedback. $190. Toomim may be contacted directly: The Alpha Center, 10480 Santa Monica Blvd., Los Angeles, Calif. 90025. Aquarius Electronics may be contacted at 737 Buena Vista West, San Francisco, Calif. 94117.

Joe Kamiya listening to feedback of his brain waves while his wife, Joanne, monitors the computer printout

Psionics produces a number of machines under the names ETC. These Electronic Techniques for Centering are continuous and binary feedback machines. The difference is that continuous feedback has no threshold control. Without threshold control you only get a steady feedback report; with threshold control you can set the machine so that it gives feedback only when you reach specific levels of frequency and amplitude, say 9 Hz alpha at 25 microvolts. (All of the machines listed above have working threshold controls. The more expensive EEG machines are better discriminators of exact threshold.) The ETC I is $100 and has only continuous feedback. The ETC II is $150, continuous and binary. The ETC III is $500, continuous and binary and features a cassette recorder for high volume/low volume threshold switching. The ETC IV has binary only and costs $125. Psionics, P.O. Box 1919, Boulder, Colo. 80302. For EMG feedback Bio-Feedback Systems, Inc., P.O. Box 1459, Boulder, Colo. 80302, offers two models; both are excellent. The professional BIFS–Research model is $2,000. A less expensive PE–2 EMG Feedback System is $450.

Psychophysics Labs also offers two additional feedback systems. One, the Bio-Sensor, gives the subject feedback (on a needle-dial) of respiration, GSR, blood pulse, and EKG. The price is $140. The other, called the Hang-Up meter, feeds back GSR in a weird, audible tone. It costs $40.

The alpha-wave without machines groups include Silva Mind Control (hypnosis for $150, complete); and Mind Dynamics, Inc., also known as MDI. Both are attempts to cash in on the brain-wave feedback fad. Neither has much to do with brain waves or physiological feedback.

Annett's *Feedback and Human Behavior* is a good book on applications of feedback control to learning. It does not, however, discuss the visceral learning potential of feedback.

Frequently the machine usage is eventually replaced by meditation in one form or another.

Edward Wortz

250   Brain music

Using a brain-wave feedback device, David Rosenboom let his own brain waves determine the kind of music he would make. This concert/experiment occurred in December, 1970. It was the first public demonstration of the use of brain-wave feedback to produce an art form. This form of art was first proposed by Charles Ives. Rosenboom links his brain waves to an input device of his own musical synthesizer, the Neurona.

ACCESS

Rosenboom gave his performance at Automation House. He teaches and heads an interdisciplinary program at York University in Toronto, Canada.

251 ESB

Electrical stimulation of the brain (ESB) is, along with bio-feedback, the area with the greatest potential for future control, understanding, and expansion of consciousness. ESB is now being used in two major ways. One, to investigate the actual make-up and operation of the brain. Two, to control behavior through implantation electrical communicating devices.

As noted above, measuring the brain's spontaneous electrical activity by means of surface electrodes (EEG) does not reflect the actual activity of the brain. A new procedure is now being developed and tested which will be able to tell us where specific types of cerebral activity initiate from and how they function. This method involves the surgical implantation of intracerebral electrodes which will monitor electrical activity at source points. Taking a reading of electrical brain activity from the temples or the occipital is quite different from taking a reading from within the brain septum. Knowledge of the actual location of the brain's different centers will speed conscious control over brain usage, much in the same way that brain-wave feedback enables rapid learning of control over reported brain-wave activity.

The control of behavior through implantation of radio-activated communicating devices is already a fact, not just with humans but with animals. Radio remote control by an experimenter over a subject has already been accomplished in the regulation of epileptic seizures, memory stimulation, facilitation and inhibition of selected speech patterns, and stimulation and inhibition of sexual drive and desires.

The key to control of the brain centers which guide motives and their expression is the key to absolute control over behavior.

Perry London

ACCESS

ESB is discussed in London's *Behavior Control* and in Calder's *The Mind of Man*. More detailed description is included in Delgado's *Physical Control of the Mind*, Sheer's collection of papers, *Electrical Stimulation of the Brain*, and in *Control of Human Behavior*, edited by R. Ulrich, T. Stachnick and J. Mabry. All of J. Z. Young's books on the brain are essential for an understanding of the future of ESB, but especially his *Doubt and Certainty in Science*.

A collection of preserved brains at Cornell University

Bibliography

Many of the works cited in this bibliography may be found in more than one edition. No attempt is made to guess which edition may be the most readily available, but the original copyright date is given where it can be determined.

Aaronson, Bernard (ed.). *Workshops of the Mind*. Garden City, N.Y.: Doubleday, 1973.

Aaronson, B., & Osmond, H. *Psychedelics*. Garden City, N.Y.: Anchor, 1970.

Adams, Henry. *Mont-Saint-Michel and Chartres*. Garden city, N.Y.: Anchor, 1959.

Ahsen, Akhter. *Basic Concepts in Eidetic Psychotherapy*. Yonkers, N.Y.: Eidetic Publishing House, 1968.

Ahsen, Akhter. *Eidetic Analysis*. Yonkers, N.Y.: Eidetic Publishing House, 1973.

Ahsen, Akhter. *Eidetic Behavior*. Yonkers, N.Y.: Eidetic Publishing House, 1973.

Alexander, F. Matthias. *The Resurrection of the Body*. New York: Dell, 1971.

Alexander, Rolf. *Creative Realism*. New York: Pageant, 1954.

Al-Gahazali. *The Niche for Lights* (W. H. T. Gairdner, trans.). Lahore, Pakistan: Ashraf, 1924.

Alpert, Richard (Baba Ram Dass) & The Lama Foundation. *Be Here Now*. New York: Crown, 1971.

Ames, Adelbert Jr. *An Interpretative Manual*. New York: Hafner, 1968.

Ames, Adelbert Jr. *The Morning Notes of Adelbert Ames, Jr.* New Brunswick, N.J.: Rutgers University Press, 1960.

Andersen, Per, & Andersson, Sven. *Physiological Basis of the Alpha Rhythm*. New York: Appleton-Century-Crofts, 1968.

Anderson, E. W. "Abnormal Mental States in Survivors, with Special Reference to Collective Hallucinations." *Journal of the Royal Naval Medical Service, 28* (1942).

Anderson, Nels. *The Hobo*. Chicago: University of Chicago Press, 1923.

Annett, John. *Feedback and Human Behavior*. Baltimore: Penguin, 1969.

Arasteh, A. Reza. "Final Integration in the Adult Personality." *American Journal of Psychoanalysis, 25,* 61–73, 1965.

Arasteh, A. Reza. *Final Integration in the Adult Personality*. Leiden, Netherlands: E. J. Brill, 1965.

Arasteh, A. Reza. *Rumi the Persian: Rebirth in Creativity and Love*. Lahore, Pakistan: Ashraf, 1965.

Arberry, A. J. *Sufism: An Account of the Mystics of Islam*. New York: Harper & Row, 1950.

Arguilles, Jose, & Arguilles, Mirium. *Mandala*. Berkeley, Calif.: Shambala, 1972.

Arnheim, Rudolf. *Art and Visual Perception*. Berkeley, Calif.: University of California Press, 1954.

Asimov, Isaac. *The Human Brain*. New York: New American Library, 1963.

Assagioli, Roberto. *Psychosynthesis*. New York: Viking, 1965.

Attar, Farid ud-Din. *Parliament of the Birds* (C. S. Nott, trans.). Berkeley, Calif.: Shambala, 1954.

Awakawa, Yasuichi. *Zen Painting*. Palo Alto, Calif.: Kodansha, 1970.

Babbitt, Irving (trans.). *The Dhammapada*. New York: New Directions, 1936.

Bahm, Archie J. *The Heart of Confucius*. New York: Harper & Row, 1969.

Bahm, Archie J. *Yoga: Union with the Ultimate*. New York: Ungar, 1961.

Bapat, P. V. (ed.). *2500 Years of Buddhism*. Delhi: Govenment of India, 1956.

Barber, T. X. *Hypnosis: A Scientific Approach*. New York: Van Nostrand Reinhold, 1969.

Barber, T. X. *LSD, Marihuana, Yoga and Hypnosis*. Chicago: Aldine, 1970.

Barber, T. X., et al. (eds.). *Bio-Feedback and Self-Control*. Chicago: Aldine, 1971.

Barber, T. X., et al. (eds.). *Bio-Feedback and Self-Control, 1970* (Annual). Chicago: Aldine, 1971.

Bardon, Franz. *Initiation into Hermetics*. Kettig über Koblenz, Germany: Osiris-Verlag, 1962.

Barlow, Wilfred. "Psychosomatic Problems in Postural Re-education." *The Lancet,* Sept. 24, 1955, 659–664.

Bartley, S. Howard. *The Human Organism as a Person*. Philadelphia: Chilton, 1967.

Basham, A. L. *The Wonder That Was India*. New York: Grove, 1954.

Basho, M. *The Narrow Road to the Deep North and Other Travel Sketches*. Baltimore: Penguin, 1966.

Bates, W. H. *Better Eyesight Without Glasses*. New York: Pyramid, 1940.

Beard, G., & Wood, E. C. *Massage: Principles and Techniques*. Philadelphia: W. B. Saunders, 1964.

Becker, Ernest. *Zen: A Rational Critique*. New York: Norton, 1961.

Beckett, L. C. *Neti-Neti (Not This–Not That)*. London: J. M. Watkins, 1955.

Becker, L. C. *Unbounded Worlds*. London: Ark Press, 1959.

Beech, H. R. *Changing Man's Behavior*. Baltimore: Pelican, 1969.

Bennett, John G. *Concerning Subud*. London: Coombe Springs Press.

Bennett, John G. *The Dramatic Universe* (4 vols.). London: Coombe Springs Press.

Bennett, John G. *Energies*. London: Coombe Springs Press.

Benoit, Hubert. *Let Go!: Theory and Practice of Detachment According to Zen*. London: George Allen & Unwin, 1954.

Benoit, Hubert. *The Supreme Doctrine: Psychological Studies in Zen Thought*. New York: Viking, 1951.

Bergamini, David. *The Universe*. New York: Time-Life Books, 1962.

(Bhagavad-Gita) *The Song of God* (C. Isherwood & Prabhavananda, trans.). New York: New American Library, 1944.

The Bhagavadgita (Radhakrishnan, trans.). London: George Allen & Unwin, 1948.

The (Bhagavad) Gita (Sri Aurobindo, trans.). Pondicherry, India: Sri Aurobindo Ashram, 1946.

Bharati, Agehananda. *The Tantric Tradition*. New York: Doubleday, 1965.

Binswanger, Ludwig. *Being-in-the-World*. New York: Harper & Row, 1963.

Birdwhistell, Ray L. *Kinesics and Context: Essays on Body Motion Communication*. Philadelphia: University of Pennsylvania Press, 1970.

Blackshaw, Alan. *Mountaineering*. Baltimore: Penguin, 1965.

Blakney, Raymond B. (trans.). *Meister Eckhart*. New York: Harper & Row, 1941.

Blewett, Duncan B. *The Frontiers of Being*. New York: Award, 1969.

Bleibtreu, John N. *The Parable of the Beast*. New York: Collier, 1968.

Blofeld, John (trans.). *The Zen Teaching of Huang Po on the Transmission of Mind*. New York: Grove, 1958.

Blofeld, John (trans.). *The Zen Teaching of Hui Hai on Sudden Illumination*. London: Rider, 1962.

Blyth, R. H. *Buddhist Sermons on Christian Texts*. Tokyo: Kokudosha, 1952.

Blyth, R. H. *Easy Poems: Book One, Book Two* (2 vols.). Tokyo: Hokuseido, 1959.

Blyth, R. H. *Edo Satirical Verse Anthologies*. Tokyo: Hokuseido, 1961.

Blyth, R. H. *Haiku* (4 vols.): 1. *Eastern Culture*; 2. *Spring*; 3. *Summer-Autumn*; 4. *Autumn-Winter*. Tokyo: Hokuseido, 1949, 1950, 1952.

Blyth, R. H. *A History of Haiku* (2 vols.). Tokyo: Hokuseido, 1963, 1964.

Blyth, R. H. *Humor in English Literature*. Tokyo: Hokuseido, 1959.

Blyth, R. H. *Japanese Humor*. Tokyo: Japan Travel Bureau, 1957.

Blyth, R. H. *Japanese Life and Character in Senryu*. Tokyo: Hokuseido, 1960.

Blyth, R. H. *Mutamagawa*. Tokyo: Hokuseido.

Blyth, R. H. *Oriental Humor*. Tokyo: Hokuseido, 1959.

Blyth, R. H. *Senryu—Japanese Satirical Verses*. Tokyo: Hokuseido, 1949.

Blyth, R. H. *Zen and Zen Classics* (5 vols.): 1. *General Introduction From the Upanishads to Huineng*; 2. *History of Zen*; 3. *History of Zen (Nangaku Branch)*; 4. *Mumonkan*; 5. *Twenty-four Essays*. Tokyo: Hokuseido, 1960, 1962, 1964, 1966, 1970.

Blyth, R. H. *Zen in English Literature and Oriental Classics*. New York: Dutton, 1942.

Boeke, Kees. *Cosmic View: The Universe in Forty Jumps*. New York: John Day, 1957.

Bohr, Niels. *Essays 1958–1962 on Atomic Physics and Human Knowledge*. New York: Vintage, 1963.

Bois, J. S. *Breeds of Men*. New York: Harper & Row, 1969.

Boisen, Anton, T. *The Exploration of the Inner World*. New York: Harper & Row, 1936.

Borges, Jorge Luis. *The Book of Imaginary Beings*. New York: Avon, 1967.

Bouquet, A. C. *Sacred Books of the World*. Baltimore: Penguin, 1954.

Bowers, M. "Friend or Traitor: Hypnosis in the Service of Religion." *International Journal of Clinical Experimental Hypnosis*, 1959.

Bradford, L. P., Gibb, J. R., & Benne, K. D. (eds.). *T-Group Theory and Laboratory Method*. New York: Wiley, 1964.

Brand, Stewart (ed.). *The Last Whole Earth Catalog*. New York: Random House, 1971.

Brener, H. Charles, & Williams, Richard. *Abilitism: A New Religion*. Lucerne Valley, Calif., 1970.

Bridges, Hal. *American Mysticism*. New York: Harper & Row, 1970.

Bridgman, P. W. *The Way Things Are*. New York: Viking, 1959.

Briggs, William (ed.). *Anthology of Zen*. New York: Grove, 1961.

Bro, Harmon. *High Play*. New York: Coward-McCann, 1970.

Brockman, John. *Afterwords*. Garden City, N.Y.: Doubleday, 1973.

Brockman, John. *By The Late John Brockman*. New York: Macmillan, 1969.

Brockman, John. *37*. New York: Holt, Rinehart & Winston, 1970.

Brockman, John, & Rosenfeld, Edward (eds.). *Real Time, 1 & 2*. Garden City, N.Y.: Doubleday, 1973.

Brunton, Paul. *The Hidden Teaching Beyond Yoga*. New York: Dutton, 1941.

Buber, Martin. *Between Man and Man*. New York: Macmillan, 1947.

Buber, Martin. *I and Thou*. New York: Scribner's, 1958.

Buber, Martin. *Pointing the Way*. New York: Harper & Row, 1957.

Buber, Martin. *Tales of the Hasidim* (2 vols.): 1. *Early Masters*; 2. *Later Masters*. New York: Schocken, 1947, 1948.

Bucke, Richard Maurice. *Cosmic Consciousness*. New York: Dutton, 1969.

Budge, E. A. Wallis. *Amulets and Talismans*. New York: Collier, 1930.

Budge, E. A. Wallis. *Egyptian Magic*. New York: Dover, 1901.

Bulfinch, Thomas. *Bulfinch's Mythology*. London: Spring, 1964.

Bull, Nina. *The Attitude Theory of Emotion*. New York: Johnson Reprint, 1951.

Bull, Nina. *The Body and Its Mind*. New York: Las Americas, 1962.

Burgess, Anthony. *Rejoyce*. New York: Ballantine, 1965.

Burckhardt, Titus. *An Introduction to Sufi Doctrine*. Lahore: Ashraf, 1969.

Burckhardt, Titus. *Letters of a Sufi Master*. London: Perennial, 1969.

Burland, C. A. *Beyond Science*. New York: Grosset & Dunlap, 1972.

Byrd, C. *Alone*. New York: Putnam's, 1938.

Cage, John. *Silence*. Middletown, Conn.: Wesleyan University Press, 1961.

Calder, Nigel. *The Mind of Man*. New York: Viking, 1970.

Campbell, Joseph. *The Hero With a Thousand Faces*. Cleveland: Meridian, 1949.

Campbell, Joseph. *The Masks of God* (4 vols.). New York: Viking, 1968.

Campbell, Joseph (ed.). *Papers from the Eranos Yearbooks* (6 vols. to date): 1. *Spirit & Nature*; 2. *The Mysteries*; 3. *Man & Time*; 4. *Spiritual Disciplines*; 5. *Man & Transformation*; 6. *The Mystic Vision*. Princeton: Princeton University Press, 1954, 1955, 1957, 1960, 1964, 1969.

Campbell, Joseph, & Robinson, Henry M. *A Skeleton Key to Finnegans Wake*. New York: Viking, 1944.

Canadian Whole Earth Almanac, Shelter Issue. Winter, 1970.

Canetti, Elias. *Crowds and Power*. New York: Viking, 1960.

Cantril, Hadley. *The "Why" of Man's Experience*. New York: Macmillan, 1950.

Caron, M., & Hutin, S. *The Alchemists*. New York: Grove, 1961

Carpenter, Edmund. *Eskimo*. Toronto: University of Toronto Press, 1960.

Carroll, Lewis. *The Annotated Alice*. Cleveland: World, 1960.

Castaneda, Carlos. *Journey to Ixtlan*. New York: Simon & Schuster, 1972.

Castaneda, Carlos. *A Separate Reality*. New York: Simon & Schuster, 1971.

Castaneda, Carlos. *The Teachings of Don Juan*. New York: Ballantine, 1968.

Chai, Ch'u, & Chai, Winberg (eds.). *The Humanist Way in Ancient China: Essential Works of Confucianism*. New York: Bantam, 1965.

Chang, Chen-Chi. *The Practice of Zen*. London: Rider, 1959.

Chang, Chung-Yuan. *Creativity and Taoism*. New York: Julian, 1963.

Chang, Chung-Yuan. *Original Teachings of Ch'an Buddhism*. New York: Pantheon, 1969.

Chaudhuri, Haridas. *Integral Yoga*. London: George Allen & Unwin, 1965.

Chen, C. M. *The Light-House in the Ocean of Ch'an*. New York: Buddhist Association of the United States, 1965.

Cheng, Man-ching, & Smith, Robert W. *Tai-Chi*. Rutland, Vt., 1966.

Chiang, Yee. *Chinese Calligraphy*. Cambridge, Mass.: Harvard University Press, 1938.

Chicago Review, Zen Issue. Summer 1958.

Chinmoy, Ghose. *Meditations*. New York: Harper & Row, 1970.

Chogyam, Trungpa. *Born in Tibet*. Baltimore: Penguin, 1966.

Chogyam, Trungpa. *Meditation in Action*. Berkeley, Calif.: Shambala, 1969.

Chou, Hsiang-Kuang. *Dhyana Buddhism in China*. Allahabad, India: Indo-Chinese Literature, 1960.

Chou, Hsiang-Kuang. *T'ai Hsu: His Life and Teachings*. Allahabad, India: Indo-Chinese Literature, 1957.

Christian, P. *The History and Practice of Magic*. Hackensack, N.J.: Wehman.

Clarke, Arthur C. *Childhood's End*. New York: Ballantine, 1953.

Clarke, Arthur C. *Profiles of the Future*. New York: Bantam, 1963.

Clarke, Arthur C. *Report on Planet Three*. New York: Harper & Row, 1972.

Clébert, Jean-Paul. *The Gypsies*. Baltimore: Penguin, 1961.

Clement, Christopher. *The Alpha*Theta Brain Wave Training Papers*. San Francisco: C. C. Clement, 1972.

Coe, G. *The Psychology of Religion*. Chicago: University of Chicago Press, 1916.

Coe, Ralph T. *The Magic Theatre*. Kansas City, Mo.: Circle, 1970.

Comfort, Alex. *The Joy of Sex*. New York: Crown, 1972.

Commoner, Barry. *The Closing Circle*. New York: Random House, 1971.

Conze, Edward. *Buddhism*. New York: Harper & Row, 1951.

Conze, Edward (trans.). *Buddhist Wisdom Books: The Diamond Sutra—The Heart Sutra*. London: George Allen & Unwin, 1958.

Conze, Edward, et al. (eds.). *Buddhist Texts Through the Ages*. New York: Harper & Row, 1954.

Coomaraswamy, Ananda K. *Buddha and the Gospel of Buddhism*. New York: Harper & Row, 1916.

Cooper, Kenneth H. *The New Aerobics*. New York: Bantam, 1970.

Cooper, L., & Erikson, M. *Time Distortion in Hypnosis*. Baltimore: Williams & Wilkins, 1954.

Cooper, Paulette. *The Scandal of Scientology*. New York: Tower, 1971.

Corbin, Henry. *Creative Imagination in the Sufism of Ibn 'Arabi*. Princeton, N.J.: Princeton University Press, 1958.

Corso, John F. *The Experimental Psychology of Sensory Behavior*. New York: Holt, Rinehart & Winston, 1967.

Cortright, Edgar M. *Exploring Space With a Camera*. Washington, D.C.: NASA, 1968.

Creel, Herrlee G. *What is Taoism and Other Studies in Chinese Cultural History*. Chicago: University of Chicago Press, 1970.

Da Lui. *T'ai Chi Chu'an and I Ching*. New York: Harper & Row, 1972.

Daniélou, Alain. *Hindu Polytheism*. New York: Pantheon, 1964.

Daniélou, Alain. *Yoga: The Method of Re-Integration*. New York: University, 1949.

Daraul, Arkon, *A History of Secret Societies*. New York: Simon & Schuster, 1962.

Dasgupta, Surendranath. *A History of Indian Philosophy,* vol. I. Cambridge, Eng.: Cambridge University Press, 1922.

Daumal, Rene. *Mount Analogue*. San Francisco: City Lights, 1952.

David-Neel, Alexandra. *Initiations and Initiates in Tibet*. New York: University, 1931.

Davids, Rhys. *The Birth of Indian Psychology and its Development in Buddhism*. London: Luzac, 1936.

Davis, Doris W. "Bibliographic Afterthoughts on the Alexandrian Movement." *Bulletin of Structural Integration,* Winter 1969–70.

deBary, William T. (ed.). *Sources of Chinese Tradition*. New York: Columbia University Press, 1960.

deBary, William T. (ed.). *Sources of Indian Tradition*. New York: Columbia University Press, 1958.

deBary, William T. (ed.). *Sources of Japanese Tradition*. New York: Columbia University Press, 1958.

Delgado, Jose. *Physical Control of the Mind*. New York: Harper & Row, 1969.

DeRopp, Robert S. *The Master Game*. New York: Delta, 1968.

DeRopp, Robert S. *Sex Energy*. New York: Delta, 1969.

Dick, Philip K. *Ubik*. New York: Ballantine, 1970.

Dixon, Peter L. *Soaring*. New York: Ballantine, 1970.

Dogen. *A Primer of Soto Zen*. Honolulu: East-West Center, 1971.

Doughty, Charles M. *Travels in Arabia Deserta*. New York: Random House, 1970.

Downing, George. *The Massage Book*. New York: Random House, 1972.

Dumoulin, Heinrich. *A History of Zen Buddhism*. New York: McGraw-Hill, 1959.

Dumoulin, Heinrich, & Sasaki, Ruth Fuller. *The Development of Chinese Zen*. New York: The First Zen Institute of America, 1953.

Dunne, J. W. *An Experiment With Time*. London: Faber & Faber, 1927.

Dunstan, M., & Garlan, P. W. *Worlds in the Making*. Englewood Cliffs, N.J.: Prentice-Hall, 1970.

Durckheim, Karlfried. *Hara*. London: George Allen & Unwin, 1956.

Durckheim, Karlfried. *The Japanese Cult of Tranquility.* London: Rider, 1960.

Egyptian Book of the Dead (E. A. Budge, trans.). Gloucester, Mass.: P. Smith.

Ehrets, Arnold. *A Guide to Rational Fasting.* New York: Lustrum, 1972.

Eliade, Mircea. *Shamanism: Archaic Techniques of Ecstacy.* New York: Pantheon, 1964.

Eliade, Mircea. *Yoga: Immortality and Freedom.* New York: Pantheon, 1958.

Elliott, H. Chandler. *The Shape of Intelligence.* New York: Scribner's, 1969.

Ellis, Albert. *A Guide To Rational Living.* Englewood Cliffs, N.J.: Prentice-Hall, 1961.

Ellis, Albert. *How To Live With a Neurotic.* New York: Crown, 1957.

Ellis, Albert. *Reason and Emotion in Psychotherapy.* New York: Lyle Stuart, 1962.

Erickson, Milton. See Cooper, L.

Evans-Wentz, W. Y. (ed.). *Tibet's Great Yogi Milarepa.* New York: Oxford, 1928.

Evans-Wentz, W. Y. (ed.). *The Tibetan Book of the Dead* (*Bardo Thodol*). New York: Oxford, 1927.

Evans-Wentz, W. Y. (ed.). *The Tibetan Book of the Great Liberation.* New York: Oxford, 1954.

Evans-Wentz, W. Y. (ed.) *Tibetan Yoga and Secret Doctrines.* New York: Oxford, 1935.

Fagan, Joen, & Shepherd, Irma Lee (eds.). *Gestalt Therapy Now.* New York: Harper & Row, 1970.

Farber, Seymour M., & Wilson, Roger H. L. (eds.). *Control of the Mind.* New York: McGraw-Hill, 1961.

Fast, Julius. *Body Language.* New York: Simon & Schuster, 1970.

Feldenkrais, M. *Body and Mature Behavior.* New York: International Universities, 1949.

Feldman, Gene, & Gartenberg, Max (eds.). *The Beat Generation and the Angry Young Men.* New York: Dell, 1958.

Feldman, Sandor S. *Mannerisms of Speech and Gestures in Everyday Life.* New York: International Universities, 1959.

Feng, Gai-Fu. *Tai Chi—A Way of Centering & I Ching.* New York: Macmillan, 1970.

Finegan, Jack. *The Archeology of World Religions* (3 vols.). Princeton, N.J.: Princeton University Press, 1952.

Fontein, Jan, & Hickman, Money. *Zen Painting and Calligraphy.* Boston: Museum of Fine Arts, 1970.

Foucault, Michel. *Madness and Civilization.* New York: New American Library, 1965.

Fowles, John. *The Aristos.* New York: New American Library, 1964.

Fowles, John. *The Magus.* New York: Dell, 1965.

Frankl, Victor. *The Doctor and the Soul.* New York: Knopf, 1955.

Frankl, Victor. *Man's Search for Meaning.* Boston: Beacon, 1962.

Fraser, J. T. (ed.). *The Voices of Time.* New York: George Braziller, 1966.

Frazer, James. *The New Golden Bough* (T. H. Gaster, ed.). New York: New American Library, 1959.

Freud, Sigmund. *The Basic Writings of Sigmund Freud.* New York: Modern Library, 1938.

Friedlander, Ira (ed.). *Year One Catalog.* New York: Harper & Row, 1972.

Fujimoto, Rindo-Roshi. *The Way of Zazen.* Cambridge, Mass.: Cambridge Buddhist Association, 1969.

Fuller, R. B. *Utopia or Oblivion.* New York: Bantam, 1969.

Fuller, R. B., & McHale, John. *World Design Science Decade.* Carbondale, Ill.: World Resources Inventory, 1967. Six vols.

Fung, Paul F., & George D. *The Sutra of the Sixth Patriarch.* San Francisco: Buddha's Universal Church, 1964.

Garrison, Omar. *Tantra: The Yoga of Sex.* New York: Julian, 1964.

Garrison, Webb. "Electricity and Physiology." *Popular Electronics,* Jan. 1971.

Geiger, Rudolf, *The Climate Near the Ground.* Cambridge, Mass.: Harvard University Press, 1966.

George, L. *A To Z Horoscope Maker and Delineator.* St. Paul, Minn.: Llewellyn, 1910.

Gewurz, Elias. *The Mysteries of the Qabalah.* Chicago: Yogi Publications Society, 1922.

Gibson, W. *The Boat.* Boston: Houghton Mifflin, 1953.

Ginsberg, Allen. "The Interview." *Paris Review,* Spring 1966.

Goble, Frank. *The Third Force.* New York: Simon & Schuster, 1970.

Goldstein, Kurt. *Human Nature in the Light of Psychopathology.* New York: Schocken, 1940.

Goldstein, Kurt. *The Organism.* Boston: Beacon, 1963.

Gombrich, E. H. *Art and Illusion.* New York: Pantheon, 1960.

Goodman, Paul & Percival. *Communitas.* New York: Vintage, 1960.

Gordon, William J. J. *Synectics.* New York: Collier, 1961.

Govinda, Anagarika. *Foundations of Tibetan Mysticism*. New York: Dutton, 1959.

Govinda, Anagarika. *The Psychological Attitude of Early Buddhist Philosophy*. London: Rider, 1961.

Govinda, Anagarika. *The White Clouds*, Berkeley, Calif.: Shambala.

Graham, Aelred. *Conversations: Christian and Buddhist Encounters in Japan*. New York: Harcourt Brace Jovanovich, 1968.

Graham, Aelred. *Zen Catholicism: A Suggestion*. New York: Harcourt Brace Jovanovich.

Graves, Robert. *The Greek Myths* (2 vols.). Baltimore: Penguin, 1955.

Graves, Robert, & Shah, Omar Ali (trans.). *The Rubaiyat of Omar Khayyam*. London: Cassell, 1967

Gray, Eden. *A Complete Guide to the Tarot*. New York: Bantam, 1971.

Gray, Henry. *Anatomy of the Human Body*. Philadelphia: Lea & Febiger, 1966.

Gregory, Richard L. *Eye and Brain*. New York: McGraw-Hill, 1966.

Gregory, Richard L. *The Intelligent Eye*. New York: McGraw-Hill, 1970.

Guenther, H. V. *The Life and Teaching of Naropa*. New York: Oxford, 1963.

Guenther, H. V. *Philosophy and Psychology in the Abhidharma*. Lucknow, India: Buddha Vihara, 1957.

Gunther, Bernard. *How the West is One*. New York: Macmillan, 1972.

Gunther, Bernard. *Keep in Touch with Massage*. Big Sur, Calif.: Esalen, 1967.

Gunther, Bernard. *Sense Relaxation: Below Your Mind*. New York: Macmillan, 1968.

Gunther, Bernard. *What to Do Until the Messiah Comes*. New York: Macmillan, 1971.

Gurdjieff, Georges. *All and Everything*. New York: Harcourt Brace Jovanovich, 1950.

Gurdjieff, Georges. *Herald of Coming Good*. New York: Weiser's, 1972.

Gurdjieff, Georges. *Meetings with Remarkable Men*. New York: Dutton, 1963.

Gustaitis, Rasa. *Turning On*. New York: Macmillan, 1969.

Gysin, Brion. "The Dream Machine." *Olympia, 2,* Jan. 1962.

Hackett, James. *The Way of Haiku*. Tokyo: Japan Publications, 1969.

Haifiz, Khoja. *The Diwan*.

Haikai and Haiku. Tokyo: The Nippon Gakujutsu Shinkokai, 1958.

Haile, B., Oakes, M., & Wyman, L. C. (trans.). *Beautyway: A Navaho Ceremonial*. New York: Pantheon, 1957.

Hakuin Zenji. *The Embossed Tea Kettle and Other Stories*. London: George Allen & Unwin, 1963.

Hall, Calvin S., & Lindzey, Gardner. *Theories of Personality*. New York: Wiley, 1957.

Hall, Edward T. *The Hidden Dimension*. Garden City, N.Y.: Doubleday, 1966.

Hall, Edward T. *The Silent Language*. New York: Fawcett, 1959.

Harding, D. E. *On Having No Head: A Contribution of Zen in the West*. London: Buddhist Society, 1961.

Harper, Robert A. *Psychoanalysis and Psychotherapy: 36 Systems*. Englewood Cliffs, N.J.: Prentice-Hall, 1959.

Haultain, Arnold. *The Mystery Golf*. Berkeley, Calif.: Serendipity Press, 1965.

Hayakawa, S. I. (ed.). *The Use and Misuse of Language*. New York: Fawcett, 1962.

Henderson, Harold. *Haiku in English*. Rutland, Vt.: Tuttle, 1967.

Henderson, Harold. *An Introduction to Haiku: An Anthology of Poems and Poets from Basho to Shiki*. Garden City, N.Y.: Doubleday, 1958.

Heron, W. "The Pathology of Boredom." *Scientific American, 196,* 1957.

Herrigel, Eugen. *Zen*. New York: McGraw-Hill, 1953.

Herrigel, Gertrude. *Zen and the Art of Flower Arrangement*. Japan, 1954.

Hesse, Hermann. *Journey to the East*. New York: Noonday, 1956.

Hesse, Hermann. *Magister Ludi*. New York: Bantam, 1943.

Hesse, Hermann. *Steppenwolf*. New York: Bantam, 1929.

Hills, Christopher, and Stone, Robert B. *Conduct Your Own Awareness Sessions*. New York: New American Library, 1970.

Hoffer, Abram, & Osmond, Humphrey. *How to Live With Schizophrenia*. New York: University, 1966.

Hogg, James (ed.). *Psychology and the Visual Arts*. Baltimore: Penguin, 1969.

Hook, Sidney (ed.). *Dimensions of Mind*. New York: Collier, 1960.

Horney, Karen. *The Neurotic Personality of Our Time*. New York: Norton, 1937.

Horney, Karen. *Self-Analysis*. New York: Norton, 1942.

Howard, Jane. *Please Touch*. New York: Dell, 1970.

Hubbard, L. Ron. *The Creation of Human Ability*. Sussex, Eng., 1954.

Hubbard, L. Ron. *Dianetics*. New York: Paperback Library, 1968.

Hubbard, L. Ron. *Scientology*. New York: Church of Scientology, 1965.

Huber, Jack. *Through an Eastern Window*. New York: Bantam, 1967.

Humphreys, Christmas. *Buddhism*. Baltimore: Penguin, 1951.

Humphreys, Christmas. *Concentration and Meditation: A Manual of Mind Development*. Baltimore: Penguin, 1935.

Hunter, Robert. *The Storming of the Mind*. Garden City, N.Y.: Doubleday, 1971.

Huxley, Aldous. *The Art of Seeing*. New York: Harper & Row.

Huxley, Aldous. *The Devils of Loudun*. New York: Harper & Row, 1952.

Huxley, Aldous. *The Doors of Perception*. New York: Harper & Row, 1956.

Huxley, Aldous. *Heaven and Hell*. New York: Harper & Row, 1956.

Huxley, Aldous. *The Letters of Aldous Huxley* (Grover Smith, ed.). New York: Harper & Row, 1969.

Huxley, Aldous. *The Perennial Philosophy*. Cleveland: World, 1944.

Huxley, Laura Archer. *You Are Not the Target*. North Hollywood, Calif.: Wilshire, 1963.

I Ching (John Blofeld, trans.). New York: Dutton, 1965.

I Ching (James Legge, trans.). New York: Dover, 1899.

I Ching (James Legge, trans.; Chai Ch'u, ed.). New York: University, 1964.

I Ching (*The Symbols* and *The Changes of the Yi King*, Z. D. Sung, trans.; 2 vols.). Shanghai: China Modern Education, 1934.

I Ching (R. Wilhelm, C. F. Baynes, trans.). Princeton, N.J.: Princeton University Press, 1950.

Issa. *The Autumn Wind*. London: John Murray, 1957.

Issa. *The Year of My Life* (*Oraga Haru*). Los Angeles: University of California Press, 1960.

Ittleson, William H. *The Ames Demonstrations in Perception*. New York: Hafner, 1968.

Iyengar, B. K. S. *Light on Yoga*. New York: Schocken, 1965.

Jacobi, Jolande (ed.). *Psychological Reflections*. New York: Harper & Row, 1953.

Jacobson, Edmund. *Progressive Relaxation*. Chicago: University of Chicago Press, 1926.

James, William. *The Varieties of Religious Experience*. New York: New American Library.

Janov, Arthur. *The Primal Revolution*. New York: Simon & Schuster, 1972.

Janov, Arthur. *The Primal Scream*. New York: Delta, 1970.

Jodorowsky, Alessandro. "Sacramental Melodrama." *City Lights Journal, 3,* 1966.

Johansson, Rune E. A. *The Psychology of Nirvana*. Garden City, N.Y.: Doubleday, 1969.

Jones, Ernest. *The Life and Work of Sigmund Freud*. New York: Basic Books, 1955.

Jones, F. P. "Method for Changing Stereotyped Response Patterns by the Inhibition of Certain Postural Sets." *Psychological Review, 72,* No. 3, May 1965.

Jourard, Sydney. *Transparent Self*. New York: Van Nostrand, 1964.

Jourard, Sydney, & Overlade, Dan. *Reconciliation*. New York: Van Nostrand, 1966.

Joyce, James. *Finnegans Wake*. New York: Viking, 1939.

Joyce, James. *Finnegans Wake* (A. Burgess, ed.). New York: Viking, 1970.

Jung, C. G. *The Archetypes of the Collective Unconscious*. New York: Pantheon, 1959.

Jung, C. G. (ed.). *Man and His Symbols*. Garden City, N.Y.: Doubleday, 1964.

Jung, C. G. *Mandala Symbolism*. Princeton, N.J.: Princeton University Press, 1959.

Jung, C. G. *Memories, Dreams, Reflections*. New York: Vintage, 1961.

Jung, C. G. *Mysterium Coniunctionis*. New York: Pantheon, 1963.

Jung, C. G. *Psychological Types*. Princeton, N.J.: Princeton University Press, 1971.

Jung, C. G., & Pauli, W. *The Interpretation and Nature of the Psyche*. New York: Pantheon, 1955.

Kamiya, Joe. "Conscious Control of Brain Waves." *Psychology Today,* April 1968.

Kantor, Robert E. "The Affective Domain and Beyond." *The Journal for the Study of Consciousness, 3,* No. 1, Jan.–June 1970.

Kapleau, Philip. *The Three Pillars of Zen: Teaching/Practice/Enlightenment*. New York: Harper & Row, 1965.

Kapleau, Philip. *The Wheel of Death*. New York: Harper & Row, 1971.

Kaprow, Alan. *Happenings*. New York: Abrams, 1966.

Keleman, Stanley. *Bio-Energetic Concepts of Grounding*. San Francisco: Lodestar, 1970.

Keleman, Stanley. *The Body, Energy and Groups*. San Diego, Calif.: Kairos, 1970.

Keleman, Stanley. *Sexuality, Self and Survival*. New York: Random House, 1971.

Khan, Hazrat Inayat. *The Sufi Message of Hazrat Inayat Khan* (12 vols.). London: Barrie and Rockliff.

Kilpatrick, Franklin P. (ed.). *Explorations in Transactional Psychology*. New York: New York University Press, 1961.

King, C. Daly. *The States of Human Consciousness*. New York: University, 1963.

Kinsey, A. C. et al. *Sexual Behavior in the Human Female*. Philadelphia: W. B. Saunders, 1953.

Kinsey, A. C. et al. *Sexual Behavior in the Human Male*. Philadelphia: W. B. Saunders, 1948.

Kirkpatrick, C. *Religion in Human Affairs*. New York: John Urley, 1929.

Kleps, Art. *The Boo Hoo Bible: The Neo-American Church Catechism*. San Cristobal, N.M.: Toad Books, 1971.

Koestler, Arthur. *The Act of Creation*. New York: Dell, 1964.

Koestler, Arthur. *The Ghost in the Machine*. Chicago: Henry Regnery, 1967.

Kohl, Herbert. *The Age of Complexity*. New York: New American Library, 1965.

Korzybski, Alfred. *Science and Sanity*. Lakeville, Conn.: International Non-Aristotelian Library, 1933.

Krishnamurti. *Education and the Significance of Life*. New York: Harper & Row, 1953.

Krishnamurti. *The Only Revolution*. New York: Harper & Row.

Kroeber, A. L. *Handbook of the Indians of California*. Berkeley: California Book, 1953.

Laban, Rudolf. *The Mastery of Movement*. London: MacDonald & Evans, 1960.

LaBarre, Weston. *The Ghost Dance: The Origins of Religion*. Garden City, N.Y.: Doubleday, 1970.

LaBarre, Weston. *They Shall Take Up Serpents*. New York: Schocken, 1969.

Laing, R. D. *The Divided Self*. New York: Pantheon, 1960.

Laing, R. D. *Knots*. New York: Pantheon, 1971.

Laing, R. D. *The Politics of Experience*. New York: Pantheon, 1967.

Laing, R. D. *Self and Others*. New York: Pantheon, 1961.

Lane, Frank W. *The Elements Rage*. Philadelphia: Chilton, 1965.

Langer, Susanne. *Philosophy in a New Key*. New York: New American Library, 1942.

Lao Tzu. *Tao Teh Ching* (John C. H. Wu, trans.). New York: St. John's University Press, 1961.

Lashley, Karl S. *The Neuropsychology of Lashley*. New York: McGraw-Hill, 1960.

Laverne, D. T. *Stoned For Life*. New York: M.I.H., 1970.

Leadbeater, C. W. *The Chakras*. Madras, India: Theosophical, 1927.

LeBon, G. *The Crowd*. London: Ernest Benn, 1896.

LeCron, Leslie M. *Self Hypnotism*. New York: New American Library, 1964.

Lederman, Janet. *Anger in the Rocking Chair: Gestalt Awareness With Children*. New York: McGraw-Hill, 1969.

Lefort, Raphael. *Teachers of Gurdjieff*. London: Victor Gollancz, 1966.

Legge, James (trans.). *The Works of Mencius*. Hong Kong: Hong Kong University, 1895.

Leggett, Trevor. *A First Zen Reader*. Rutland, Vt.: Tuttle, 1960.

Leggett, Trevor. *The Tiger's Cave*. London: Rider, 1964.

Leibowitz, Judith. "The Alexander Technique." *Dance Scope*, 4, No. 1.

Leiderman, H. "Sensory Deprivation: Clinical Aspects." *Archives of Internal Medicine*, 101, 1958.

Levenson, Joseph R. *Confucian China and its Modern Fate* (3 vols.). Los Angeles: University of California, 1958, 1964, 1965.

Leverant, Robert, *Zen in the Art of Photography*. San Francisco: Images, 1969.

Levin, Harry. *James Joyce*. Norfolk, Conn., 1941.

Lewi, Grant. *Heaven Knows What*. St. Paul, Minn.: Llewellyn, 1935.

Lewis, Samuel L. *The Rejected Avatar*. Bolinas, Calif.: Prophecy Pressworks, 1968.

Lilly, John C. *The Center of the Cyclone*. New York: Julian, 1972.

Lilly, John C. *Man and Dolphin*. New York: Pyramid, 1961.

Lilly, John C. *The Mind of the Dolphin*. New York: Avon, 1967.

Lilly, John C. *Programming and Metaprogramming in the Human Biocomputer: Theory and Experiments*. New York: Julian, 1972.

Linssen, Robert. *Living Zen*. New York: Grove, 1958.

London, Perry. *Behavior Control*. New York: Harper & Row, 1969.

Lorenz, Konrad. *On Aggression*. New York: Harcourt Brace Jovanovich, 1963.

Lounsbery, G. Constant. *Buddhist Meditation in the Southern School*. London: Luzac, 1936.

Lowen, Alexander. *The Betrayal of the Body.* New York: Macmillan, 1967.

Lowen, Alexander. *The Language of the Body.* New York: Collier, 1958.

Lowen, Alexander. *Love and Orgasm.* New York: Macmillan, 1965.

Lowen, Alexander. *Pleasure.* New York: Lancer, 1970.

Lowenstein, Otto. *The Senses.* Baltimore: Penguin, 1966.

Luce, Gay Gaer. *Biological Rhythms in Psychiatry and Medicine.* Chevy Chase, Md.: NIMH, Public Health Service Publication No. 2088.

Luce, Gay Gaer. *Body Time.* New York: Pantheon, 1971.

Luce, Gay Gaer & Segal, Julius. *Insomnia.* Garden City, N.Y.: Doubleday, 1969.

Luce, Gay Gaer & Segal, Julius. *Sleep.* New York: Lancer, 1966.

Luk, Charles. *Ch'an and Zen Teaching* (3 vols.). London: Rider, 1960, 1961, 1962.

Luk, Charles. *The Secrets of Chinese Meditation.* London: Rider, 1964.

Luk, Charles (trans.). *The Surangama Sutra.* London: Rider, 1966.

Luk, Charles. *Taoist Yoga: Alchemy and Immortality.* New York: S. Weiser's, 1970.

MacNeice, Louis. *Astrology.* Garden City, N.Y.: Doubleday, 1964.

Maharishi Mahesh Yogi. *The Science of Being and the Art of Living.* Students International Meditation Society, 1966.

Mairet, Philip. *A. R. Orage: A Memoir.* New York: University, 1966.

Malinowski, Bronislaw. *Magic, Science and Religion.* Garden City, N.Y.: Doubleday, 1948.

Malko, George. *Scientology: The Now Religion.* New York: Delta, 1970.

Margolin, S., & Kubie, L. "An Apparatus for the Use of Breath Sounds as a Hypnogogic Stimulus." *American Journal of Psychiatry, 100,* 1944.

Maslow, Abraham H. *The Farthest Reaches of Human Nature.* New York: Viking, 1972.

Maslow, Abraham H. *Motivation and Personality.* New York: Harper & Row, 1970.

Maslow, Abraham H. *The Psychology of Science.* Chicago: Henry Regnery, 1966.

Maslow, Abraham H. *Religions, Values and Peak-Experiences.* Columbus: Ohio State University Press, 1964.

Maslow, Abraham H. *Towards a Psychology of Being.* Princeton, N.J.: D. Van Nostrand, 1962.

Masters, Robert E. L. (ed.). *Sexual Self-Stimulation.* Los Angeles: Shelbourne, 1967.

Masters, Robert E. L., & Houston, Jean. *Mind Games.* New York: Viking, 1972.

Masters, Robert E. L., & Houston, Jean. *New Ways of Being.* New York: Viking. In press.

Masters, Robert E. L., & Houston, Jean. *Psychedelic Art.* New York: Grove, 1968.

Masters, Robert E. L., & Houston, Jean. "Subjective Realities." *Yale Scientific Review.* In press.

Masters, William, & Johnson, Virginia. *Human Sexual Inadequacy.* Boston: Little, Brown, 1970.

Masters, William, & Johnson, Virginia. *Human Sexual Response.* Boston: Little, Brown, 1966.

May, Rollo (ed.). *Existence.* New York: Clarion, 1958.

May, Rollo. (ed.). *Existential Psychology.* New York: Random House, 1961.

McClure, Michael. *Meat Science Essays.* San Francisco: City Lights, 1963.

McGlashan, Alan. *The Savage and Beautiful Country.* Boston: Houghton Mifflin, 1966.

McHale, John. *The Future of the Future.* New York: George Braziller, 1969.

McLuhan, Eric. *What the Thunder Said: Joyce's Guide to the Media.* (unpublished manuscript).

McLuhan, Marshall, & Fiore, Quentin. *War and Peace in the Global Village.* New York: Bantam, 1968.

Meher Baba. *God Speaks.* New York: Dodd, Mead, 1962.

Mellen. "Hole in the Head." *Other Scenes,* Nov. 1970.

Mencius (D. C. Lau, trans.). Baltimore: Penguin, 1970.

Mendelson, J., et al. "Hallucinations of Poliomyelitis Patients During Treatment in a Respirator." *Journal of Nervous and Mental Diseases, 126,* 1958.

Merton, Louis (Thomas). "Final Integration: Toward a 'Monastic Therapy'." *Monastic Studies, 6,* 1968.

Merton, Thomas. *Mystics and Zen Masters.* New York: Delta, 1967.

Merton, Thomas. *Zen and the Birds of Appetite.* New York: New Directions, 1968.

Metzner, Ralph. *Maps of Consciousness.* New York: Collier, 1971.

Mishra, Rammurti. *Fundamentals of Yoga.* New York: Julian, 1959.

Miura, Isshu, & Sasaki, Ruth Fuller. *Zen Dust.* New York: Harcourt Brace Jovanovich, 1966.

Miura, Isshu, Sasaki, Ruth Fuller. *The Zen Koan*. New York: Harcourt Brace Jovanovich, 1965.

Moreno, J. L. *Psychodrama*. Beacon, N.Y.: Beacon House.

Moreno, J. L. *Who Shall Survive*. Beacon, N.Y.: Beacon House, 1953.

Moseley, A. L. "Hypnogogic Hallucinations in Relation to Accidents." *American Psychologist, 8*, 1953.

Muller, Kal. "Land Diving With the Pentecost Islanders." *National Geographic,* Dec. 1970.

Muller, Paul. *Le Livre Rose du Hippy*. Paris: Union Générale d'Editions, 1968.

Murphy, Gardner, & Lois B. (eds.). *Asian Psychology*. New York: Basic Books, 1968.

Murphy, Michael. *Golf in the Kingdom*. New York: Viking, 1972.

Musés, Charles. "Altering States of Consciousness by Mathematics." *Journal for the Study of Consciousness, 3,* No. 1, Jan.–June 1970.

Musés, Charles, and Young, Arthur M. (eds.). *Consciousness and Reality*. New York: Outerbridge and Lazard, 1972.

Naranjo, Claudio. *The One Quest*. New York: Viking, 1972.

Naranjo, Claudio, & Ornstein, Robert E. *On the Psychology of Meditation*. New York: Viking, 1971.

Neal, A. H. *Jungle Magic*. New York: Paperback Library, 1966.

Neale, Tom. *An Island to Myself*. New York: Avon, 1966.

Needham, Joseph. *Science and Civilization in China*. Vol. I: *Introductory Orientations;* Vol. II: *History of Scientific Thought*. Cambridge, Eng.: Cambridge University, 1954, 1956.

Needleman, Jacob. *The New Religions*. Garden City, N.Y.: Doubleday, 1970.

Neisser, Ulric. *Cognitive Psychology*. New York: Appleton-Century-Crofts, 1967.

Netter, Frank H. *Nervous System*. Summit, N.J.: CIBA, 1962.

Neumann, Erich. *The Origins and History of Consciousness*. New York: Harper & Row, 1954.

"New Habits for Old: The Alexander Method." *Prevention, 23,* No. 3, March 1971.

Nicholson, R. A. *The Idea of Personality in Sufism*. Lahore, Pakistan: Ashraf, 1922.

Nicks, Oran W. *This Island Earth*. Washington, D.C.: NASA, 1970.

Nicoll, Maurice. *Living Time*. London: Vincent Stuart, 1952.

Nicoll, Maurice. *The Mark*. London: Vincent Stuart, 1954.

Nicoll, Maurice. *The New Man*. London: Vincent Stuart, 1967.

Nicoll, Maurice. *Psychological Commentaries on the Teaching of Gurdjieff and Ouspensky* (5 vols.). London: Vincent Stuart.

Northrop, F. S. C. *The Meeting of East and West*. New York: Macmillan, 1946.

Nott, C. S. *Journey Through this World: The Second Journal of a Pupil*. New York: S. Weiser's, 1970.

Nott, C. S. *Teachings of Gurdjieff: The Journal of a Pupil*. New York: S. Weiser's, 1969.

Noyle, Ken. *Gone Tomorrow*. Rutland, Vt.: Tuttle, 1966.

Noyle, Ken. *Here Today: Zen Inspired Poetry*. Rutland, Vt.: Tuttle, 1969.

O'Brien, Elmer. *Varieties of Mystic Experience*. New York: New American Library, 1964.

Ogata, Sohaku. *Zen for the West*. London: Rider, 1959.

Ogden, C. K., & Richards, I. A. *The Meaning of Meaning*. New York: Harcourt Brace Jovanovich, 1923.

Okakura, Kakuzo. *The Book of Tea*. New York: Dover, 1906.

Orage, A. R. *Psychological Exercises*. New York: S. Weiser's, 1930.

Ornstein, Robert E. *On the Experience of Time*. Baltimore: Penguin, 1969.

Oster, Gerald. "Phosphenes." *Scientific American, 222,* No. 2, Feb. 1970.

Oster, Gerald. *The Science of Moiré Patterns*. Barrington, N.J.: Edmund Scientific, 1964.

Oster, Gerald & Nishijima. "Moiré Patterns." *Scientific American,* May 1963.

Ostrander, Sheila, & Schroeder, Lynn. *Psychic Discoveries Behind the Iron Curtain*. Englewood Cliffs, N.J.: Prentice-Hall, 1970.

Otsu, D. R. *The Ox and His Herdsman: A Chinese Zen Text*. Tokyo: Hokuseido, 1969.

Otto, Herbert (ed.). *Explorations in Human Potentialities*. Springfield, Ill.: C. C. Thomas, 1966.

Otto, Herbert, & Mann, John (eds.). *Ways of Growth*. New York: Viking, 1968.

Otto, Rudolph. *Mysticism East and West*. New York: Collier, 1932.

Ouspensky, P. D. *The Fourth Way*. New York: Knopf, 1959.

Ouspensky, P. D. *In Search of the Miraculous*. New York: Harcourt Brace Jovanovich, 1949.

Ouspensky, P. D. *The Psychology of Man's Possible Evolution*. New York: Bantam, 1950.

Pallis, Mario. *Peaks and Lamas*. London: Peter Owen.

Pandit, M. P. *Mystic Approach to the Veda and the Upanishad*. Madras, India: Sri Aurobindo Library, 1952.

Pauwels, Louis. *Gurdjieff*. New York: S. Weiser's, 1954.

Pauwels, Louis, & Bergier, Jacques. *The Morning of the Magicians*. New York: Avon, 1960.

Pearce, Joseph Chilton. *The Crack in the Cosmic Egg*. New York: Julian, 1971.

Perls, Frederick S. *Ego, Hunger and Aggression*. New York: Random House, 1947.

Perls, Frederick S. *Gestalt Therapy Verbatim*. New York: Bantam, 1969.

Perls, Frederick S. *In and Out the Garbage Pail*. New York: Bantam, 1969.

Perls, Frederick S., Hefferline, Ralph F., & Goodman, Paul. *Gestalt Therapy*. New York: Julian, 1951.

Perry, Whitall N. *A Treasury of Traditional Wisdom*. New York: Simon & Schuster, 1971.

Pesso, Albert. *Movement in Psychotherapy: Psychomotor Techniques and Training*. New York: New York University, 1969.

Peterson, Severin. *A Catalog of the Ways People Grow*. New York: Ballantine, 1971.

Phelan, Nancy, and Volin, Michael. *Sex and Yoga*. New York: Harper & Row, 1971.

Phillips, Bernard (ed.). *The Essentials of Zen Buddhism: An Anthology of the Writings of Daisetz T. Suzuki*. London: Rider, 1962.

Pickthall, Mohammed Marmaduke (trans.). *The Meaning of the Glorious Koran*. New York: New American Library.

Pound, Ezra. *The Confucian Odes*. New York: New Directions, 1954.

Pribram, Karl H. (ed.). *Brain and Behavior* (4 vols.). I. *Mood, States and Mind*; II. *Perception and Action*; III. *Memory Mechanisms*; IV. *Adaptation*. Baltimore: Penguin, 1969.

Price, A. F., & Wong Mou-lam (trans.). *The Diamond Sutra and The Sutra of Hui Neng*. Berkeley, Calif.: Shambala, 1969.

Progoff, Ira. *Jung's Psychology and Its Social Meaning*. New York, Grove, 1953.

Pursglove, Paul David (ed.). *Recognitions in Gestalt Therapy*. New York: Funk & Wagnalls, 1968.

Ramacharaka. *Hatha Yoga*. Chicago: Yogi Publication Society, 1904.

Ramacharaka. *Raja Yoga*. Chicago: Yogi Publication Society, 1906.

Rampa, T. Lobsong. *The Third Eye*. New York: Ballantine.

Rank, Otto. *Beyond Psychology*. New York: Dover, 1941.

Rank, Otto. *The Myth of the Birth of the Hero*. New York: Vintage, 1959.

Rank, Otto. *Will Therapy and Truth and Reality*. New York: Knopf, 1947.

Reich, Ilse Ollendorf. *Wilhelm Reich*. New York: Avon, 1969.

Reich, Wilhelm. *Character Analysis*. New York: Noonday, 1949.

Reich, Wilhelm. *The Discovery of the Orgone*: Vol. I, *The Function of the Orgasm*. New York: Noonday, 1942.

Reich, Wilhelm. *Selected Writings*. New York: Noonday, 1960.

Reich, Wilhelm. *The Sexual Revolution*. New York: Noonday, 1945.

Reps, Paul. *Ask a Potato*. New York: Doric, 1967.

Reps, Paul. *Big Bath*. Hong Kong: Liu Shih Chieh, 1960.

Reps, Paul. *Gold and Fish Signatures*. Rutland, Vt.: Tuttle, 1969.

Reps, Paul. *Picture Poem Primer*. New York: American Fabric, 1969.

Reps, Paul. *Square Sun Square Moon*. Rutland, Vt.: Tuttle, 1967.

Reps, Paul. *Ten Ways to Meditate*. New York: Walker/Weatherhill, 1969.

Reps, Paul (ed.). *Zen Flesh, Zen Bones*. Rutland, Vt.: Tuttle, 1957.

Reps, Paul. *Zen Telegrams*. Rutland, Vt.: Tuttle, 1959.

Rhine, J. B. *Extra-Sensory Perception*. Boston: Bruce Humphries, 1964.

Richards, I. A. *Mencius on the Mind: Experiments in Multiple Definition*. London: Routledge & Kegan Paul, 1932.

Richards, Whitman. "The Fortification Illusions of Migraines." *Scientific American*, May 1971.

Rigaud, Milo. *Secrets of Voodoo*. New York: Simon & Schuster, 1969.

Ritter, Christiane. *A Woman in the Polar Night*. New York: Dutton, 1954.

Roerich, Helen. *Agni Yoga*. 1929.

Roerich, Nicholas. *Altai-Himalaya*. New York: Frederick A. Stokes, 1929.

Rogers, Carl. *Client Centered Therapy*. Boston: Houghton Mifflin, 1951.

Rogers, Carl. *Counseling and Psychotherapy*. Boston: Houghton Mifflin, 1942.

Rogers, Carl. *Freedom to Learn*. Chicago: Merrill, 1969.

Rogers, Carl. *On Becoming a Person*. Boston: Houghton Mifflin, 1961.

Rogers, Carl, & Stevens, Barry (eds.). *Person to Person*. Lafayette, Calif.: Real People Press, 1967.

Rokeach, Milton. *The Three Christs of Ypsilanti*. New York: Vintage, 1964.

Rolf, Ida P. "Structural Integration." *Journal of the Institute for the Comparative Study of History, Philosophy and the Sciences, 1*, No. 1, June, 1963.

Rosenblith, Walter A. (ed.). *Sensory Communication*. Cambridge, Mass.: MIT, 1961.

Rosenfeld, Edward. "Planetary People." *Last Supplement to the Last Whole Earth Catalog,* March 1971.

Rosenfeld, Edward, & Brockman, John (eds.). *Real Time, I & II*. Garden City, N.Y.: Doubleday, 1973.

Rosenfeld, Edward, & Rubenfeld, Ilana. "The Alexander Technique." In Aaronson, B. (ed.), *Workshops of the Mind*.

Ross, Nancy Wilson (ed.). *The World of Zen*. New York: Random House, 1960.

Ross, Shirley. *The Interior Ecology Cookbook*. San Francisco: Straight Arrow, 1970.

Roszak, Theodore. *The Making of a Counter Culture*. Garden City, N.Y.: Doubleday, 1969.

Rothblatt, Ben (ed.). *Changing Perspectives on Man*. Chicago: University of Chicago Press, 1968.

Rowley, Peter. *New Gods in America*. New York: David McKay, 1971.

Royce, Joseph. *Surface Anatomy*. Philadelphia: F. A. Davis, 1965.

Royce, Joseph R. *The Encapsulated Man*. Princeton, N.J.: D. Van Nostrand, 1964.

Rudhyar, Dane. *The Astrology of Personality*. Garden City, N.Y.: Doubleday, 1970.

Rudhyar, Dane. *The Planetarization of Consciousness*. New York: Harper & Row, 1972.

Ruitenbeek, Hendrik M. *The New Group Therapies*. New York: Avon, 1970.

Ruitenbeek, Hendrik M. (ed.). *Psychoanalysis and Existential Philosophy*. New York: Dutton, 1962.

Rumi. *Mathnawi*.

Rund, J. "Prayer and Hypnosis." *International Journal of Clinical Experimental Hypnosis,* 1957.

Russell, Bertrand. *A History of Western Philosophy*. New York: Simon & Schuster, 1945.

de Sade, D. A. F. *Juliette*. New York: Grove, 1968.

de Sade, D. A. F. *Justine*. New York: Grove, 1965.

de Sade, D. A. F. *120 Days of Sodom*. New York: Grove, 1966.

de Sade, D. A. F. *Philosophy in the Bedroom*. New York: Grove, 1965.

Sadhu, Mouni. *The Tarot*. North Hollywood, Calif.: Wilshire, 1962.

Sadler, A. L. *Cha-No-Yu: The Japanese Tea Ceremony*. Rutland, Vt.: Tuttle, 1933.

Sanders, Ed. *The Family*. New York: Dutton, 1971.

Sargant, William. *Battle for the Mind*. Garden City, N.Y.: Doubleday, 1957.

Sasaki, Ruth Fuller. *Zen* (3 vols.). New York: First Zen Institute of America, 1958.

Satchidanada. *Integral Hatha Yoga*. New York: Holt, Rinehart & Winston, 1970.

Satir, Virginia. *Conjoint Family Therapy*. Palo Alto, Calif.: Science & Behavior, 1967.

Saunders, E. Dale. *Mudra*. New York: Pantheon, 1960.

Schiffman, Muriel. *Gestalt Self-Therapy*. Menlo Park, Calif.: Self Therapy, 1971.

Schiffman, Muriel. *Self-Therapy*. Menlo Park, Calif.: 1967.

Schofield, Russell Paul. *The Actual Design of Cosmic Man*. Los Angeles.

Schofield, Russell Paul. *Imprint Unmistakable*. Los Angeles, 1969.

Scholem, Gershom G. *Major Trends in Jewish Mysticism*. New York: Schocken, 1941.

Scholem, Gershom G. *On the Kabbalah and Its Symbolism*. New York: Schocken, 1960.

Schuon, Frithjof. *Understanding Islam*. Baltimore: Penguin, 1961.

Schultz, J., & Luthe, W. *Autogenic Training*. New York: Grune & Stratton, 1959.

Schutz, William. *Joy*. New York: Grove, 1967.

Schwenk, Theodor. *Sensitive Chaos*. London: Rudolf Steiner, 1965.

Selver, Charlotte, & Brooks, Charles V. W. "Report on Work in Sensory Awareness and Total Functioning." In Otto, Herbert (ed.), *Explorations in Human Potentialities*.

Selye, Hans. *The Stress of Life*. New York: McGraw-Hill, 1956.

Senzaki, Nyogen, & McCandless, Ruth S. (trans.). *The Iron Flute: 100 Zen Koans*. Rutland, Vt.: Tuttle, 1961.

Sesshu's Long Scroll: A Zen Landscape Journey. Rutland, Vt.: Tuttle, 1959.

Shabistari, Mahmud. *The Secret Garden*. London: Octagon, 1969.

Shah, Idries. *The Book of the Book*. London: Octagon.

Shah, Idries. *Caravan of Dreams*. London: Octagon, 1968.

Shah, Idries. *The Dermis Probe*. New York: Dutton, 1970.

Shah, Idries. *The Diffusion of Sufi Ideas in the West* (L. Lewin, ed.). Boulder, Colo.: Keysign, 1972.

Shah, Idries. *The Exploits of the Incomparable Mulla Nasrudin*. London: Jonathan Cape, 1966.

Shah, Idries. *The Magic Monastery*. New York: Dutton, 1972.

Shah, Idries. *Oriental Magic*. London: Octagon.

Shah, Idries. *The Pleasantries of the Incredible Mulla Nasrudin*. London: Jonathan Cape, 1968.

Shah, Idries. *Reflections*. London: Zenith, 1968.

Shah, Idries. *The Secret Lore of Magic*. London: Octagon.

Shah, Idries. *The Sufis*. Garden City, N.Y.: Doubleday, 1964.

Shah, Idries. *Tales of the Dervishes*. New York: Dutton, 1967.

Shah, Idries. *The Way of the Sufi*. New York: Dutton, 1968.

Shah, Idries. *Wisdom of the Idiots*. London: Octagon, 1969.

Shaw, R. D. M. (trans.). *The Blue Cliff Records: The Hekigan Roku*. London: Michael Joseph, 1961.

Sheer, Daniel E. (ed.). *Electrical Stimulation of the Brain*. Austin, Tex.: University of Texas, 1961.

Shepard, Paul, & McKinley, Daniel (eds.). *The Subversive Science*. Boston: Houghton Mifflin, 1969.

Shibayama, Zenkei. *A Flower Does Not Talk: Zen Essays*. Rutland, Vt.: Tuttle, 1970.

Shimano, Eido Tai. *Zen: Endless Treasure*. New York: Zen Center.

Singer, Jerome. *Daydreaming*. New York: Random House, 1966.

Sinha, Jadunath. *Indian Psychology* (2 vols.). I. *Cognition;* II. *Emotion and Will*. Calcutta, India: Sinha, 1958, 1961.

Slocum, J. *Sailing Alone Around the World*. London: Rupert Hart-Davis, 1943.

Smith, Huston. *The Religions of Man*. New York: Harper & Row, 1958.

Smithsonian Institution Center for Short-Lived Phenomena. *The Pulse of the Planet*. New York: Crown, 1972.

Smuts, Jan C. *Holism and Evolution*. New York: Viking, 1926.

Snyder, Gary. *Earth House Hold*. New York: New Directions, 1969.

Sohl, Robert & Carr, Audrey (eds.), *The Gospel According to Zen*. New York: New American Library, 1970.

Solomon, P. et al. (eds.). *Sensory Deprivation*. Cambridge, Mass.: Harvard University, 1961.

Sommerville, Ian. "Flicker." *Olympia, 2*. Jan. 1962.

Sonnemann, Ulrich. *Existence and Therapy*. New York: Grune & Stratton, 1954.

Sparks, Laurence. *Self-Hypnosis*. North Hollywood, Calif.: Wilshire, 1962.

Spiritual Community Guide for North America. San Rafael, Calif.: 1972.

Spolin, Viola. *Improvisations for the Theatre*. Evanston, Ill.: Northwestern, 1963.

Stace, Walter T. *The Teachings of the Mystics*. New York: New American Library, 1960.

Stcherbatsky, F. Th. *Buddhist Logic* (2 vols.). New York: Dover, 1930.

Stcherbatsky, F. Th. *The Central Conception of Buddhism and the Meaning of the Word "Dharma."* Calcutta, India: Susil Gupta, 1923.

Stcherbatsky, F. Th. *The Conception of Buddhist Nirvana*. The Hague, Netherlands: Mouton, 1927.

Steiner, Rudolf. *Knowledge of the Higher World and Its Attainment*. New York: Anthroposophic.

Steiner, Rudolf. *Occult Science: An Outline*. New York: Anthroposophic.

Steiner, Rudolf. *Theosophy: An Introduction*. New York: Anthroposophic.

Stevens, Barry. *Don't Push the River*. Lafayette, Calif.: Real People, 1970.

Stevens, John O. *Awareness*. Lafayette, Calif.: Real People, 1971.

Strong, C. L. "Generating Visual Illusions with Two Kinds of Apparatus." *Scientific American,* March 1971.

Stryk, Lucien, & Ikemoto, Takashi (eds.). *Zen: Poems, Prayers, Sermons, Anecdotes, Interviews*. Garden City, N.Y.: Doubleday, 1965.

Subuh, Mohammed. *Subud in the World*. Subud Brotherhood, 1965.

The Sutra of Wei Lang (or Hui Neng). London: Luzac, 1944.

Suzuki, Beatrice Lane. *Mahayana Buddhism: A Brief Outline*. New York: Collier, 1956.

Suzuki, D. T. *Essays in Zen Buddhism, First, Second & Third Series* (3 vols.). London: Rider, 1949, 1950, 1953.

Suzuki, D. T. *The Field of Zen*. New York: Harper & Row, 1969.

Suzuki, D. T. *An Introduction to Zen Buddhism*. New York: Grove, 1934.

Suzuki, D. T. (trans.). *The Lankavatara Sutra: A Mahayana Text*. London: Routledge & Kegan Paul, 1932.

Suzuki, D. T. *Manual of Zen Buddhism*. New York: Grove, 1935.

Suzuki, D. T. *Mysticism, Christian and Buddhist: The Eastern and Western Way*. New York: Collier, 1957.

Suzuki, D. T. *On Indian Mahayana Buddhism*. New York: Harper & Row, 1968.

Suzuki, D. T. *Studies in Zen*. New York: Delta, 1955.

Suzuki, D. T. *The Training of a Zen Buddhist Monk*. New York: University, 1934.

Suzuki, D. T. *Zen and Japanese Buddhism*. Tokyo Japan Travel Bureau, 1958.

Suzuki, D. T. *Zen and Japanese Culture*. New York: Pantheon, 1959.

Suzuki, D. T. *Zen Buddhism*. Garden City, N.Y.: Doubleday, 1956.

Suzuki, D. T. *The Zen Doctrine of No Mind*. London: Rider, 1949.

Suzuki, D. T., Fromm, Erich, & DeMartino, Richard. *Zen Buddhism and Psychoanalysis*. New York: Grove, 1960.

Suzuki, Shunryu. *Zen Mind, Beginner's Mind*. New York: Walker/Weatherhill, 1970.

Symonds, John, & Grant, Kenneth. *The Confessions of Aleister Crowley*. New York: Hill & Wang, 1969.

Tagore, Rabindranath. *The Religion of Man*. Boston: Beacon, 1931.

Takakusu, Junjiro. *The Essentials of Buddhist Philosophy*. Honolulu: University of Hawaii, 1947.

Tart, Charles T. (ed.). *Altered States of Consciousness*. Garden City, N.Y.: Anchor, 1969.

Taylor, F. Sherwood. *The Alchemists*. New York: Collier, 1949.

Taylor, John G. *The Shape of Minds to Come*. New York: Weybright & Talley, 1971.

Taylor, Renee. *Hunza Health Secrets*. New York: Award, 1964.

Teilhard de Chardin, Pierre. *Building the Earth*. New York: Avon, 1965.

Teilhard de Chardin, Pierre. *The Divine Milieu*. New York: Harper & Row.

Teilhard de Chardin, Pierre. *The Future of Man*. New York: Harper & Row, 1969.

Teilhard de Chardin, Pierre. *The Phenomenon of Man*. New York: Harper & Row, 1959.

Thomas, E. S. "The Fire Walk." *Proceedings of Social Psychological Research*, 1934.

Thommen, George. *Is This Your Day?* (Biorhythm). New York: Award, 1964.

Thornton, R. J. *The Philosophy of Medicine*. 1813.

Timmons, B., & Kamiya, J. "The Psychology and Physiology of Meditation and Related Phenomena: a Bibliography." *Journal of Transpersonal Psychology*, 1, 1970.

Tindall, William Y. *A Reader's Guide to James Joyce*. New York, 1959.

Todd, Mabel E. *The Thinking Body*. Brooklyn: Dance Horizons, 1937.

Toffler, Alvin. *Future Shock*. New York: Random House, 1970.

Tomkins, William. *Indian Sign Language*. New York: Dover, 1931.

Tucci, Giuseppe. *The Theory and Practice of Mandala*. New York: S. Weiser.

Ueda, Daisuke. *Zen and Science*. Tokyo: Risosha, 1963.

The Upanishads (F. Manchester & Probhavananda, trans.). New York: New American Library, 1948.

Van Hein, Edward. *What is Subud*. London: Rider, 1963.

Vernon, Jack. *Inside the Black Room*. New York: Clarkson N. Potter, 1963.

Vernon, M. D. *The Psychology of Perception*. Baltimore: Penguin, 1962.

Viherjuuri, H. J. *Sauna: The Finnish Bath*. Brattleboro, Vt.: Stephen Greene, 1965.

Vithaldas. *The Yoga System of Health and Relief from Tension*. New York: Outlet, 1957.

Von Foerster, H. et al. *Purposive Systems*. New York: Spartan, 1968.

Waite, A. E. *The Pictorial Key to the Tarot*. New York: University, 1959.

Waley, Arthur (trans.). *The Analects of Confucius*. New York: Random House, 1938.

Waley, Arthur. *Three Ways of Thought in Ancient China*. London: George Allen & Unwin, 1939.

Waley, Arthur. *The Way and Its Power: A Study of the Tao Te Ching and its Place in Chinese Thought*. New York: Macmillan, 1934.

Walker, Kenneth. *Diagnosis of Man*. Baltimore: Penguin, 1942.

Walker, Kenneth. *A Study of Gurdjieff's Teaching*. London: Jonathan Cape, 1957.

Wallace, R. K. "Physiological Effects of Transcendental Meditation." *Science, 167*, March 27, 1970.

Walter, W. Grey. *The Living Brain*. New York: Norton, 1963.

Ward, Ritchie R. *The Living Clocks*. New York: New American Library, 1972.

Ware, James R. (trans.). *The Sayings of Mencius*. New York: Mentor, 1960.

Warren, Richard & Rosalyn. "Auditory Illusions and Confusions." *Scientific American, 223,* Dec. 1970.

Waters, Frank. *Book of the Hopi*. New York: Ballantine, 1963.

Waters, Frank. *Masked Gods: Navaho and Pueblo Ceremonialism*. New York: Ballantine, 1950.

Watson, Burton (trans.). *Chuang Tzu*. New York: Columbia University, 1964.

Watson, Burton (trans.). *Cold Mountain: 100 Poems by the T'ang Poet Han-shan*. New York: Columbia University, 1962.

Watson, Burton (trans.). *Mo Tzu: Basic Writings*. New York: Columbia University, 1963.

Watts, Alan. *Beyond Theology: The Art of Godsmanship*. New York: Pantheon, 1964.

Watts, Alan. *The Book: On the Taboo Against Knowing Who You Are*. New York: Collier, 1966.

Watts, Alan. *The "Deep-In" View*. El Cerrito, Calif.: Dust Books, 1965.

Watts, Alan. *Does it Matter?: Essays on Man's Relation to Materiality*. New York: Pantheon, 1970.

Watts, Alan. *Nature, Man and Woman*. New York: Mentor, 1958.

Watts, Alan. *Nonsense*. San Francisco: Stolen Paper Editions, 1967.

Watts, Alan. *Psychotherapy East and West*. New York: Mentor, 1961.

Watts, Alan. *The Spirit of Zen: A Way of Life, Work, and Art in the Far East*. New York: Grove, 1958.

Watts, Alan. *This Is It and Other Essays on Zen and Spiritual Experience*. New York: Pantheon, 1960.

Watts, Alan. *The Two Hands of God: The Myths of Polarity*. New York: Collier, 1963.

Watts, Alan. *The Way of Zen*. New York: Mentor, 1957.

Wavell, Stewart et al. *Trances*. New York: Dutton, 1966.

Weil, Andrew. *The Natural Mind*. Boston: Houghton Mifflin, 1970.

Weil, Gunther, et al. (eds.). *The Psychedelic Reader*. New York: Citadel, 1965.

Weisel, Elie. *Souls on Fire*. New York: Knopf, 1972.

Welbon, Guy Richard. *The Buddhist Nirvana and its Western Interpreters*. Chicago: University of Chicago Press, 1968.

Wertheimer, Max. *Productive Thinking*. New York: Harper & Row, 1959.

Westbrook, A., & Ratti, O. *Aikido and the Dynamic Sphere*. Rutland, Vt.: Tuttle, 1970.

White, John. *The Highest State of Consciousness*. Garden City, N.Y.: Anchor, 1972.

White, T. H. *The Bestiary*. New York: Putnam, 1954.

Whitehead, Alfred N. *Adventures of Ideas*. New York: New American Library, 1933.

Whitehead, Alfred N. *Process and Reality*. New York: Harper & Row, 1929.

Whitehead, Alfred N. *Symbolism: Its Meaning and Effect*. New York: Macmillian, 1927.

Whorf, Benjamin L. *Language, Thought and Reality*. Cambridge, Mass.: MIT, 1956.

Whyte, Lancelot L. *The Next Development in Man*. New York: New American Library, 1950.

Whyte, Lancelot L. *The Unconscious Before Freud*. London: Tavistock, 1960.

Whyte, Lancelot L. *The Unitary Principle in Physics and Biology*. New York: Holt, Rinehart & Winston, 1949.

Wienpahl, Paul. *The Matter of Zen: A Brief Account of Zazen*. New York: New York University, 1964.

Wienpahl, Paul. "Zen and the Work of Wittgenstein." *Chicago Review, 12,* 67–72, Summer 1958.

Wienpahl, Paul. *Zen Diary*. New York: Harper & Row, 1970.

Wilentz, Joan S. *The Senses of Man*. New York: Apollo, 1968.

Wilhelm, Hellmut. *Change: Eight Lectures on the I Ching*. New York: Pantheon, 1960.

Wilhelm, Richard (trans.). *The Secret of the Golden Flower: A Chinese Book of Life*. New York: Harcourt Brace Jovanovich, 1931.

Wilhelm, Richard. *A Short History of Chinese Civilization*. New York: Viking, 1929.

Wilhelm, Richard. *The Soul of China*. New York: Harcourt Brace Jovanovich, 1928.

Williams, G. W. "Hypnosis in Perspective." In *Experimental Hypnosis* (L. Cron, ed.). New York: Macmillan, 1956.

Wilson, Colin. *Beyond the Outsider*. Boston: Houghton Mifflin, 1965.

Wilson, Colin. *Introduction to the New Existentialism*. Boston: Houghton Mifflin, 1967.

Wilson, Colin. *The Mind Parasites*. Oakland, Calif.: Oneiric Press, 1967.

Wilson, Colin. *New Pathways in Psychology*. New York: Taplinger, 1972.

Wilson, Colin. *The Occult: A History*. New York: Random House, 1971.

Wilson, Colin. *The Outsider*. New York: Delta, 1956.

Wilson, Colin. *The Philosopher's Stone*. New York: Crown, 1969.

Wilson, Colin. *Poetry and Mysticism*. San Francisco: City Lights, 1969.

Wilson, Colin. *Sex Diary of Gerard Sorme*, New York: Simon & Schuster, 1963.

Wilson, John R. et al. *The Mind*. New York: Time-Life Books, 1964.

Wine, William A. *Alternatives: Altered States of Consciousness and Countercultural Games*. Canadian Government Report Monograph, 1970.

Wissler, Clark. *Indians of the United States*. Garden City, N.Y.: Doubleday, 1940.

Wittgenstein, Ludwig. *The Blue and Brown Books*. New York: Harper & Row, 1958.

Wittgenstein, Ludwig. *Lectures and Conversations*. Oxford: Basil Blackwell, 1966.

Wittgenstein, Ludwig. *Notebooks, 1914–1916*. New York: Harper & Row, 1961.

Wittgenstein, Ludwig. *On Certainty*. New York: Harper & Row, 1969.

Wittgenstein, Ludwig. *Philosophical Investigations*. New York: Macmillan, 1958.

Wittgenstein, Ludwig. *Remarks on the Foundations of Mathematics*. Cambridge, Mass.: MIT Press, 1956.

Wittgenstein, Ludwig. *Tractatus Logico-Philosophicus*. New York: Humanities, 1922.

Wittgenstein, Ludwig. *Zettel*. Berkeley: University of California, 1967.

Wolf, Adolf H. *Good Medicine: Life in Harmony with Nature*. British Columbia, Canada: Good Medicine, 1970.

Wope, J., & Lazarus, A. *Behavior Therapy Techniques*. New York: Pergamon, 1966.

Woodburne, Lloyd S. *The Neural Basis of Behavior*. Cleveland: Chas. E. Merrill, 1967.

Woodroffe, John (Arthur Avalon). *Principles of Tantra (Tantra Tattra)*. Madras, India: Ganesh, 1914.

Woodroffe, John (Arthur Avalon). *The Serpent Power*. Madras, India, Ganesh, 1918.

Wu, John C. H. *The Golden Age of Zen*. Formosa: National War College, 1967.

Yablonsky, Lewis. *Synanon: The Tunnel Book*. Baltimore: Pelican, 1965.

Yaker, H., et al. *The Future of Time*. Garden City, N.Y. Doubleday, 1971.

Yasuda, Kenneth. *The Japanese Haiku: Its Essential Nature, History, and Possibilities in English with Selected Examples*. Rutland, Vt.: Tuttle, 1957.

Yokochi, Chihiro. *Photographic Anatomy of the Human Body*. Baltimore: University Park Press, 1971.

Young, J. Z. *Doubt and Certainty in Science*. Oxford: Oxford University Press, 1950.

Young, J. Z. *An Introduction to the Study of Man*. Oxford: Oxford University Press, 1971.

Young, J. Z. *The Memory System of the Brain*. Oxford: Oxford University Press, 1966.

Young, J. Z. *A Model of the Brain*. Oxford: Oxford University Press, 1964.

Young, La Monte, & Zazeela, Marian. *Selected Writings*. Munich: Heiner Friedrich, 1969.

Youngblood, Gene. *Expanded Cinema*. New York: Dutton, 1970.

Zimmer, Heinrich. *Myths and Symbols in Indian Art and Civilization*. New York: Harper & Row, 1946.

Zimmer, Heinrich. *Philosophies of India*. Cleveland: World, 1951.

Zubek, John P. (ed.). *Sensory Deprivation: Fifteen Years of Research*. New York: Appleton-Century-Crofts, 1969.

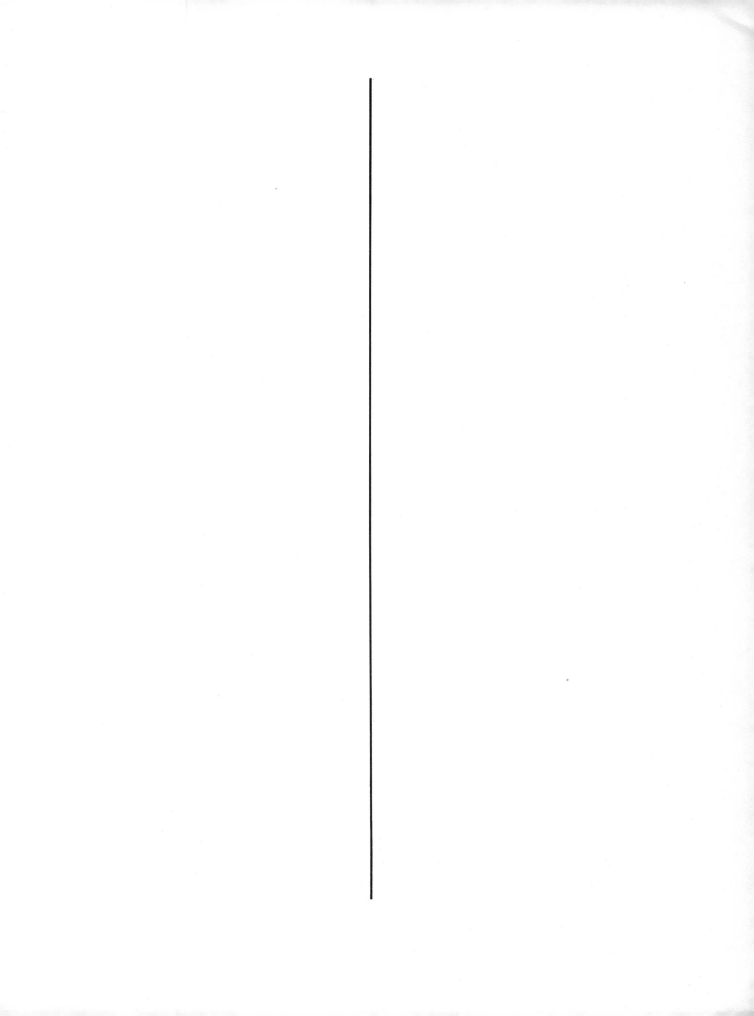

INDEX